# DESIGNING QUALITATIVE RESEARCH
## 3rd Edition

P9-ELO-328

# DESIGNING QUALITATIVE RESEARCH
## 3rd Edition

CATHERINE MARSHALL
GRETCHEN B. ROSSMAN

SAGE Publications
*International Educational and Professional Publisher*
Thousand Oaks   London   New Delhi

*For information:*

 SAGE Publications, Inc.
2455 Teller Road
Thousand Oaks, California 91320
E-mail: order@sagepub.com

SAGE Publications Ltd.
6 Bonhill Street
London EC2A 4PU
United Kingdom

SAGE Publications India Pvt. Ltd.
M-32 Market
Greater Kailash I
New Delhi 110 048 India

Printed in the United States of America

**Library of Congress Cataloging-in-Publication Data**

Marshall, Catherine
    Designing qualitative research / Catherine Marshall, Gretchen
  B. Rossman.—3rd ed.
       p.   cm.
    Includes bibliographical references and index.
    ISBN 0-7619-1339-4 (acid-free paper)
    ISBN 0-7619-1340-8 (pbk.: acid-free paper)
      1. Social sciences—Research—Methodology.   I. Rossman, Gretchen B.
  II. Title.
  H62 .M277   1999
  300'.72—dc21                                                         98-40148

99  00  01  02  03  04  05  7  6  5  4  3  2  1

*Acquisition Editor:*      Peter Labella
*Production Editor:*       Astrid Virding
*Editorial Assistant:*     Nevair Kabakian
*Copyeditor:*              Linda Gray
*Typesetter:*              Lynn Miyata
*Cover Designer:*          Ravi Balasuriya

# Contents

# List of Tables

# List of Figures

# List of Vignettes

---

# Preface to Third Edition

Qualitative research methodology is maturing now, and this third edition addresses the advances and challenges presented by provocative developments and new applications. The book originally met the need for advice on designing such research, given the complexity, the flexibility, and the controversies of qualitative approaches. That need persists: Doctoral students, research managers, policy analysts, and researchers anticipating multimethod team research will find clear and direct guidance in our book. Now, qualitative designs are used in health behavior, education, urban planning, public relations and communications, sociology, psychology, management, social work, nursing, and more.

Originally, *Designing Qualitative Research* was written because qualitative reports were intriguing but mystical. Earthy, evocative ethnographies seemed to just appear by magic. Researchers and students had no guidance for imitating such work. A few researchers provided chapters or appendixes recounting their procedures. Texts extolled the philosophical stances and the cultural premises for qualitative research. We wrote this book to fill the void, to provide specific advice on design. Then, and now in this third edition, we benefit from the research experience of those who first documented their systematic design and also from the probing questions of our doctoral students. Thus, we provide readers connections to the classics of ethnography as well as presenting the issues and design dilemmas of researchers with new questions for the new century. Furthermore, this edition demonstrates how to incorporate qualitative methodology with the challenges posed by postmodernists, feminists, and those who demand that research be directly useful to the researched.

The third edition provides vignettes to illustrate the methodological challenges posed by the intellectual, ethical, political, and technological advances affecting qualitative research design. New vignettes include, for example, researchers' political stance toward promoting democracy while conducting evaluations of community development, and critical theorists' puzzling over reporting research without colonizing those who allowed them into their lives. Because qualitative design is not linear, different pedagogical strategies are required; the vignettes, we hope, assist readers in transferring our words about design to applications in their own research.

Nothing keeps us attuned to qualitative research dilemmas more than the challenges our students present in classes and dissertations. We wish to thank the hundreds who have continuously pressed for innovative approaches and research questions fresh from real-life problems; many have graciously agreed for us to use their questions in vignettes. Finally, we, and our readers, benefit from the contributions of reviewers in scholarly journals and in anonymous reviews as well as from critical suggestions from our own students. In particular, we appreciate specific editorial contributions of Cindy Gerstl-Pepin and Dara Tomlin Rossman as we incorporated our substantial revisions for this new edition. We hope our efforts will continue to provide a practical guide, assisting researchers as they craft sound, thoughtful, and sensitive qualitative research proposals.

# 1 Introduction

Qualitative research genres have become increasingly important modes of inquiry for the social sciences and applied fields such as education, regional planning, nursing, social work, community development, and management. Long dominated by techniques borrowed from the experimental sciences, the social sciences now present a sometimes confusing array of alternative research methods. From anthropology come ethnomethodology, ethnoscience, and the more familiar ethnography. Sociology has yielded symbolic interactionism and the Chicago School. Philosophers would have us engage in concept analysis, and interdisciplinary work has spawned sociolinguistics, discourse analysis, life histories, narrative analysis, and clinical methodology. The critical traditions and postmodern perspectives bring feminist research and critical ethnography as well as action and participatory research—often explicitly ideological with emancipatory goals, intended to radically change fundamental social structures and processes and to reconceptualize the entire research enterprise.

Each of these disciplinary traditions rests on somewhat different assumptions about what constitutes proper inquiry within the qualitative, or interpretive, paradigm. Throughout this text, we refer to *qualitative research* and *qualitative methodology* as if they were one agreed-on approach. Although this might be reassuring to the novice researcher, unfortunately it is not the case. As Denzin and Lincoln (1994) note, "qualitative research . . . crosscuts disciplines, fields, and subject matter. A complex, interconnected family of terms, concepts, and assumptions surround [*sic*] the term *qualitative research*" (p. 1).

A wide variety of qualitative research genres exists, and many excellent texts serve as guides to their assumptions and approaches. Despite this variety, however, there are some common considerations and procedures for its conduct and certain "habits of mind and heart" (Rossman & Rallis, 1998) that most qualitative researchers espouse. Qualitative researchers are intrigued with the complexity of social interactions as expressed in daily life and with the meanings the participants themselves attribute to these interactions. This interest takes qualitative researchers into natural settings rather than laboratories and fosters pragmatism in using multiple methods for exploring the topic of interest. Thus, qualitative research is pragmatic, interpretive, and grounded in the lived experiences of people. Rossman and Rallis (1998) offer eight characteristics of qualitative research and researchers: It (a) is naturalistic, (b) draws on multiple methods that respect the humanity of participants in the study, (c) is emergent and evolving, and (d) is interpretive. Qualitative researchers (e) view social worlds as holistic or seamless, (f) engage in systematic reflection on their own roles in the research, (g) are sensitive to their personal biographies and how these shape the study, and (h) rely on complex reasoning that moves dialectically between deduction and induction (see Table 1.1).

Qualitative research, then, is a broad approach to the study of social phenomena; its various genres are naturalistic and interpretive, and they draw on multiple methods of inquiry. This book is intended to be a guide to researchers who have chosen some genre of qualitative methods to understand—and perhaps change—a complex social phenomenon and who seek to develop solid, ethical proposals as they plan their inquiry.

## Qualitative Research Genres

Many typologies of qualitative research have been offered. With a specific focus on education, Jacob (1987, 1988) describes six qualitative traditions: human ethology, ecological psychology, holistic ethnography, cognitive an-

**Table 1.1  Characteristics of Qualitative Research**

| |
|---|
| *Qualitative research* |
| Takes place in the natural world |
| Uses multiple methods that are interactive and humanistic |
| Is emergent rather than tightly prefigured |
| Is fundamentally interpretive |
| |
| *The qualitative researcher* |
| Views social phenomenon holistically |
| Systematically reflects on who she is in the inquiry |
| Is sensitive to her personal biography and how it shapes the study |
| Uses complex reasoning that is multifaceted and iterative |

SOURCE: Rossman and Rallis (1998, p. 9). Reprinted by permission.

thropology, ethnography of communication, and symbolic interactionism (see Table 1.2). Atkinson, Delamont, and Hammersley (1988) critique Jacob's typology and offer seven somewhat differing ones: symbolic interactionism, anthropology, sociolinguistics, ethnomethodology, democratic evaluation, neo-Marxist ethnography, and feminism. Denzin and Lincoln (1994) provide chapters on major paradigms and approaches to qualitative inquiry. The paradigms they list are constructivism and interpretivism, critical theory, feminism, ethnic studies, and cultural studies. The approaches include case studies, ethnography and participant observation, phenomenology and eth-nomethodology, grounded theory, biographical method, historical social sci-ence, participative inquiry, and clinical research. Analysis of these lists yields three major genres, following the discussion provided in Gall, Borg, and Gall (1996): (a) a focus on *individual lived experience* exemplified by phenome-nological approaches, some feminist inquiry, and narrative analysis; (b) a focus on *society and culture* as seen in ethnography and qualitative sociology; and (c) a focus on *language and communication* expressed by sociolinguistic and semiotic approaches.

In the past few decades, some qualitative researchers have espoused post-modern arguments that critique traditional social science (see Denzin & Lincoln, 1994; Rosenau, 1992). These researchers challenge historic assumptions of neutrality in inquiry and assert that *all* research is interpretive, "guided by a set of beliefs and feelings about the world and how it should be understood and studied" (Denzin & Lincoln, 1994, p. 13). They further argue that research

**Table 1.2  Typologies of Qualitative Research**

| Jacob (1987, 1988) | Atkinson, Delamont, and Hammersley (1988) | Denzin and Lincoln (1994) |
|---|---|---|
| Human ethology | Symbolic interactionism | Case studies |
| Ecological psychology | Anthropology | Ethnography |
| Holistic ethnography | Sociolinguistics | Phenomenology and ethnomethodology |
| Cognitive anthropology | Ethnomethodology | Grounded theory |
| Ethnography of communication | Democratic evaluation | Biographical method |
| Symbolic interactionism | Neo-Marxist ethnography | Historical social science |
|  | Feminism | Participative inquiry |
|  |  | Clinical research |

involves issues of power: Traditionally conducted social science research has silenced many groups marginalized and oppressed in society by making them the passive object of inquiry. Those espousing critical perspectives have developed research strategies that are openly ideological and that have empowering and democratizing goals.

Each genre, we argue, can be undergirded by either traditional or more critical and postmodern assumptions. "Traditional" qualitative research assumes (a) that knowledge is subjective rather than being the objective Truth, (b) that the researcher learns from participants to understand the meaning of their lives but should maintain a certain stance of neutrality, and (c) that society is structured and orderly.[1] Critical theory, critical race theory, feminist theory, and postmodern perspectives also assume that knowledge is subjective, but they view society as essentially conflictual and oppressive. These positions critique traditional modes of knowledge production (i.e., research) because they have evolved in settings structured to legitimize elite social scientists and exclude other forms of knowing. Critical race theorists and feminists, particularly, point to knowledges and truths excluded from traditional knowledge production (Harding, 1987; LeCompte, 1993; Matsuda, Delgado, Lawrence, & Crenshaw, 1993). Through such challenges, it becomes clear that questions must be dismantled and reframed (Marshall, 1997; Scheurich, 1997). Such researchers view inquiry as leading to radical change or emancipation from oppressive social structures, either through a sustained critique or through direct advocacy and action taken by the researcher, often in collaboration with participants in the study. These critiques share four assumptions:

> (a) Research fundamentally involves issues of power; (b) the research report is not transparent but, rather, is authored by a raced, gendered, classed, and politically oriented individual; (c) race, class, and gender [among other social identities] are crucial for understanding experience; and (d) historic, traditional research has silenced members of oppressed and marginalized groups. (Rossman & Rallis, 1998, p. 66)

Three injunctions are embedded in these newer perspectives on qualitative research: (a) We, as researchers, must examine closely how we represent the participants in our work—the Other; (b) we should carefully scrutinize the "complex interplay of our own personal biography, power and status, inter-actions with participants, and written word" (Rossman & Rallis, 1998, p. 67); and (c) we must be vigilant about the dynamics of ethics and politics in our work. One implication of these concerns is that qualitative researchers pay close attention to their participants' reactions to the research and to the *voice* used in writing up their work, as a representation of the relationship between researcher and participants.[2]

Much of the critique of traditional qualitative research finds expression in narrative analysis, action research, critical ethnography, participatory action research, and feminist research. Each has the change of existing social struc-tures and processes as a primary purpose. Critical ethnography, participatory action research, and feminist research often have explicit emancipatory goals.

An interdisciplinary approach with many guises, *narrative analysis,* seeks to describe the meaning of experience for individuals, frequently those who are socially marginalized or oppressed, as they construct stories (narratives) about their lives. Life histories, biographies and autobiographies; oral histo-ries; and personal narratives are all forms of narrative analysis. Each specific approach assumes that storytelling is integral to understanding lives and that all people engage in the construction of narratives. Some approaches focus on the sociolinguistic techniques that the narrator uses; others focus on life events and the narrator's meaning making. When framed by feminist or critical theory, the purpose of narrative analysis may be emancipatory (Bloom & Munro, 1995; Lather, 1991).

*Action research* challenges the claims of neutrality and objectivity of tradi-tional social science and seeks full collaborative inquiry by all participants, often to engage in sustained change in organizational, community, or institutional contexts (Stringer, 1996). It seeks to "decentralize" traditional research by maintaining a commitment to local contexts rather than to the quest for Truth and to liberate research from its excessive reliance on the "restrictive conventional rules of the research game" (Guba, in Stringer, 1996, p. x). When ideally executed, the distinctions between researcher and participants blur, creating a democratic inquiry process. Much action research is found in education, where teachers collaboratively inquire into their own practice, make changes, and assess the effects of those changes (Kemmis & McTaggart, 1982; McKernan, 1991; Miller, 1990). Action research, also used in social work, business management, and community development (Hollingsworth, 1997), typically involves practitioners who engage in research to improve their practice.

*Critical ethnography* is grounded in critical theories that assume that society is structured by class and status, as well as by race, ethnicity, gender, and sexual orientation, to maintain the oppression of marginalized groups. In education, critical ethnography developed from a commitment to radical schooling that found expression in several works sharply critical of accepted teaching practice (Keddie, 1971; Sharp & Green, 1975; Young, 1971). Later work of this type focused on constraints on the adoption of radical teaching practices (Atkinson et al., 1988). Critical ethnography can go beyond the classroom to ask questions about fundamental policy, power, and dominance issues and dilemmas in schooling, including the role of the school in reproducing and reinforcing gender, race, and other social inequities (Anderson, 1989; Anderson & Herr, 1993; Kelly & Gaskell, 1996; Marshall, 1991, 1997).

More visible in international than domestic work, *participatory action research* draws on the precepts of emancipation articulated by Friere (1970). It assumes that sustainable empowerment and development must begin from the concerns of the marginalized (Park, Brydon-Miller, Hall, & Jackson, 1993). In addition to an explicit commitment to action, full collaboration between researcher and participants in posing the questions to be pursued and gathering data to respond to them is the hallmark of participatory action research. Participatory action research entails a cycle of research, reflection, and action. Examples of this work include Maguire's (1987) research on battered women, Phaik-Lah's (1997) work in Malaysia, and Titchen & Bennie's (1993) study on training for nursing; it is well described by McTaggart (1997).

*Feminist theories* frame research ranging across issues and disciplines. They put women at the center and identify patriarchy as central to understanding experience. They "uncover cultural and institutional sources and forces of oppression. . . . They name and value women's subjective experience" (Marshall, 1997, p. 12). Different feminisms frame different research goals (Collins, 1990; Marshall, 1997; Tong, 1989), but many draw on the positions exemplified in the work of hooks (1989). Feminist work ranges from examining gender differences in schools (Clarricoates, 1980, 1987) to the development of adolescent girls (Griffin, 1985; Lees, 1986) to Indonesian women's challenges to male dominance of shaman rituals (Tsing, 1990). Marshall (1997) combines feminist and critical perspectives to dismantle traditional policy analysis that has failed to incorporate women, as does Lather (1991) who advocates agendas that challenge the legitimacy of the dominant order and turn critical thought into emancipating action (p. xv). Socialist, "women's ways" feminisms may frame research on women in leadership positions to expand leadership theory; "power and politics" feminisms frame examinations of, for example, state-imposed oppression of women in welfare, medical, and other state-regulated systems, grounding "research, policy and action [in] the political choices and power-driven ideologies and embedded forces that categorize, oppress, and exclude" (Marshall, 1997, p. 13).

The preceding discussion is intended to provide ways of categorizing some of the variety of qualitative research genres and approaches as well as to depict the current critical, feminist, and postmodern critiques. As we note, each genre assumes that systematic inquiry must occur in a natural setting rather than an artificially constrained one, such as a laboratory. The approaches vary, however, depending on the role of theory and ideology, the focus of interest (individual, group or organization, or communicative interaction), the degree of interaction between researcher and participants in gathering data, and the participants' role in the research. The discussion above should have provided some sense of the array of paradigms and approaches subsumed under the qualitative research umbrella. This text, however, cannot do justice to the details and nuances of the variety of qualitative methods; we refer you to additional sources at the end of this chapter. Some of these sources are classic—the grandmothers and grandfathers in the field; others are more current, reflecting emergent perspectives. Our purpose in this book is to describe the generic process of designing qualitative research; it entails immersion in the everyday life of the setting chosen for study, values and seeks to discover participants' perspectives on their worlds, views inquiry as an interactive process between the researcher and the participants, is both descriptive and analytic, and relies on people's words and observable behavior as the primary data. Whether some particular methodological refinement is qualitative or not is a debate for another arena. We hope to give practical guidance to those embarking on an exciting, sometimes frustrating, and ultimately rewarding journey into qualitative inquiry.

*    *    *    *    *

The evocative case study, the rich description of ethnography, and the narratives of complex personal journeys are all the products of systematic inquiry. In their beginnings, however, they were once modest research proposals. Qualitative researchers have had to search hard to find useful guidelines for writing thorough, convincing research proposals.[3] Too often, policy studies offer findings and recommendations with little sense of how the research led to those recommendations. Some written reports of qualitative research lack sufficient detail to provide strong examples of how they were designed; beginning qualitative researchers have difficulty learning how to write proposals from such reports. Other research reports are written as if the process unfolded smoothly, with none of the messiness inherent in qualitative research; these versions are also difficult to learn from. This book provides specific guidance for writing strong, convincing proposals for research grounded in the assumptions of qualitative methodology.

Although qualitative research has an accepted place in formal research arenas, dissertation committees and reviewers for funding agencies need to see proposals that are well developed, sound, rigorous, and ethical. This book is organized as a guide through the process of writing a qualitative research proposal, demonstrating how to write a proposal that reassures reviewers by defining explicit steps to follow, principles to adhere to, and rationales for the strengths of qualitative research.

Sociologists, community psychologists, criminologists, anthropologists, political scientists, regional planners, and others from a range of the social sciences and applied fields will find this guide useful. Although many of the examples come from the field of education (because of our own backgrounds), the principles, challenges, and opportunities are transferable across disciplines and into other applied fields.

This book does not replace the numerous texts, readers, and journal articles that are important for learning qualitative methodology. It is meant to complement the numerous existing texts that explicate the philosophical bases, history, and findings of qualitative studies. Its purpose is to give practical, useful guidance for writing proposals that fit within the qualitative paradigm and that are successful.

## The Challenges

Researchers who would conduct qualitative research face three challenges: (a) developing a conceptual framework for the study that is thorough, concise, and elegant; (b) planning a design that is systematic and manageable, yet flexible; and (c) integrating these into a coherent document that convinces the proposal readers—a funding agency or a dissertation committee—that the study should be done, can be done, and will be done.

### Should-Do-Ability

The first challenge is to build an argument both that the study will contribute to theory and research—the ongoing conversation in a particular social science discipline or applied field—and that it will be significant for policy and practice. This consideration addresses the familiar "So what?" question about why the study should be conducted, to which the researcher should respond cogently and knowledgeably.

### Do-Ability

The second challenge is to demonstrate the feasibility, or do-ability, of the study. This depends on judgments about sufficiency of available resources (time, money), access to the site or population of interest or both, ethical considerations, and the researcher's knowledge and skills. Both proposals seeking external funding and those for dissertation research *must* include a discussion of resources. The researcher should also discuss strategies for access to a specific site or to identify participants for the study. Ethical considerations should be thoughtfully and sensitively analyzed, both the generic ethical issues in qualitative research and those specific to the site or the participants. Finally, throughout the proposal, the researcher demonstrates her[4] competence to conduct a thorough, ethical qualitative research study. In citing the methodological literature and discussing pilot studies or previous research, the researcher reveals experience in conducting qualitative research and familiarity with the ongoing methodological discourse.

*Want-to-Do-Ability*

In contrast, the want-to-do-ability is solely a function of the researcher's engagement in the topic. Far removed from the dispassionate scientist of the past, the qualitative researcher cares deeply about the substance of the inquiry at hand. This should not suggest that qualitative research is naively subjectivist and biased—all-too-common criticisms. Rather, qualitative inquiry acknowledges that *all* social science research may well be subjective and shifts the discourse to a discussion of epistemology and strategies for ensuring trustworthy and credible studies. The proposal, then, is an argument that makes the case that the study can and should be done and that there is sufficient energy and interest to sustain it.

## Developing an Argument

Central to this book is the premise that proposal development is a process of building an *argument* supporting the proposed work. Not unlike the logic of formal debate or the reasoning of a position paper, a research proposal is intended to convince the reader that the research holds potential significance and relevance, that the design of the study is sound, and that the researcher is capable of conducting the study successfully. The proposal writer must, therefore, build a logical argument for the endeavor, amass evidence in support of each point, and show how the entire enterprise is integrated conceptually.

Research proposals have two major sections: (a) the conceptual framework and (b) the design and research methods. Roughly corresponding to the *what*—the substantive focus of the inquiry—and the *how*—the means for conducting that inquiry—these two sections of the proposal detail the specific topic or issue to be explored and the proposed means for that exploration. In a sound, well-developed, and well-argued proposal, the sections are integrally related: They share common epistemological assumptions; the research questions and methods chosen to explore the topic are congruent and have an organic relation to one another.

*Conceptual Framework*

The first section of the proposal—the conceptual framework—demands a solid rationale. In examining a specific setting or set of individuals, the writer should show how she is studying a case of a larger phenomenon. By linking the specific research questions to larger theoretical constructs or to important policy issues, the writer shows that the particulars of the study serve to illuminate larger issues and, therefore, hold potential significance for that field. The economics doctoral student, for example, who demonstrates that his qualitative case studies of five families' financial decision making are relevant for understanding larger marketplace forces, while focusing at the individual level, has met this condition. The case studies are significant because they illuminate in detail larger economic forces.

Similarly, the university research team that designs a teacher induction project evaluation component stipulating phenomenological, in-depth interviewing as the sole data collection method and that links this approach to socialization theory has begun to build a case for the proposal that grounds it in important theoretical and empirical literatures. We develop the logic undergirding the conceptual framework in Chapter 2.

*Design Soundness*

The second area for building a sound argument in favor of the proposal is its design. The writer should show that the design is the result of a series of decisions she has made based on knowledge gained from the methodological literature and previous work. Justification for those decisions should derive not only from the methodological literature; it should also flow logically from the research questions and the conceptual framework surrounding those questions.

Because qualitative research proposals are at times unfamiliar to reviewers, the logic supporting the choice of those methods must be sound. Ensuring a clear, logical rationale in support of qualitative methods entails attention to seven topics:

1. The assumptions of qualitative approaches;
2. The logic for selecting a site, a sample, participants, or any combination of these;
3. The choice of overall design and data collection methods;
4. An acknowledgment of the intensive aspects of fieldwork;
5. A consideration of ethical issues;

6. The resource needs; and

7. Attention to the trustworthiness of the overall design.

The first five of these areas are considered in detail in Chapters 3, 4, and 5; the sixth, resource needs, is discussed in Chapter 6, and ensuring the trustworthiness of the study is elaborated in Chapter 7.

### Researcher Competence

Finally, in developing an argument to support the proposal, the writer should explicitly and implicitly demonstrate competence. The exact standard of competence applied for evaluating the proposal depends on the purpose and scope of the research; most likely, the standards applied to a dissertation proposal will differ from those used to evaluate a multiyear funded project written by established researchers. Paradoxically, because dissertation research is intended to provide an opportunity for learning the craft of research, careful scrutiny will be given to all portions of the proposal. The dissertation proposal writer will be expected to show his capability by thorough attention to every facet of the conceptual framework and the research design. Established researchers, on the other hand, may not receive such careful scrutiny because their record of previous work engenders trust, and the logic of good faith preserves standards for research. Although this may seem unfair, it nevertheless reflects the reality of proposal evaluation.

Demonstrating competence, then, involves reference to the proposal writer's previous work, discussion of a pilot study's strengths and weaknesses, discussion of the proposal writer's course work and other relevant educational experiences, and the overall high quality of the proposal's organization, conceptual framework, discussion of relevant literature, and design.

Next, we present two vignettes to illuminate this process of building an argument to support qualitative research. The first describes a doctoral student in sociology trying to convince her dissertation committee that qualitative methods are best suited for exploratory research on the culture of a hospital. She intends to uncover patterns in the work life of participants that will lead to important improvements in the treatment of patients. Vignette 2 shows researchers building a rationale around the strengths of qualitative methods for policy analysis. The researchers had to convince legislators that qualitative methods would yield useful, vivid analyses that could inform the policy-making process. We develop the implications for building an argument in support of qualitative proposals after the vignettes and then provide an overview of the rest of the book.

*    *    *    *    *

### Vignette 1

## Justifying Fieldwork to Explore Organizational Culture[5]

As O'Brien reviewed the notes she had written to help with the proposal defense, she realized that her strongest argument rested on two aspects of the proposed study's significance: its exploratory purpose and its commitment to improving patient treatment in large urban hospitals. She realized that the latter aspect might be construed as biased, but if she kept the rationale grounded in the need to better understand complex interactions, tacit processes, and often hidden beliefs and values, she could demonstrate the study's clear potential to improve practice.

Her committee was composed of two quantitatively trained sociologists and a medical anthropologist. She knew she had the support of the anthropologist, whose advice had been crucial during the several proposal drafts she had written. The two sociologists, however, were more likely to be critical of the design.

O'Brien decided to begin her presentation with an explication of the four purposes of research (exploration, explanation, description, and prediction) to link the purpose of her proposed study to general principles regarding the conduct of inquiry. She could then proceed quite logically to a discussion of the ways in which exploratory research could serve to identify important variables for subsequent explanatory or predictive research. This logic could allay the concerns of the two quantitatively oriented sociologists, who would search the proposal for testable hypotheses, instrumentation and operationalization of variables, and tests of reliability.

The second major justification of the study would develop from its significance for practice. O'Brien recalled how she had reviewed empirical studies indicating that organizational conditions had a significant effect on wellness and hospital leaving rates. What had not been identified in those studies were the specific interactions between hospital staff and patients, the widely shared beliefs about patients among the staff, and the organizational norms governing patient treatment. Her research, she would argue, would help identify those tacit, often hidden, aspects of organizational life. This, in turn, could have usefulness both for policy regarding health care and for practice in health care facilities.

That O'Brien would be engaging in exploratory research where the relevant variables had not been identified and uncovering the tacit aspects of organizational life strongly suggested qualitative methods. Fieldwork would be most appropriate for discovering the relevant variables and building a thorough, rich, detailed description of hospital culture. By linking her proposed research to concepts familiar to the quantitative sociologists, O'Brien hoped to draw the sociologists into the logic supporting her proposal and to convince them of its sound design.

\*   \*   \*   \*   \*

A researcher's first task, even before the formulation of the proposal, is quite often to convince critics that the research will be useful. O'Brien faces this challenge in the preceding vignette and develops a rationale supporting her choice of qualitative research methods. In many cases, and especially in policy research, one can appeal to policymakers' frustration with previous research. The researcher should convince policymakers that qualitative research will lead to strong, detailed conclusions and recommendations. The next vignette shows how two policy analysts convinced their superiors that they could answer pressing policy questions with qualitative methods.

\*   \*   \*   \*   \*

### *Vignette 2*

*Convincing Policymakers of the Utility of Qualitative Methods*[6]

Why, 6 months after state legislators had allocated $10 million to provide temporary shelters, were homeless families still sleeping in cars? Keppel and Wilson, researchers in the legislative analyst's office, knew that the question demanded qualitative research methodology. Their superiors, however, would be skeptical. They prepared the following memo:

Memorandum Re: Analysis of Homeless Family Shelter Policy

This memo is to explain the usefulness of qualitative research for answering policy questions. At tomorrow's meeting, we will show you how this approach to an analysis of the Homeless Family Shelter Policy will provide the insights we need.

Studies and evaluations that tell you, after the fact, that things have *already* gone wrong, give too little too late. To understand homelessness, in all its complexity, to identify areas we can influence, and to see the consequences of policy intervention in real life, we need a different approach to policy analysis. We can do little with studies that tell us that policies have had little or no effect. In addition, we need information that will enable us to see beyond simple dependent variables. Thus, we believe that this agency's approach to policy analysis ought to include qualitative research methods. We believe that the benefits for doing so in formulating policy include the following:

1. Qualitative methods identify and describe the complexity of social problems like homelessness.
2. Qualitative methods identify the unanticipated outcomes of policies.
3. Qualitative methods help debug policy—they find inconsistencies and conflicts built into policies.
4. Qualitative methods identify how policies are changed as they are implemented at various levels.
5. Qualitative methods help find the natural solutions to problems—the solutions that people devise without policy intervention.
6. Qualitative methods provide a way to study problems in cases in which experiments would be unethical. (Marshall, 1987)

We hope that you will give us the opportunity to demonstrate the viability of qualitative research and to build the capacity of the legislative analyst's office in that direction. Too often, our research and evaluations miss the mark. It is far better to have an approximate answer to the right question than an exact answer to the wrong question. We look forward to tomorrow's discussion.

In their 30-minute presentation, Keppel and Wilson built their argument around two major points. The first was that there were numerous implementation questions concerning homelessness to be explored in the real-world setting, and the second was that certain subtleties of the policy implementation process had to be explored to understand fully what was happening. They spoke of needing to discover the right questions to ask, followed by the systematic collection of data. Keppel and Wilson convinced their superiors that their findings would help define the important questions, describe patterns of implementation, and identify the challenges and barriers that could lead to more effective policy outcomes.

Keppel and Wilson's strategy called for site visits to shelters and social service agencies and for interviews with members of homeless families, with the intent of uncovering the complex interactions of bureaucracy, money, implementing agents' goals and motivations, and local site interpretation of policy and homeless family situations.

*   *   *   *   *

In Vignette 2, we see researchers convincing others that a qualitative study was needed. This underscores the notion that researchers proposing qualitative inquiry do best by emphasizing the promise of quality, depth, and richness in the findings. They may, however, encounter puzzlement and resistance from those accustomed to survey and quasi-experimental research; they may need to translate between qualitative and quantitative paradigms. Researchers who are convinced that a qualitative approach is best for the question or problem at hand should make a case that "thick description" (Geertz, 1973, p. 5) and systematic and detailed analysis will yield valuable explanations of processes.

## Overview of the Book

The remainder of the book takes the reader through the sections of a qualitative research proposal. Chapter 2 discusses the complex task of building a conceptual framework around the study. Such a process entails moving beyond the initial puzzle or intriguing paradox and embedding it in appropriate traditions of research; it links the specific case to larger theoretical domains. This argument also should demonstrate the proposed study's significance to larger social policy issues, concerns of practice, and people's everyday lives or to some combination of these. Thus, the study's general focus and research questions, related literature, and significance are interrelated aspects of the conceptual framework. We call this the substance of the study—*the what*.

Chapter 3 presents a detailed discussion of *the how* of the study. Having focused on a research topic with a set of questions or a domain to explore, the proposal should next describe how systematic inquiry will yield data that will respond to the questions. The writer should discuss the logic and assumptions of the overall design and methods, linking these directly to the focus of the study. Here, the choice of qualitative methods should be justified.

Chapter 4 describes primary and secondary data collection methods. This chapter is not intended to replace the many exemplary texts that deal in great detail with methods; rather, we present a brief discussion of various alternatives and their strengths and weaknesses. Chapter 5 then describes procedures for managing, recording, and analyzing qualitative data. This discussion is necessarily brief because the writer cannot precisely stipulate the exact categories and themes for analysis at the proposal stage. He can, however, describe the strategy he will use and link this to the conceptual framework of the study.

Chapter 6 describes the complex, dialectical process of projecting the resources necessary for the study. Time, personnel, and financial resources should be considered. Finally, Chapter 7 revisits the image introduced here of the proposal as an argument. We discuss criteria for evaluating the soundness and competence of a qualitative proposal, with special attention to building a logical rationale and answering challenges from critics.

Throughout the book, we use vignettes to illustrate our points. Most of these are drawn from our own work and that of other social scientists; a few are fictitious with no references to published work. The principles depicted in the vignettes are applicable to research grounded in several disciplines as well as in the applied fields; they challenge you, the reader, to apply them to your own design.

Two themes run through this book. The first is that design flexibility is a crucial feature of qualitative inquiry; demands for specificity in design and method selection, however, seem to preclude such flexibility. We urge the researcher to think of the proposal as an initial plan; one that is thorough, sound, well thought-out, and based on current knowledge. The proposal reveals the researcher's sensitivity to the setting, the issues to be explored, and the ethical dilemmas sure to be encountered, but it also reminds the reader that considerations as yet unforeseen may well dictate changes in this initial plan. The language of the design and methods discussion is sure, positive, and active, while reserving the right to modify what is currently proposed.

· The second theme, which we have already introduced, is that the proposal is an argument. Because the proposal's primary purpose is to convince the reader that the research is substantive, will contribute to the field, and is well conceived and that the researcher is capable of conducting the research, it should rely on supportive reasoning, marshal evidence sufficient to convince the reader of the points, and argue the logic undergirding the proposal carefully. All this will demonstrate a thorough knowledge of both the topic to be explored and the methods to be used. At times, we give guidance and use terminology that should assist in translating qualitative design assumptions for more quantitatively oriented audiences. Finally, in thinking of the proposal as an argument, we often mention the reader (of the proposal) to remind you, the reader (of this book), that a sense of audience is critically important in crafting a solid research proposal.

## Notes

1. Burrell and Morgan (1979) provide one useful way for understanding research paradigms and the assumptions they embrace; Rossman and Rallis (1998) rely on their conceptualization to help situate various qualitative research genres. The discussion here draws on Rossman and Rallis's work.

2. We address this more fully in Chapters 3 and 7, but here we note that participants may disagree with the researcher's report and that passive constructions ("the research was conducted") suggest anonymity and distance, whereas active ones ("we conducted the research") claim agency.

3. Recent works provide guidance, in addition to this text. See, for example, *Research Design: Qualitative and Quantitative Approaches,* by J. W. Creswell (1994), and *Qualitative Research Design: An Interactive Approach,* by J. A. Maxwell (1996).

4. Throughout the text, we alternate between *he* and *she* when referring to the qualitative researcher.

5. This vignette is fictitious.

6. This vignette is fictitious.

## Further Reading

### Introductions to Qualitative Research

Bogdan, R. C., & Biklen, S. K. (1998). *Qualitative research for education: An introduction to theory and methods* (3rd ed.). Boston: Allyn & Bacon.

Eisner, E. W. (1991). *The enlightened eye: Qualitative inquiry and the enhancement of educational practice.* New York: Macmillan.

Glesne, C., & Peshkin, A. (1992). *Becoming qualitative researchers: An introduction.* White Plains, NY: Longman.

Lincoln, Y. S., & Guba, E. G. (1985). *Naturalistic inquiry.* Beverly Hills, CA: Sage.

Rossman, G. B., & Rallis, S. F. (1998). *Learning in the field: An introduction to qualitative research.* Thousand Oaks, CA: Sage.

Schatzman, L., & Strauss, A. L. (1973). *Field research: Strategies for a natural sociology.* Englewood Cliffs, NJ: Prentice Hall.

Schwartz, H., & Jacobs, J. (1979). *Qualitative sociology: A method to the madness.* New York: Free Press.

Strauss, A., & Corbin, J. (1990). *Basics of qualitative research.* Newbury Park, CA: Sage.

Taylor, J. J., & Bogdan, R. (1984). *An introduction to qualitative research: The search for meanings* (2nd ed.). New York: John Wiley.

### On Narrative Analysis

Hatch, J. A., & Wisniewski, R. (Eds.). (1995). *Life history and narrative.* London: Falmer.

Josselson, R. (Ed.). (1996). *Ethics and process in the narrative study of lives.* Thousand Oaks, CA: Sage.

Josselson, R., & Lieblich, A. (Eds.). (1993). *The narrative study of lives.* Newbury Park, CA: Sage.

Riessman, C. (1993). *Narrative analysis.* Newbury Park, CA: Sage.

### On Action Research

Heron, J. (1996). *Co-operative inquiry: Research into the human condition.* Thousand Oaks, CA: Sage.

Hollingsworth, S. (Ed.). (1997). *International action research: A casebook for educational reform.* London: Falmer.

Stringer, E. T. (1996). *Action research: A handbook for practitioners.* Thousand Oaks, CA: Sage.

### On Critical Ethnography

Carspecken, P. F. (1996). *Critical ethnography in educational research: A theoretical and practical guide.* New York: Routledge.

Gitlin, A. (Ed.). (1994). *Power and method: Political activism and educational research.* New York: Routledge.

Marcus, G., & Fischer, M. (1986). *Anthropology as cultural critique: An experimental moment in the human sciences.* Chicago: University of Chicago Press.

Morrow, R. A., with D. D. Brown. (1994). *Critical theory and methodology.* Thousand Oaks, CA: Sage.

### On Participatory Action Research

Maguire, P. (1987). *Doing participatory research: A feminist approach.* Amherst, MA: Center for International Education.

McTaggart, R. (Ed.). (1997). *Participatory action research: International contexts and consequences.* Albany: State University of New York Press.

Park, P., Brydon-Miller, M., Hall, B., & Jackson, T. (Eds.). (1993). *Voices of change: Participatory research in the United States and Canada.* Ontario, Canada: Ontario Institute for Studies in Education Press.

Whyte, W. F. (Ed.). (1991). *Participatory action research.* Newbury Park, CA: Sage.

### On Feminist Research

Harding, S. (Ed.). (1987). *Feminism and methodology.* Bloomington: Indiana University Press.

Lather, P. (1991). *Getting smart: Feminist research and pedagogy with/in the postmodern.* New York: Routledge.

Marshall, C. (1997). Dismantling and reconstructing policy analysis. In C. Marshall (Ed.), *Feminist critical policy analysis: A perspective from primary and secondary schooling* (Vol. 1, pp. 1-39). London: Falmer.

Nielson, J. (Ed.). (1990). *Feminist research methods: Exemplary readings in the social sciences.* Boulder, CO: Westview.

# 2

# The "What" of the Study

## BUILDING THE CONCEPTUAL FRAMEWORK

---

What is research? What is a research proposal? How do the two relate to each other? For the social scientist or researcher in applied fields, research is a process of trying to gain a better understanding of the complexities of human experience and, in some genres of research, to take action based on that understanding. Through systematic and sometimes collaborative strategies, the researcher gathers information about actions and interactions, reflects on their meaning, arrives at and evaluates conclusions, and eventually puts forward an interpretation, most frequently in written form. Quite unlike its pristine and logical presentation in journal articles—"the reconstructed logic of science" (Kaplan, 1964)—real research is often confusing, messy, intensely frustrating, and fundamentally nonlinear. In critiquing the way journal articles display research as a supremely sequential and objective endeavor, Bargar and Duncan (1982) describe how, "through such highly standardized reporting practices, scientists inadvertently hide from view the real inner drama of their work, with its intuitive base, its halting time-line, and its extensive recycling of concepts and perspectives" (p. 2).

The researcher begins with interesting, curious, or anomalous phenomena that he observes, discovers, or stumbles across. Not unlike the detective work of Sherlock Holmes or the best traditions in investigative reporting, research seeks to explain, describe, or explore the phenomenon chosen for study. Emancipatory genres, such as those represented by some critical, feminist, or postmodern work, also make explicit their intent to act to change oppressive circumstances. The research proposal is *a plan for engaging in systematic inquiry* to bring about a better understanding of the phenomenon and, increasingly, to change problematic social circumstances. As discussed in Chapter 1, the finished proposal should demonstrate that (a) the research is worth doing, (b) the researcher is competent to conduct the study, and (c) the study is carefully planned and can be executed successfully.

A proposal for the conduct of any research represents *decisions* the researcher has made that a particular theoretical framework, design, and methodology will generate data appropriate for responding to the research questions. These decisions emerge through intuition, complex reasoning, and weighing a number of possible research questions, possible conceptual frameworks, and alternative designs and strategies for gathering data. Throughout, the researcher considers the should-do-ability, do-ability, and want-to-do-ability of the proposed project (discussed in Chapter 1). This is the complex, dialectic process of designing a qualitative study. This chapter demonstrates how, in qualitative design, you are deciding among possible research questions, frameworks, approaches, sites, and data collection methods. Building the research proposal demands that the researcher consider all elements of the proposal *at the same time.* But how to begin? This is often the most challenging aspect of developing a solid proposal.

## Sections of the Proposal

Proposals for qualitative research vary in format but typically include the following three sections: (a) *the introduction,* which includes an overview of the proposal, a discussion of the topic or focus of the inquiry and the general research questions, the study's purpose and potential significance, and its limitations; (b) *a discussion of related literature,* which situates the study in the ongoing discourse about the topic and develops the specific intellectual traditions to which the study links; and (c) *the research design and methods,* which details the overall design, the site or population of interest, the specific methods for gathering data, a preliminary discussion of strategies for analyzing the data, how the study's trustworthiness will be ensured, the personal biography of the researcher, and ethical and political issues that may arise in the conduct of the study. In all research, these sections are interrelated, each one building on the others. These sections are listed in Table 2.1. In qualitative inquiry, the proposal should reserve some flexibility in research questions and design because these are likely to change during the research process. The next section provides some strategies for building a clear conceptual framework while retaining the flexibility to allow the unanticipated to emerge.

## Building the Conceptual Framework: Topic, Purpose, and Significance

The purposes of this section of the proposal are (a) to describe the substantive focus of the research—the topic—and its purpose; (b) to frame it in larger theoretical, policy, social, or practical domains and thereby develop its significance; (c) to pose initial research questions; (d) to forecast the literature to be discussed in the review of related literature; and (e) to discuss the limitations of the study. The proposal writer should organize the information so that a reader can clearly ascertain the essence of the research study. This section, along with the review of related literature, forms the conceptual framework of the study and tells the reader the study's substantive focus and purpose. The design section then describes how the study will be conducted and displays the writer's ability to conduct the study.

Although separated into discrete sections through convention, the narrative of the first two sections—the introduction and the review of related literature—is derived from a thorough familiarity with literature on relevant theory, empirical studies, reviews of research, and informed essays by knowledgeable experts. A careful reading of related literature serves two purposes. First, it establishes evidence for the significance of the study for practice and policy and as a contribution to the ongoing discourse about the topic (often referred to as contributing to "knowledge"). Second, it identifies the important intellectual traditions that guide the study, thereby developing a conceptual framework and refining an important and viable research question.

**Table 2.1  Sections of a Qualitative Research Proposal**

---

**Introduction**
  Overview
  Topic and purpose
  Potential significance
  Framework and general research questions
  Limitations
**Review of Related Literature**
  Theoretical traditions
  Essays by informed experts
  Related research
**Design and Methodology**
  Overall approach and rationale
  Site or population selection
  Data-gathering methods
  Data analysis procedures
  Trustworthiness
  Personal biography
  Ethical and political considerations
**Appendixes**

---

Because of the interrelatedness of the sections and because writing is a developmental, recursive task, the writer may find it necessary to rewrite the research questions or problem statement after reviewing the literature or to refocus the significance after the research design is developed. Bargar and Duncan's (1982) description of "extensive recycling of concepts and perspectives" (p. 2), quoted earlier, captures this dialectic process. Our advice is that the writer be sensitive to the need for change and flexibility and not rush to closure too soon. Sound ideas for research may come in a moment of inspiration, but the hard work comes next as the idea, the intellectual traditions that surround the idea, and the methods for exploring it are developed, refined, and polished.

### Overview

The first section of the proposal provides an overview of the study for the reader. It introduces the topic or problem and purpose of the study, the general research questions, and design of the study. This section should be crisply written, engage the reader's interest, and forecast the sections to follow. First, the topic or problem that the study will address is introduced, linking this to practice, policy, social issues, and/or theory, and forecasting the study's significance. Next, the broad areas of theory and related research to be discussed in the literature review are outlined. Then the design of the study is sketched in which the particular approach, major data collection techniques, and unique features of the design are noted. Finally, the introduction provides a transition to a more detailed discussion of the topic, the study's significance, and the research questions.

## The Topic

In qualitative inquiry, initial curiosities for research often come from real-world observations, emerging from the interplay of the researcher's direct experience, tacit theories, political commitments, interests in practice, and growing scholarly interests. At other times, the topic of interest derives from theoretical traditions and their attendant empirical research. Beginning researchers should examine reviews of literature found in journals specifically committed to publishing extensive review articles (e.g., *Review of Educational Research*), peruse policy-oriented publications to learn about current or emerging issues in their fields, and talk with experts for their judgments about crucial issues. They might also reflect on the intersection of their personal, professional, and political interests to ascertain what particular topics or issues capture their imaginations.

Figure 2.1 provides a schematic description of the dialectic relationship between theory, practice, research questions, and personal experience. We call this the *cycle of inquiry*; the figure suggests that a research project may begin at any point in this complex process. For example, as a focus for the study emerges (the general topic), possible research questions, potential sites, and individuals or groups to invite to participate in the research may be considered. Imagining potential sites or groups of people to work with may, in turn, reshape the focus of the study. Thinking about sites or people for the study also encourages the researcher to think about her role in the setting and possible strategies for gathering data. Alternatively, the researcher may know of a site where intriguing issues of practice capture her imagination. Thinking about this site and the issues and people in it will foster analysis about what research questions are likely to be significant for practice. The research questions then shape decisions about gathering data. Developing the research

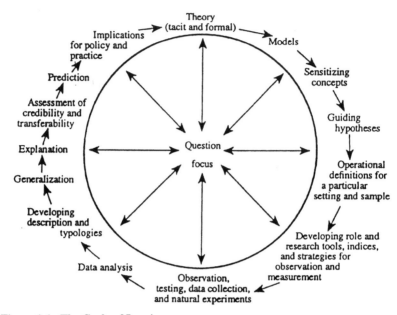

**Figure 2.1. The Cycle of Inquiry**

project proceeds dialectically as possible research focuses, questions, sites, and strategies for gathering data are considered.

Crabtree and Miller (1992) offer refinements of this generic cycle of inquiry. They argue that the process of much qualitative research can be captured by "Shiva's circle of constructivist inquiry" (p. 10)—Shiva is the Hindu god of dance and death (see Figure 2.2). The researcher enters this cycle of interpretation with exquisite sensitivity to context, seeking no ultimate truths. She must be faithful to the dance, but she also stands apart from it, discovering and interpreting the "symbolic communication and meaning . . . that helps us maintain cultural life" (p. 10). A more radical inquiry process is captured in Figure 2.3, which expresses critical, feminist, and some postmodern perspectives. These two models depict the researcher looking critically at experience and the larger social forces that shape it. She searches for expressions of domination, oppression, and power in daily life. Her goal is to unmask this "false consciousness" and create "a more empowered and emancipated consciousness by reducing the illusions" of experience (pp. 10-11). Figures 2.2 and 2.3 provide alternative conceptualizations of the cycle of inquiry; note, however, that each entails question posing, design, data collection, analysis, and interpretation.

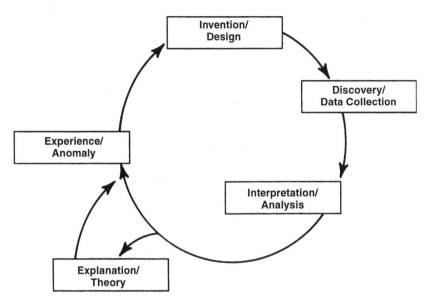

**Figure 2.2. Shiva's Circle of Constructivist Inquiry**

SOURCE: Crabtree and Miller (1992, p. 10). Reprinted by permission.
NOTE: Hx = hypotheses.

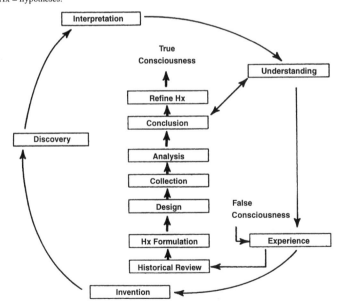

**Figure 2.3. Global Eye of Critical/Ecological Inquiry**

SOURCE: Crabtree and Miller (1992, p. 11). Reprinted by permission.

Especially in applied fields, such as management, nursing, community development, education, and clinical psychology, a strong autobiographical element often drives the research interest. For example, a doctoral student in family counseling psychology studied bereaved mothers because of her own experience with the loss of a teenaged son (Oliver, 1990). A student in social psychology, deeply committed to the protection of the environment, studied environmental attitudes from an adult development theoretical perspective (Greenwald, 1992). A student in organizational development investigated male and female physicians' espoused moral principles of care and justice in compensation issues, as a way of exploring Gilligan's (1982b) theory, because of her deep commitment to ethical practice (Cormier, 1993). A student in international development education studied Indonesian farmers' views on land use because of her political commitment to indigenous peoples (Campbell-Nelson, 1997).

The qualitative researcher's challenge is to demonstrate that this personal interest will not bias the study. A sensitive awareness of the methodological literature about *the self* in conducting inquiry, interpreting data, and constructing the final narrative helps, as does knowledge of the epistemological debate about what constitutes knowledge and knowledge claims, especially the critique of power and dominance in traditional research (see the discussion in Chapter 1 about critical ethnography, feminist research, action research, and postmodern perspectives). If direct experience stimulates the initial curiosity, moreover, the researcher needs to link that curiosity to general research questions. The large end of the conceptual funnel, if you will, contains the general, or "grand tour," questions that the study will explore; the small end depicts the specific focus for the proposed study.

Figure 2.4 illustrates this funnel metaphor, drawing from the study by Benbow (1994) about the development of commitment to social action. The large end of the funnel represents the general conceptual focus—the issue of social activism and its role in ameliorating oppressive circumstances. Midway down the funnel, the focus narrows to a concern with individuals who have demonstrated and lived an intense commitment to social causes. An alternative choice at this point would have been to focus on social movements as group phenomena rather than on individuals whose lived experiences embody social consciousness. The small end of the conceptual funnel focuses even more closely on a research question (or set of questions) about how life experiences helped shape and develop a lifelong, intensive commitment to social activism.

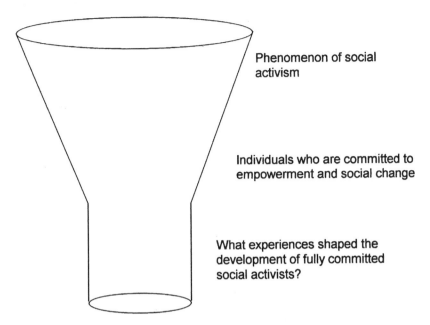

Phenomenon of social
activism

Individuals who are committed to
empowerment and social change

What experiences shaped the
development of fully committed
social activists?

**Figure 2.4. The Conceptual Funnel**

People develop personal theories (theories-in-use or tacit theories; Argyris
& Schön, 1974) about events as ways of reducing ambiguity and explaining
paradox. When they decide to conduct inquiry, however, they should be guided
by systematic considerations, such as existing theory and empirical research.
Tacit theory (one's personal understanding) and formal theory (from a literature review) help to bring the question, the curious phenomenon, or the
problematic issue into focus and raise it to a more general level. The potential
research moves from a troubling or intriguing real-world observation (e.g.,
these kids won't volunteer in class no matter how much it's rewarded!), to
personal theory (these kids care more about what other kids think than they
do about grades), to formal theory, concepts, and models from literature
(students' behavior is a function of the formal classroom expectations as
mediated by the informal expectations of the student subculture). These
coalesce to frame a focus for the study in the form of a research question:
What are the expectations of the student subculture vis-à-vis class participation?

This complex process of conceptualizing, framing, and focusing a study is
depicted in Figure 2.5. It shows the interplay of personal observation with a

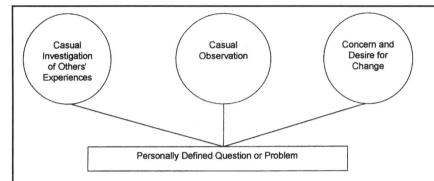

## Personal Theories, Hunches, Curiosities

How do I move from casual perturbations to systematic inquiry? What previous research, existing theoretical frames, expressions of concern, and calls for change from people affected by the problem should focus my research?

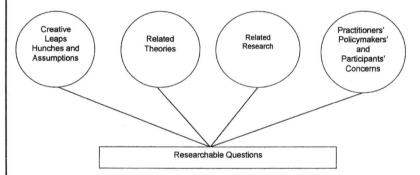

## Grounding in Social Science Literatures

*Guiding Questions and Hypotheses*

Now that the literature review has revealed an array of settings, populations, and methodological traditions used in previous research on similar questions, what is my focus? What will be the most creative and useful questions? What do I assume or guess I will see? What settings and populations can I observe and gather data from to explore these questions? What will I look at? How do I connect the concepts in the literature to behaviors and interactions in natural settings? How can I gain access? Record data? Decide whether to move to other settings or other data collection strategies?

**Figure 2.5.  Framing the Research Process**

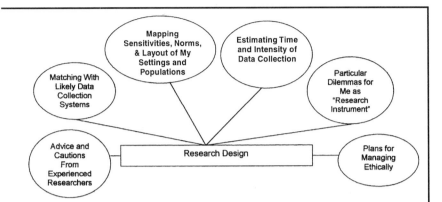

## Data Collection Management and Analysis

As I move into the actual research, what strategies will I use to store my data, move toward identifying patterns, and work systematically to ensure that I am working toward identifying useful and significant "truths."

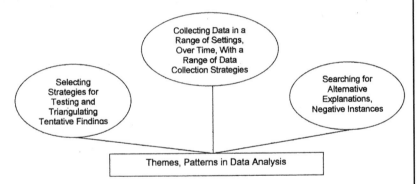

## Reporting Findings, Conclusions

What modes of reporting are ethical, useful for my career, useful for helping people? How inventive should I be? What traditions in qualitative reporting make the most sense for my purposes? How do I demonstrate to readers the transferability of my findings, the limitations, and the new research challenges uncovered by my research? Should I provide specific recommendations for change based on my research?

Reports and Publications

theoretical rationale that leads to focusing the research question and making decisions about where to go, what to look for, and how to move to real-world observations. It identifies the kinds of questions the researcher should ask at each stage. This framework is intended to be generic and, therefore, transferrable to research in an urban neighborhood, with a legislative body, in a rural village in West Timor, Indonesia, or with newly arrived immigrant groups.

This early conceptualization work is the most difficult and intellectually rigorous of the entire process of proposal writing. It is messy and dialectic, as alternative frames (scholarly traditions) are examined for their power to illuminate and sharpen the research focus. As noted earlier, exploring possible designs and strategies for gathering data also enters into this initial process. The researcher must let go of topics and captivating questions as he fine-tunes and focuses the study to ensure its do-ability. Although this entails loss, it bounds the study and protects the researcher from impractical ventures.

The role of intuition in this phase of the research process cannot be underestimated. Studies of eminent scientists reveal the central role of creative insight—intuition—in their thought processes (Hoffman, 1972; Libby, 1922; Mooney, 1951). By allowing ideas to incubate and through maintaining a healthy respect for the mind's capacity to reorganize and reconstruct, the researcher finds that richer research questions evolve. This observation is not intended to devalue the analytic process but, instead, to give the creative act its proper due. Bargar and Duncan (1982) note that research is a process "that religiously uses logical analysis as a critical tool in the *refinement* of ideas, but which often begins at a very different place, where imagery, metaphor and analogy, intuitive hunches, kinesthetic feeling states, and even dreams and dream-like states are prepotent" (p. 3).

Initial insights and the recycling of concepts begin the process of bounding and framing the research by defining the larger theoretical, policy, or social problem or issue of practice that the study will address. This complex thinking also begins to establish the study's parameters (what it is and what it is *not*) and to develop the conceptual framework that will ground the study in ongoing research traditions.

*Purpose of the Study*

The researcher should also describe her intent in conducting the research— its purpose. Generally embedded in the discussion of the topic (often only a sentence or two but nonetheless important), a statement of the purpose of the

**Table 2.2  Matching Research Questions and Purpose**

| *Purpose of the Study* | *General Research Questions* |
|---|---|
| **Exploratory:** | |
| To investigate little-understood phenomena | What is happening in this social program? |
| To identify or discover important categories of meaning | What are the salient themes, patterns, or categories of meaning for participants? |
| To generate hypotheses for further research | How are these patterns linked with one another? |
| **Explanatory:** | |
| To explain the patterns related to the phenomenon in question | What events, beliefs, attitudes, or policies shape this phenomenon? |
| To identify plausible relationships shaping the phenomenon | How do these forces interact to result in the phenomenon? |
| **Descriptive:** | |
| To document and describe the phenomenon of interest | What are the salient actions, events, beliefs, attitudes, and social structures and processes occurring in this phenomenon? |
| **Emancipatory:** | |
| To create opportunities and the will to engage in social action | How do participants problematize their circumstances and take positive social action? |

study tells the reader what the results of the research are likely to accomplish. Historically, qualitative methodologists have described three major purposes for research: *to explore, explain,* or *describe* the phenomenon of interest. Synonyms for these terms could include *to understand, to develop,* or *to discover.* Many qualitative studies are descriptive and exploratory: They build rich descriptions of complex circumstances that are unexplored in the literature. Others are explicitly explanatory: These studies show relationships (frequently as perceived by the participants in the study) between events and the meaning these relationships have. These traditional discussions of purpose, however, do not mention action, advocacy, empowerment, or emancipation—the purposes often found in studies grounded in critical, feminist, or postmodern assumptions. The researcher can assert *taking action* as part of the intention of the proposed study, as in action research. He can assert *empowerment* (the goal of participatory action research) as a goal—although he can, at best, discuss how the inquiry *may* create opportunities for empowerment (see Table 2.2).

The discussion of the topic and purpose also articulates the *unit of analysis*—the level of inquiry on which the study will focus. Qualitative studies typically focus on individuals, dyads, groups, processes, or organizations. Discussing the level of inquiry helps focus subsequent decisions about data gathering.

### Significance and Potential Contributions

Convincing the reader that the study is significant and should be conducted entails building an argument that links the research to important theoretical perspectives, policy issues, concerns of practice, or persistent social issues that affect people's everyday lives. Think of the study's significance as discussing ways that the study is likely to contribute. Who might be interested in the results? With what groups might they be shared: Scholars? Policymakers? Practitioners? Members of similar groups? Individuals or groups usually silenced or marginalized? The challenge here is to situate the study as addressing a particular, important problem; defining the problem shapes the study's significance. For instance, a clinical psychologist identifies a theoretical gap in the literature about isolation and defines the topic for an ethnography of long-distance truck drivers as contributing to theory. The study may be relatively unconcerned with policy or practice; its contributions to theory are preordinate. On the other hand, a feminist sociologist frames a study of discriminatory thinking among business executives as addressing the policy and practice problems of persistent sexism in the workplace. A study of the impact of welfare reform on the lives of adult basic education learners could focus either on policy issues or on how this recurring social problem plays out in the learners' lives. Here, theoretical problems are less significant. The researcher develops the significance of the study through a definition of the problem to be addressed.

Funding opportunities often focus a question. A welfare-to-work grants program calling for a multisite evaluation of programs for the "hard to employ" provides opportunities for the researcher. It also provides policy-oriented significance. Be cautious about such opportunities, however, because policy-delineated foci may seduce the researcher into agendas serving primarily the powerful elite (Anderson, 1989; Marshall, 1997; Scheurich, 1997). Recall the discussion of explicitly ideological research in Chapter 1. For further discussion of these issues, see Smith (1988).

A study may well be able to contribute understanding and action in all four domains, but it is unlikely to contribute equally to all four; the statement of the topic should thus emphasize one particular domain. For example, a study of the integration of children with disabilities into the regular classroom could be significant for both policy and practice. Framing this study as a policy study requires that the topic be situated in national and state policy debates on special education. Alternatively, framing the study as most significant for practice would require the researcher to focus on structures supporting inclusive classrooms. Either frame is legitimate and defensible; the researcher's challenge is to argue for the study's potential contributions to the domains in which he is most interested. This, in turn, has implications for the literature review and the design of the study.

### Significance for Theory

The discussion of the study's significance for theory is often an intellectual odyssey for the researcher that is more fully developed in the review of related literature. At this point in the proposal, the researcher should outline the project's potential contribution to fundamental knowledge by describing how the study fits into theoretical traditions in the social sciences or applied fields in ways that will be new, insightful, or creative. The significance statement should show how the study will contribute to research traditions or foundational literatures in new ways.

Often, the proposal identifies gaps in the literature to which the study will contribute. If the research is in an area for which theory is well developed, the study may be a significant test or expansion of the theory. The researcher may use concepts developed by previous researchers and formulate questions similar to those used in previous research. Data collection, however, may be in a different setting, with a different group, and certainly at a different time. Thus, the results of the research will constitute an extension of theory that will expand the generalizations or more finely tune theoretical propositions. The contribution of such research is the expansion of previous theory. For example, the study cited earlier by Cormier (1993) contributed primarily to theory by extending Gilligan's (1982b) notions of gendered moral reasoning to a new population—physicians.

When researchers conceptualize the focus of the study and generate the research questions, they may draw on a body of theory and related research that is different from previous research. Significance of this sort, however, generally derives from an extensive and creative review of related literature. Having developed that section of the proposal, the writer then incorporates references to and summaries of it in the significance section. This type of significance is treated fully in the next section on the review of related literature. Generally, by answering the question, How is this research important? the researcher can demonstrate the creative aspects of the work.

The development of theory takes place by incremental advances and small contributions to knowledge through well-conducted and well-conceptualized research. Most researchers use theory to guide their own work, to locate their studies in larger theoretical traditions, or to map the topography of the specific concepts they will explore in detail. In addition, some very creative research can emerge when a researcher breaks theoretical boundaries and reconceptualizes a problem or relocates the problem area. For example, Bronfenbrenner (1980) reconceptualized children's learning processes by applying the concept of *ecology* to child development theory. Weick's (1976) metaphor of schools as *loosely coupled systems* profoundly altered theoretical conceptualizations of educational organizations. Often we follow a theoretical pragmatism, being "shamelessly eclectic" in the creative application of concepts from one discipline to another (Rossman & Wilson, 1994).

Significance for Policy

The significance of a study for policy can be developed by discussing formal policy development in that area and presenting data that show how often the problem occurs and how costly it can be. For example, to demonstrate the significance of a study of the careers of women faculty, the researcher could present statistics documenting persistently lower salaries for women than men at comparable ranks; this is the problem that the study will address. The study's potential contributions for university compensation policies could then be spelled out. Enrollment data depicting increasing adult participation in off-campus degree programs would establish that this is an increasing trend in university enrollments and therefore worthy of inquiry. Contributions to university degree program policy could then be articulated. In another example, the researcher could describe recent changes in welfare law and discuss how this reform was developed with little regard for those most affected—the problem the study will address. Potential contributions of the study to further reform of welfare law could then be described. In developing the topic and how the study might contribute to policy in that area, the researcher would demonstrate that the general topic is one of significant proportions that should be studied systematically.

A study's importance can also be argued through summaries of the writings of policymakers and informed experts who identify the topic as important and call for research pursuing the general questions. Both statistical presentations of incidence and persistence of the problem and calls for research by experts demonstrate that the study addresses an important topic, one of concern to policymakers in that area. In applied fields such as education, health policy, management, regional planning, and clinical psychology, for example, demonstrating a study's significance to policy—whether international, national, state, regional, or institutional—may be especially important.

### Significance for Practice

Situating a study as significant for practice follows the same logic as developing significance for policy. The argument here should rely on a discussion of the concerns or problems articulated in the literature. This will involve citing experts, prior research, and summarizing incidence data. Recall the preceding discussion of a study about the inclusion of children with disabilities. Should the researcher want this study to focus on issues of practice, she would discuss the literature detailing the concerns of teachers about meeting the needs of children with disabilities in their classrooms. The study's potential contributions, then, would be to improve teachers' classroom practice. Shadduck-Hernandez's (1997) proposal for a study exploring how participation in community service classes affects immigrant and refugee college students' sense of ethnic identity summarized incidence data on the increasing enrollment of these students and the paucity of culturally relevant experiences the college curriculum offered them. She then detailed the study's potential contributions to pedagogical practice in university classrooms.

### Significance for Social Issues and Action

Finally, a study may be significant for its detailed description of life circumstances that express particular social issues. The contribution of such a study may not be to try to influence policy, contribute to scholarly literature, or improve practice; it might be to illuminate the lived experiences of interest by providing rich description and to foster taking action. Action research and participatory action research genres stipulate *taking action* as central to their work. In these cases, researchers should argue that the proposed inquiry and its attendant action will likely be valuable to those who participate, as well as to others committed to the issue. The challenge here is to identify how and in what ways.

Maguire's (1987) study with battered women was a participatory action research project. Her study's primary contributions were not intended to be to scholarly traditions, policy, or practice per se; rather, they were for the women involved in the work and for others committed to alleviating the abuse of women. The work was important because it focused on a major social issue. Lather and Smithies's (1997) study, collaborating with HIV-positive women, invites the reader to enter into the women's lives so as to create new connections and the possibilities for action.

In sum, through a discussion of relevant literature, this section articulates the topic to be studied and argues that further investigation of this problem has the potential to contribute to scholarship, policy, practice, or a better understanding of recurring social issues. This section defines who is likely to have an interest in this topic and therefore how and in what ways the study will contribute.

Of course, researchers preparing proposals for funding should adjust their statements about significance to the needs and priorities of the funding agencies. The foundation that takes pride in funding action projects or interventions will want to see statements about how the proposed research will directly help people or change a problematic situation. On the other hand, when seeking funds from an agency with goals of expanding knowledge and theory (e.g., the National Science Foundation), the researcher should emphasize the undeveloped or unsolved theoretical puzzles to be addressed to demonstrate the significance of the research.

## Posing Research Questions

The qualitative approach to research is uniquely suited to uncovering the unexpected and exploring new avenues. This demands flexibility in the proposal so that data gathering can respond to increasingly refined research questions. Herein lies a dilemma, however. The proposal should be sufficiently clear both in research questions and design so that the reader can evaluate its do-ability; on the other hand, the proposal should reserve the flexibility that is the hallmark of qualitative methods. This suggests that the research questions should be general enough to permit exploration but focused enough to delimit the study. Not an easy task.

Focusing the study and posing general research questions are best addressed in a developmental manner, relying on discussions of related literature to help frame and refine the specific topic. Often, the primary research goal is to discover those very questions that are most probing and insightful. Most likely, the relevant concepts will be developed during the research process, but the research proposal must suggest themes, based on knowledge of the literature.

Initial questions should be linked to the problem and significance and should forecast the literature to be reviewed in the next section. Questions may be theoretical ones, which can be researched in a number of different sites or with different samples. Or they may be focused on a particular population or class of individuals; these too can be studied in various places. Finally, the questions may be site specific because of the uniqueness of a specific program or organization. The example cited earlier in this chapter of the study of physicians' moral constructions of compensation issues (Cormier, 1993) could have been conducted in any setting that had physicians and conflict; the theoretical interest driving the research was not linked to a particular organization. A study of an exemplary sex education program, however, can be studied only at that site because the problem identified is one of practice. Thus, the questions posed are shaped by the identified problem and, in turn, constrain the design of the study.

Examples of *theoretical questions* include the following:

- How does play affect reading readiness? Through what cognitive and affective process? Do children who take certain roles—for example, play leadership roles—learn faster? If so, what makes the difference?

- How does the sponsor-protégé socialization process function in professional careers? Does it work differently for women? For minorities? What processes are operating?

Questions focused on *particular populations* could include these:

- How do neurosurgeons learn to cope with the realities that they hold the lives of people in their hands and that many of their patients die?

- What happens to women who enter elite MBA programs? What are their career paths?

- What is the life of the long-distance truck driver like?

- How do school superintendents manage relations with school board members? What influence processes do they use?

- What happens to change-agent teachers during their careers? Do organizational socialization processes change or eliminate them? Do they burn out early in their careers?

Finally, *site-specific* research questions might take the following form:

- Why is the sex education program working well in this school but not in the others? What is special about the people? The plan? The support? the context?

- How do the school-parent community relations of an elite private school differ from those in the neighboring public school? How are the differences connected with differences in educational philosophies and outcomes?

- What are the ways in which lobbying groups influence pollution control policy in the Massachusetts legislature?

- Why is there a discrepancy in the perceptions of the efficacy of affirmative action policy between university officials and groups of students of color at the University of North Carolina? What explains the discrepancy?

The above are examples of typical initial questions developed in the proposal. They serve as boundaries around the study without unduly constraining it. The questions focus on interactions and processes in sociocultural systems and in organizations and thus link to important research literature and theory, but they are grounded in everyday realities. The goal of this section of the proposal is to explicate the questions, thereby further focusing the study, and to forecast the literature to be discussed in the next section. The following vignette shows early development of an introductory statement for a proposal for a pilot study.

* * * * *

### Vignette 3

### An Initial Statement

Joseph-Collins (1997) was deeply interested in the lack of African Americans enrolling in and successfully completing college. She was particularly concerned about African American males. In developing a proposal for a pilot study for her dissertation, she developed the following discussion of the focus of the study, its purpose, the preliminary research questions, potential significance, and design:

Perspectives on the Persistence of African American Males
in Higher Education

Martin Carnoy (1995) contends that African Americans, especially African
American males, are not reaping the benefits of higher education. He cites
various studies that reveal the fact that African American males are more
likely to drop out of college than African American females and people
from other racial groups. According to Carnoy, the reasons for low enrollment include "hostile environments" on campus that lessen the incentives
for African American males to attend and graduate from college, "a century
of subordination and separation," "inherent cultural incompatibility with
white middle-class values," and the idea that African American males are
"caught up in cycles of poverty, violence, and despair" (pp. 66-67). Quali-
tatively, how can institutions of higher education support the inclusion of
African American males?

This study will focus on deepening our understanding about the experience
of African American males students in higher education so that policymakers, program developers, and teachers will be more conscious of the
factors that can positively influence the persistence of African American
males. My hope is that if people are equipped with knowledge and goodwill
they will act to help put an end to the disparities.

The overall questions that will guide the research are as follows:

1. What are some of the motivational factors that encourage African
   American males to attend and graduate from college?
2. What type of conditions within higher education can help to stimulate and
   nurture the persistence of African American males in college?
3. What other conditions (outside of higher education) might contribute to the
   success of African American males in higher education?

My general approach to this research study will be to develop greater
understanding about this issue through an in-depth, phenomenological case
study involving an African American male college student who has aspirations
of obtaining an advanced degree. The research design includes a series of four
1.5-hour videotaped interviews and at least 5 hours of classroom and campus
observations. A participant for the study has been identified and an agreement
has been reached for a collaborative approach to the study.

* * * * *

As depicted in this vignette, Joseph-Collins has introduced the topic—persistence of African American males in college—given a brief discussion of purpose, posed the preliminary general research questions, forecast the significance, and stipulated the overall design and unit of analysis. This pilot study was small, but its logic holds for larger studies.

Following are two examples of other introductory paragraphs. Each states the topic, discusses the purpose, stipulates the unit of analysis, and forecasts the study's significance:[1]

> Children with physical handicaps have unique perceptions about their "bodiedness." Grounded in phenomenological inquiry, this study will explore and describe the deep inner meaning of bodiedness for five children. The study will result in rich description through stories of these children's relationships with sports. The central concept of bodiedness will be explicated through the children's words. Those working with children with physical handicaps, as well as policymakers framing programs that affect them, will find the study of interest.

> The Neighborhood Arts Center in Orange, Massachusetts, is an award-winning program that serves all members of its community. The purpose of this study is to explain the success of this program in bringing arts to members of this low-income community. The study will use an ethnographic design, seeking detailed explanations of the program's success. The study will help decision makers and funders design similar programs that involve groups historically underrepresented in the arts.

* * * * *

## Limitations of the Study

No proposed research project is without limitations; there is no such thing as a perfectly designed study. As Patton (1990) notes, "There are no perfect research designs. There are always trade-offs" (p. 162). A discussion of the study's limitations demonstrates that the researcher understands this reality—that she will make no overweening claims about generalizability or conclusiveness relative to what she has learned.

Limitations derive from the conceptual framework and the study's design. A discussion of these limitations early on in the proposal reminds the reader what the study is and is *not*—its boundaries—and how its results can and *cannot* contribute to understanding. As discussed throughout this chapter, framing the study in specific research and theoretical traditions places limits on the research. A study of land use in Indonesia, for example, could be situated in development economics; reminding the reader that the study is framed this way helps allay criticism. The overall design, moreover, indicates how broadly applicable the study may be. Although no qualitative studies are generalizable in the statistical sense, their findings may be transferable. A discussion of these considerations reminds the reader that the study is bounded and situated in a specific context. The reader, then, can make decisions about its usefulness for other settings.

## Review of Related Literature

A thoughtful and insightful discussion of related literature builds a logical framework for the research that sets it within a tradition of inquiry and a context of related studies. The literature review serves four broad functions. First, it demonstrates the underlying assumptions behind the general research questions. If possible, it should display the research paradigm that undergirds the study and describe the assumptions and values the researcher brings to the research enterprise. Second, it demonstrates that the researcher is knowledgeable about related research and the intellectual traditions that surround and support the study. Third, it shows that the researcher has identified some gaps in previous research and that the proposed study will fill a demonstrated need. Finally, the review refines and redefines the research questions by embedding those questions in larger empirical traditions.

As the researcher conceptualizes the research problem, he locates it in a tradition of theory and related research. Initially, this may be an intuitive locating, chosen because of the underlying assumptions, how the researcher sees the world, and how he sees the research questions fitting in. As the researcher explores the literature, however, he should identify and state those assumptions in a framework of theory. This framework could be child development theory, organizational theory, learning theory, adult socialization theory, or whatever body of theory is appropriate. This section of the literature review provides the framework for the research and identifies the area of knowledge that the study is intended to expand.

The next portion of the review of literature should, quite literally, review and critique previous research that relates to the general research question.

This critical review should lead to a more precise problem statement or refined questions because it demonstrates the specific area that has not yet been adequately explored or it shows that a different design would be more appropriate. If a major aspect of the significance of the study arises from a reconceptualization of the topic, this is where that should be developed fully. Cooper (1988) provides a discussion of the focus, goal, perspective, coverage, organization, and audience for a literature review. An extended example of the integration and dovetailing of the significance and the review sections of the proposal is described in Vignette 4. Look for the ways the literature review led Marshall (1979, 1981, 1985b) to find new possibilities for pursuing the research questions.

* * * * *

## *Vignette 4*

### *Building Significance Through the Literature*

When Marshall was researching the general problem of women's unequal representation in school administration careers, she first reviewed the work of previous researchers. Many researchers before her had conducted surveys to identify the attributes, the positions, and the percentages of women in school administration. A few researchers had identified patterns of discrimination.

In a significant departure from this tradition, Marshall reconceptualized the problem. She looked at it as a problem in the area of adult socialization and looked to career socialization theory. From a review of this body of theory and related empirical research on the school administrative career, including recruitment, training, and selection processes, and on women in jobs and careers, Marshall framed a new question. She asked, "What is the career socialization process for women in school administration? What is the process through which women make career decisions, acquire training and supports, overcome obstacles, and move up in the hierarchy?"

Marshall already knew from previous research that there was discrimination and that women administrators were different from women in other roles. With a background knowledge of organizational theory emphasizing the influence of organizational norms and the power of informal processes, she created a new research question and a different research design. The literature review, therefore, determined the relevant concepts (i.e., norms, informal training) and the tentative guiding hypotheses. The need to identify how this research would be different from previous research focused this literature review. And from this review came the theoretical framework, key concepts, findings from previous research that would guide the new research, and a major aspect of the study's significance. The flow from theory to concepts to tentative hypotheses, moreover, helped focus the research questions.

Once the overall question was identified, the choice of qualitative methods was logical because this question required the exploration of a process not yet identified and not yet encompassed in theory. The research had to build in openness to the unexpected, to new findings, and it had to retain a flexible design that fostered the exploration of nuances of meaning in a complex, tacit process.

This reconceptualization came from asking the significance question: Who cares about this research? The question encouraged a review of previous research that demonstrated how other research had already answered many questions. It showed that women were as competent as men in school administration. But a critical review of this literature argued that this previous research had asked different questions. Marshall could assert that her study would be significant because it would focus on describing a process about which previous research had only guessed. The new research would add to theory by exploring career socialization of women in a profession generally dominated by men. It would also identify the relevant social, psychological, and organizational variables that are part of women's career socialization. This established the significance of the research by showing how it would add to knowledge.

The literature review also established the significance of the research for practice and policy with an overview of the issues of affirmative action and equity concerns. Thus, the research question, literature review, and research design were all tied in with the significance question. Responding to this question demanded a demonstration that this was an area of knowledge and practice that needed exploration. To ensure exploration, qualitative methods were the most appropriate for the conduct of the study.

\* \* \* \* \*

As the preceding vignette shows, the literature review can identify established knowledge and, more important, develop significance, new questions, and often turn old questions around. This "initiating function" (Rossman & Wilson, 1994) of the literature review can be quite creative. This review, moreover, provides the intellectual glue for the entire proposal, demonstrating the sections' conceptual relatedness. The researcher cannot write about the study's significance without knowledge of the literature. Similarly, she cannot describe the design without a discussion of the general research topic. The dissertation proposal is divided into sections because of tradition and convention; there is no magic to these divisions. To organize complex topics and to address the three critical questions posed at the beginning, however, the structure provided here is recommended. Another vignette illustrates how the conceptualization of a study can be creative and exciting, as the researcher forges links among historically disparate literatures.

* * * * *

### Vignette 5

### Creative Review of the Literature

When research questions explore new territory, previous literature and theory may be inadequate for constructing frameworks for the study. A case in point is that of Christman (1987), a graduate student in educational administration who searched the literature for a way to frame her study of women returning to graduate school.

Christman's forays into the literature on returning women students and her interaction with faculty and colleagues suggested a number of relevant and provocative questions for her research. Previous studies identified and described demographics about returning women and evaluated the effectiveness of support programs for these women. Many of these studies employed survey or quasi-experimental research designs focused on outcomes and/or products. It became clear that previous research failed to conceptualize the problem in terms of process. With an emphasis on experience, the meaning of experience, and development over time, a process conceptualization placed the study in the theoretical domains of adult socialization. The goal of the research then became the description and analysis of contexts, interactions, and processes.

Continuing to examine the graduate school experience of returning women students, Christman believed that placement of this experience within the context of psychosocial development would illuminate its meaning for the participant. Indeed, recent research had suggested a direct link between a woman's life stage and her understanding of her educational experience.

A curiosity about women's management of two domains—expressive/relational/domestic and instrumental/public/work—during the child-rearing years provided Christman with another set of questions about returning women students' experience. Piqued originally by Friedan's (1981) *The Second Stage,* this curiosity was then reinforced by the work of a growing number of social scientists who have called for research that explores the dynamic interaction of these domains (Giele, 1982; Kanter, 1977; Piotrkowski, 1979; Smelser & Erikson, 1980). Such interaction is complex. In some instances, the two domains may merge so completely as to render the distinction between the two largely artificial. At the same time, the construct of overlapping domains seemed useful in conceptualizing the study.

Christman quoted Kanter (1977) to describe the interplay among field data, literature, and the researcher's self-reflection:

> The other important base for this study should not be neglected. This was, of course, an extensive review of the sociological, social psychological, psychological, and organizational behavior literatures. I considered this a part of the study critical to its success. I worked back and forth between the literature and the field. I formulated hypotheses and questions from the literature, and I could test the generalizability of my field observations through the literature review. With C. Wright Mills I believe that reading can also be a valid form of research. (p. 298)

That no single strand of theoretical or empirical literature encompassed the entirety of her research questions was clear from the outset. Literature on returning women graduate students focused on the evaluation of programs designed to overcome obstacles. Literature acknowledging the interface of love and work was just emerging. With this emergence came the overthrow of the functionalists' assumptions that the institutions of family and workplace were divided into emotional and geographical units that were specialized in their separate activities, without mutual interference (Pleck, 1976, p. 179).

The relatively recent attention given to the developmental nature of adulthood by social psychology focused primarily on the life stages of men.

Critiques by Gilligan (1982a, 1982b) and Chodorow (1978) indicated that
the values and dreams of the women involved in Christman's study would
probably differ from those of men. Socialization theory pointed to role acquisition, the development of commitment to a profession, and the impact
of formal and informal structures in graduate school that affect those being
socialized in different ways.

Although Christman's literature review did not precisely set her research
question within a particular framework, it did expose missing areas and the
questions raised by existing literature. It also underscored her work as
research into unexplored territory that promised to identify new ways of
connecting previous knowledge to new grounded theory.

* * * * *

Vignette 5 shows a creative blending of several strands of literature for
framing the research. The integration of literatures helped shape a research focus
that was theoretical in interest yet could help inform policy at the organizational
level. Broad reading and knowledge of sociological role theory, adult development, organizational structures and processes, and feminist theory provided a
rich background for this creative synthesis. Rather than narrowly constructing
the study to focus on only one of the above topics, the author searched widely
for illuminating constructs from other disciplines. Such work, although at times
tedious, confusing, and ambiguous, enhances the research to follow and demonstrates that the researcher has engaged in significant intellectual work already.

Another example of integrative literature reviews comes from the proposal
for a study of the decision process of a major research university to adopt a
multimillion dollar information system (Alvarez, 1998). In developing the
conceptual framework for her study, Alvarez (1998) integrated innovation
theory and institutional theory, arguing that neither theoretical tradition with
its attendant research could adequately explain the adoption process. Excerpts
from her proposal are presented in Vignette 6.

* * * * *

## Vignette 6

### Integrating Theoretical Perspectives

Why and how do organizations evaluate, adopt, and implement innovations? An innovation is considered any idea, practice, or material artifact

perceived to be new by the adopting organization or individual (Zaltman, Duncan, & Holbeck, 1973). The question is especially relevant for information technology innovations. As organizations confront new information technologies in an atmosphere of uncertainty, they are forced to make very expensive and long-term decisions with far too little information about the product's benefits, long-term viability, and potential fit with the organization.

Much of the scholarly research [on innovation adoption] . . . is informed by innovation theory (Zaltman et al., 1973). . . . Innovation theory provides insightful explanations of relationships among task, technology, individual and work outputs to explain the successful adoption and implementation of technology. Most studies define, or operationalize, successful adoption as amount or level of technology use. Accordingly, many of the studies seek to discover independent variables, or factors, that tend to influence technology use, including the adopter's characteristics or the innovation's characteristics (cf. Kwon & Zmud, 1987). . . . Generally speaking, these studies draw on a perspective that is concerned with maximizing the use of technology and assume, implicitly at least, that adoption will enhance work activities and outputs.

Yet while this research has provided much in the way of understanding why individuals or organizations adopt a new information technology, it has done little to provide a more complete picture of the entire adoption process. As Meyer and Goes (1988) have suggested, the technology adoption process is a dynamic, multilevel, and lengthy decision process involving a host of actors and actions. However, the tools of innovation researchers, intended to capture these relationships through the discrete measurement of factors, or "snapshots," do not lend themselves to capturing the *adoption process as a whole*. For instance, we are not told how technical criteria, such as "flexible" and "integrated" systems, get on the agenda, or why decision makers believe that these criteria are important, much less why some work requirements become subordinated to technical requirements, while others compel technological adjustments. And finally, how do decisions based on these criteria diffuse over a period of time throughout the organization and its environment? The end result is that innovation research falls short of providing a complete picture of what is a considerably more complicated process of evaluating, adopting, and implementing a new technological innovation.

Institutional theory is a set of approaches to the study of organizations that seeks insight into less determinate goal-driven institutions like universities. This study will draw on institutional theory to integrate the isolated parts of technology adoption to provide a holistic picture. One of the underlying premises of institutional theory is that organizations are not merely technical systems. Instead, the theory suggests that the wider social and cultural context constitutes and shapes an organization's structures, processes, and practices (Meyer, Scott, & Deal, 1992). Institutional theory allows us to examine how organizations choose and legitimate courses of action in situations governed by formal rules and technical rationality. Much of the stability and order we associate with the existence of organizations does not flow from stable material forces such as technology or production systems but, rather, from less determinate elements such as knowledge systems, myths, rituals and beliefs. The concepts of *institutional rules* and *rational myths* (Meyer & Rowan, 1992) and *institutionalization* as a political process (DiMaggio, 1988) are used to examine why and how particular decisions leading to the adoption of a new information system are considered, selected, and diffused throughout the organization.

In this dissertation I will combine innovation theory and institutional theory to examine managers' practices and choices during the introduction of the proposal and subsequent adoption of a university-wide information system. Innovation theory is used to categorize and describe objective and perceived influencing factors that lead to successful adoptions and implementations of new information systems. I plan to use innovation theory, in this dissertation, to create an organizational framework and to identify the objective and predicted, but static, factors that tend to influence the decision to adopt a new information system. At the same time, I plan to use institutional approaches to unfold the course by which technology adoption was charted. I shall seek to chart the manner in which the decision to adopt diffused throughout the organization and its environment. In this regard, I shall examine organizational practices that sustain and continually renew the decision to adopt both internal and external to the organization.

* * * * *

In this proposal, Alvarez (1998) integrates two diverse theoretical perspectives to provide a more complete framework for her study than could be provided by either theory alone. In so doing, she defines the important questions and concepts that each perspective brings to the research.

Yet another example is offered in Vignette 7. Framed as a study of high school cultures undergoing change, the conceptual framework and research design for this study had to address fundamental definitions of change, culture, and the interaction of the two. The researchers then had to argue that these notions applied to schools. Specifically, the researchers were challenged to blend distinctive writings on organizational culture (derived from social anthropology and applied in organizational behavior studies), change in social systems (found in sociology, social psychology, and again, organizational behavior), and recent research depicting and analyzing the complex processes of what was then called school improvement (today we would call this restructuring). Vignette 7 describes this framework development.

* * * * *

## Vignette 7

### Developing Concepts Through the Literature

As part of an ongoing interest in school improvement and school change, the Applied Research Group at Research for Better Schools became interested in exploring the notion of culture as a lens for viewing school change, improvement initiatives, and mandates for reform. This interest arose because the researchers believed that a significant portion of the effective schools research expressed or implied that school culture was a significant aspect of effectiveness. More important than any one particular finding, Rossman, Corbett, and Firestone (1984) argued, was the way those elements were melded together to create a school culture that supported and encouraged learning and respect for one another.

These ideas were developed into a conceptual framework and research design (Rossman, 1985) that guided the study. The conceptual framework explored literatures from four traditions: anthropology, sociology, organization theory, and education. The first three were drawn on to build the definition of culture that guided the research, emphasizing the descriptive and prescriptive aspects of culture. Next, the researchers turned to the literatures on cultural change and transformation, some of which had been applied to the study of organizations, and the literature on educational change and innovation. These traditions were used to develop the idea that change in school culture could be conceptualized as evolutionary, additive, or transformative. Further examination of the literature on educational innovation and implementation helped refine this into the idea that change initiatives (broadly construed) could affect school culture. This search identified places where the concept of culture was relied on either directly or implicitly.

Finally, a search through the literature on successful schools and other types of organizations generated five domains, or large categories of meaning, that might well be present in schools in the process of fundamental changes in their meaning structures. These domains encompassed two basic sets of questions about organizations and organizing. First, how did those who participated in this organization relate to one another in the workplace? What were the norms governing how they interacted? The two domains identified here were *collegiality* and *community.*

The second set of questions captured how participants defined the nature of the work. How were goals and expectations for others defined? Was there a belief in taking risks that was supported by others? And what constituted knowledge among those actors? To what authorities were claims made? Three domains were described to capture this set of questions: *goals and expectations, action orientation or risk taking,* and *knowledge base.* Together, these five domains fostered a creative use of literature outside the field of education and helped frame data collection for the research project.

* * * * *

The literature review serves many purposes for the research. It supports the importance of the study's focus and may serve to validate the eventual findings in a narrowly descriptive study. It also guides the development of explanations during data collection and analysis in studies that seek to explain, evaluate, and suggest linkages between events. In grounded-theory development, the literature review provides theoretical constructs, categories, and their properties that can be used to organize the data and discover new connections between theory and real-world phenomena.

The sections of the proposal discussed thus far—introduction, discussion of the topic and purpose, significance, general research questions, and literature review—stand together as the conceptual body of the proposal. Here, the major (and minor) ideas for the proposal are developed, their intellectual roots are displayed and critiqued, and the writings and studies of other researchers are presented and critiqued. All of this endeavor is intended to tell the reader what the research is about (its subject), who ought to care about it (its significance), and what others have described and concluded about the subject (its intellectual roots). All three purposes are interwoven into these sections of the proposal.

The final major section—research design and methods—must flow conceptually and logically from all that has gone before. Here, the researcher makes a case, based on the conceptual portion of the proposal, for the particular methods, sample, data analysis techniques, and reporting format chosen for the study. Thus, the section on design and methods should build a rationale for decisions about the study's overall design and specific data collection methods. Here, the researcher should develop a case for the selection of qualitative methods.

The researcher must *not* decide to do a qualitative study and then search for a research problem. The methods should be linked epistemologically to the focus of the study and the research questions. In fact, novice researchers sometimes pose questions that demand quantitative responses and then find themselves in a quandary because they believed they were developing a proposal for qualitative work! Other times they ·suppose that qualitative research will be easier to conduct. Researchers should design the study according to the research questions they seek to answer. This suggests, of course, that there are many questions not appropriate to pursue through qualitative methods.

Although there are parallels, qualitative and more traditional quantitative proposals differ. In the development of a qualitative proposal, the researcher first orients the proposal reader to the general topic to be explored. This will not be a statement of specific research questions, propositions to be tested, or hypotheses to be examined. The discussion of the topic may be a general discussion of the puzzle, unexplored issue, or group to be studied. It becomes more precise and focused through the literature review that often includes several bodies of literature because, in exploratory studies, it is hard to predict which literature will be most relevant and encompassing.

In some cases, the literature review yields cogent and useful definitions, constructs, concepts, and even data collection strategies. These may fruitfully result in a set of preliminary guiding hypotheses. Using such a phrase—"guiding hypothesis"—may assist readers accustomed to more traditional proposals. It is essential, however, that the researcher explain that guiding hypotheses are merely tools used to generate questions and to search for patterns and may be discarded when the researcher gets into the field and finds other exciting patterns of phenomena. This approach retains the flexibility needed to allow the precise focus of the research to evolve during the research process itself.

By avoiding precise hypotheses, the researcher retains her right to explore and *generate* questions in the general area of the topic. The guiding hypotheses illustrate for the reader some possible directions the researcher may follow. The researcher, however, is still free to discover and pursue other patterns.

We do not intend to suggest that proposal development proceeds in a linear fashion. As noted in Chapter 1, conceptualizing a study and developing a design that is clear, flexible, and manageable is dialectic, messy, and just plain hard work. As the researcher plays with concepts and theoretical frames for the study, she often entertains alternative designs, assessing them for their power to address the emerging questions. Considering an ethnography, a case study, or an in-depth interview study as the overall design will in turn reshape the research questions. And so the process continues as the conceptual framework and specific design features become more and more elegantly related. The challenge is to build the logical connections between the topic, the questions, and the design and methods; we turn now to that last topic.

## Note

1. These paragraphs are adapted from Rossman and Rallis (1998).

## Further Reading

Creswell J. W. (1994). *Research design: Qualitative and quantitative approaches.* Thousand Oaks, CA: Sage.

Glesne, C., & Peshkin, A. (1992). *Becoming qualitative researchers: An introduction.* White Plains, NY: Longman.

Janesick, V. J. (1994). The dance of qualitative research design. In N. K. Denzin & Y. S. Lincoln (Eds.), *Handbook of qualitative research* (pp. 209-219). Thousand Oaks, CA: Sage.

Locke, L. F., Spirduso, W. W., & Silverman, S. J. (1993). *Proposals that work: A guide for planning dissertations and grant proposals* (3rd ed.). Newbury Park, CA: Sage.

Maxwell, J. A. (1996). *Qualitative research design: An interactive approach.* Thousand Oaks, CA: Sage.

Strauss, A., & Corbin, J. (1990). *Basics of qualitative research.* Newbury Park, CA: Sage.

# 3

## The "How" of the Study

BUILDING THE RESEARCH DESIGN

---

The section of the research proposal devoted to a description of the design and methods serves three major purposes. First, it presents a plan for the conduct of the study. Second, it demonstrates to the reader that the researcher is capable of conducting the study. And third, it preserves the design flexibility that is a hallmark of qualitative methods. This latter purpose is often the most challenging.

There are typically eight major topics addressed in this section: (a) the qualitative genre, overall strategy, and rationale; (b) site selection, population selection, or both; (c) the researcher's role; (d) data collection methods; (e) data management; (f) data analysis strategy; (g) trustworthiness features; and (h) a management plan or time line. Woven into these topics is the challenge to present a clear, doable plan—concrete, specific details—while maintaining flexibility in the implementation of that plan. After discussing this challenge, the first three topics are discussed. Chapter 4 describes data collection methods, followed by a discussion of strategies for managing, analyzing, and interpreting qualitative data in Chapter 5. Because managing the entire research process (using a management plan and time line) and trustworthiness considerations require full elaboration, they are presented in Chapters 6 and 7, respectively.

## Meeting the Challenge

How do researchers maintain the needed flexibility of research design, so that the research can "unfold, cascade, roll, and emerge" (Lincoln & Guba, 1985, p. 210), and yet present a plan that is logical, concise, thorough, and meets the criterion of do-ability? The research design section should demonstrate to the reader that the overall plan is sound and that the researcher is competent to undertake the research, capable of employing the methods arrayed, and sufficiently interested to sustain the effort necessary for the successful completion of the study.

The researcher should demonstrate to the reader that she reserves the right to make modifications in the original design as the research evolves: Building flexibility into the design is crucial. The researcher does this by (a) demonstrating the appropriateness and the logic of qualitative methods for the particular research question and (b) devising a proposal that includes many of the elements of traditional models. But she reserves the right to modify and change the implementation plan during data collection. As mentioned earlier, this section of the proposal should discuss the rationale and logic of the particular qualitative genre in which the study is grounded, the overall strategy, and the specific design elements. At times, however, the researcher may need to justify qualitative research in general before situating the proposed study in a particular genre. Given this reality, we address this issue first and then focus on specific genres and approaches.

## Justifying Qualitative Research

Given the historic domination of social science research by traditional, quantitative models, the researcher may well have to develop a justification for qualitative methods in general before describing the specific genre and approach. To accomplish this, he should show how and why the research questions will be best addressed in a natural setting, using exploratory approaches. Here, the strengths of qualitative methodology should be emphasized by elaborating the value of such studies for the following types of research (Marshall, 1985a, 1987):

- Research that delves in depth into complexities and processes.
- Research on little-known phenomena or innovative systems.
- Research that seeks to explore where and why policy and local knowledge and practice are at odds.
- Research on informal and unstructured linkages and processes in organizations.
- Research on real, as opposed to stated, organizational goals.
- Research that cannot be done experimentally for practical or ethical reasons.
- Research for which relevant variables have yet to be identified.

Further support is found in the many excellent introductory texts on qualitative methods that describe the characteristics and strengths of qualitative methods (see the list at the end of Chapter 1). Drawing on these sources, the researcher proposing a study in a particular setting (e.g., hospital ward or social service agency) could argue that human actions are significantly influenced by the setting in which they occur; thus, one should study that behavior in real-life situations. The social and physical setting—schedules, space, pay, and rewards—and internalized notions of norms, traditions, roles, and values are crucial aspects of the environment. The researcher would argue that the study should be conducted in the setting where all this complexity operates. For a study focusing on individuals' lived experience, the researcher could argue that one cannot understand human actions without understanding the meaning that participants attribute to those actions—their thoughts, feelings, beliefs, values, and assumptive worlds; the researcher, therefore, needs to understand the deeper perspectives captured through face-to-face interaction. He might argue that the objective scientist, by coding the social world into operational variables, destroys valuable data by imposing her world on the subjects. Finally, the researcher might further critique experimental models, by noting that policymakers and practitioners are sometimes unable to derive meaning and useful findings from experimental research and that the research techniques themselves have affected the findings.

The lab, the questionnaire, and so on, have become artifacts. Subjects are either suspicious and wary, or they are aware of what the researchers want and try to please them.

In short, the strengths of qualitative studies should be demonstrated for research that is exploratory or descriptive and that stresses the importance of context, setting, and the participants' frames of reference. A well-reasoned and convincing rationale for qualitative methods is presented in Vignette 8, which describes how Rossman, Wilson, and Corbett (1985) developed a concise but strong rationale for the use of qualitative methods in a proposal for a long-term study of the local implementation of state-mandated school improvement programs. The rationale was firmly grounded in the conceptual framework proposed for the study and shows how the selection of methods should flow from the research questions.

*     *     *     *     *

### Vignette 8

### Building a Rationale for Qualitative Research

"We simply cannot understand organizational phenomena without considering culture both as a cause and as a way of explaining such phenomena" (Schein, 1985, p. 311).

The significance of organizational culture as a way of understanding, describing, and explaining complex social phenomena has been increasingly acknowledged by students of organizations, consultants to organizations, and those of us who spend most of our workday lives within organizations. Moreover, students of educational organizations have found the concept of culture elusive but powerful in understanding the complexities of schools and schooling.

The research proposed here would undertake an in-depth, long-term exploration of how the cultures of 12 schools are modified and transformed as a result of state-initiated improvement programs. Underlying the proposed research is the guiding assumption that although such programs do not typically attend to the culture of schools, features of these programs can profoundly alter core values and beliefs. Cultural transformation, then, may be one of the unintended by-products of state-initiated programs. Since cultural norms and values are being increasingly recognized as crucial

for understanding organizational change and effectiveness (see, e.g.,
Schein, 1985), one benefit of this study will be to describe those unintended but critical effects.

The research approach is a longitudinal, multisite case study of improvement programs in 12 schools in four states. Sites will be selected that provide the greatest potential for revealing cultural transformation in response
to a state-initiated improvement program. Data collection will consist of
structured and unstructured interviewing and observation in the 12 schools.
Periodic site visits will allow us to track change processes over time and to
generate detailed knowledge of each school.

*Research Approach*

A cultural perspective for a study of local reactions to state-initiated
school improvement programs suggests particular methods that are congruent with the perspective's assumptions. First, a cultural perspective requires
an in-depth look into the improvement process. To fully understand the impact of the improvement on the school culture a set of twelve schools is proposed for case study. A researcher will spend at least 25 days at each site to
gain an in-depth understanding of the cultural aspects of the improvement
process. This will provide sufficient time to get beneath the surface of the
school's culture, to observe behavior, and to become familiar with key actors. It will also allow time to explore the development, maintenance, and
alteration of the school's culture over time.

Second, because it is so difficult to generalize from single cases (Kennedy,
1979), the research will focus on cross-site analyses that identify major patterns (Herriott & Firestone, 1983). This approach recognizes both the need
to inform policy-makers and the importance of local variation (Corbett,
Dawson, & Firestone, 1984) that cannot be explored unless the cases are
compared. Thus, while preserving holistic data from specific sites, it is important to conduct more general, comparative analyses concerning implementation of school improvement efforts at the local level.

Finally, the research will rely on interviews as the primary method of
data collection. The purpose of the interviews will be to have local practitioners reflect on recent behavior. In addition, it will allow the researchers
to discuss cultural changes in detail. With schools currently undergoing
these mandated improvement efforts, any changes will be fresh in people's
minds and, thus, the reconstruction of events will be possible. Interviews

will allow us to trace the development of improvement efforts as perceived by the local staff. We will be particularly interested in their accounts of events, their responses to and interpretations of those events, and how they have negotiated with the sources of changes and among themselves to create an emergent improvement orientation. In-depth interviews with multiple informants at each site will also allow us to triangulate findings across sources and test issues of reliability and validity.

*     *     *     *     *

Vignette 8 illustrates how a team of researchers effectively argued for a cultural perspective and in-depth data collection. The proposal contained detailed information about data collection that would be in sufficient depth to foster thick description of social systems undergoing substantial change. This level of detail provides answers to funding agencies' questions and concerns and guides the intensive fieldwork planned for the project. Having presented an argument for qualitative methods generally, the proposal should then discuss the specific genre and overall approach to the study.

## The Qualitative Genre and
## Overall Approach

Although acceptance of qualitative inquiry is currently widespread, at times it is necessary to provide a rationale for the particular genre of qualitative research in which the study is situated. Recall the discussion in Chapter 1 in which we argued that the many nuanced traditions of qualitative research can be categorized into (a) those focusing on *individual lived experience,* (b) those focusing on *society and culture,* and (c) those with an interest in *language and communication.* The most compelling argument is to stress the unique strengths of the genre for research that is exploratory or descriptive, that assumes the value of context and setting, and that searches for a deeper understanding of the participants' lived experiences of the phenomenon. One assumption common to all genres is a focus on the meaning that people express about some aspect of their lives. This follows Thomas's (1949) classic proposition that, in the study of human experience, it is essential to know how people define their situations: "If men *[sic]* define situations as real, they are real in their consequences" (p. 301). Explicating the logical and compelling connections—the epistemological integrity—between the genre, overall strategy, research questions, design, and methods is often quite convincing.

**Table 3.1  Qualitative Genre and Overall Strategy**

| Genre | Strategy | Focus of Inquiry |
|---|---|---|
| Individual lived experience | In-depth interviews | Individuals |
| Society and culture | Case study | Groups or organizations |
| Language and communication | Microanalysis | Speech events and interactions |

*Overall Strategies*

The richness and diversity of overall design strategies in qualitative research is evident in the vast literature detailing specific studies. Analysis of this richness, however, yields three distinct strategies, each one associated with the genres mentioned earlier (see Table 3.1). A study focusing on individual lived experience typically relies on an *in-depth interview strategy,* although this may be supplemented with journal writing by the participants in the study or other forms of data; the primary strategy is to capture the deep meaning of experience in their own words. Studies focusing on society and culture, whether a group, a program, or an organization, typically espouse some form of *case study* as an overall strategy; this entails immersion in the setting and rests on both the researcher's and the participants' worldviews. Research focusing on language and communication typically involves *microanalysis* through which speech events and subtle interactions are recorded (often through videotape) and then analyzed. Directly linked to the qualitative genre and research questions, each strategy stipulates the focus of the inquiry (individual, group, interactions) and the overall approach to collecting data.

The distinctions among these three broad strategies rest on two continua: the *complexity* of design, and the *degree of close interaction* between researcher and participants. In-depth interview strategies are elegant in design, relying on a single primary method for gathering data. Microanalyses frequently encompass more from the complexities of context than in-depth interview strategies, relying on some form of observation often complemented by interviews. A case study, the most complex strategy, may entail multiple methods—interviews, observations, document analysis, even surveys. Following the same logic, interview strategies entail close, personal interactions between researcher and participants, often over long periods of time. Case studies are less intimate than those involving participant observation (discussed in Chapter 4), which foster close relationships. With their focus on

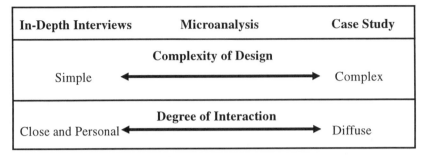

**Figure 3.1. Complexity of Design and Interaction**

observation, microanalyses tend to lie somewhere in the middle of this continuum. These continua are presented in Figure 3.1.

The strategy is a road map, an overall plan for undertaking a systematic exploration of the phenomenon of interest; the research methods are the specific tools for conducting that exploration. In-depth interview strategies stipulate the primary method for gathering data—interviewing. In contrast, case studies and microanalysis do not; the specific combination of methods proposed for responding to the research questions may be quite complex. A case study of the impact of welfare reform, for example, could rely on an array of methods ranging from in-depth interviewing to analysis of work experiences. A microanalysis study of classroom interactions might choose direct observation (through videotape) supplemented by interviews and analysis of student work. The overall strategy frames the study by placing boundaries around it, identifying the analytic focus. The research strategy thus reflects major decisions made by the researcher to determine the best approach to the research questions posed in the conceptual portion of the proposal.

In developing the overall strategy for the study, the researcher needs to anticipate ethical concerns as well as the classic criteria developed by Zelditch (1962): *informational adequacy* and *efficiency.* In discerning the adequacy of the strategy, ask if this research design can be carried out without harming people or significantly disrupting the setting. Furthermore, ask where it is likely to foster responses to the research questions thoroughly and thoughtfully. Will this strategy elicit the sought-after information? The criterion of efficiency harkens back to questions of the study's do-ability mentioned in Chapter 1. Does this plan allow adequate data to be collected, given constraints of time, financial resources, access, and cost to participants and the researcher? To these we would add ethical considerations as a critical criterion

against which to judge research strategies. Will the proposed strategy violate
the participants' privacy or unduly disrupt their everyday worlds? Are they
putting themselves in danger or at risk by participating in the study? Will the
study violate their human rights in some way? We address these ethical issues
more fully later in this chapter. The range of possible qualitative strategies is
small; choice depends on the research questions, qualitative genre, and ethics
and on the possible time frame for the study. Vignette 9 returns to the example
used in the funnel metaphor in Chapter 2 to depict decisions about strategy
and how these in turn shape the research questions.

*   *   *   *   *

### Vignette 9

### *Decisions About Strategy*

In thinking through the choices about overall strategy, Benbow (1994)
may well have considered several alternatives. Once she had determined
the topic—the development of a commitment to social justice and action—
she was at a decision point. One alternative would be to focus on the meaning individuals created about their life work of social action. This would
situate the study within the genre focusing on individual lived experience—
the phenomenological genre—and have implications for the size of her
sample and the methods for gathering data. The phenomenological genre
tends to focus in depth on the experiences of a few individuals to explore in
detail and, often, over time, their deeply held understandings of some facet
of their lives. This suggests a series of long, in-depth interviews that explore the past and the present and that integrate aspects of the individual's
experience into a coherent account.

Another equally legitimate alternative would be to focus on a social
movement—for example, a community development and empowerment
project to enhance the participation of the homeless in regional employment and housing policy. This alternative would have situated her study in
the genre interested in society and culture—perhaps a critical ethnography
of the project. This alternative, just as the first, would redefine the research
questions and suggest participant observation as the primary mode for gathering data. To help in making the decision about overall strategy, Benbow
also would have had to consider the resources available for the study (time,

money for travel) as well as her ethical stance about critical consciousness and commitment to social action. Either strategy would have been appropriate. Given limited time and financial support for the study and given her interests in the psychology of commitment to social action, she chose an indepth interview strategy.

*    *    *    *    *

To further buttress the rationale for the particular qualitative genre and overall strategy, discussion of a pilot study can be quite important. Description and assessment of a qualitative pilot study support the researcher's claim that she is capable of conducting the proposed research. Even without a pilot study, the researcher can illustrate her ability to manage qualitative research by describing initial observations or interviews. These experiences usually reveal fascinating questions and intriguing patterns. A description of initial observations demonstrates not only the ability to manage this research but also the strengths of the particular genre for generating enticing research questions. Thus, the inclusion of a description of a pilot study or initial observations strengthens the proposal.

In addition to developing a strong, supported rationale for the genre and strategy, this section of the proposal should preserve the right to modify aspects of the design as the research proceeds. Early investigations into the phenomenon can also demonstrate the benefits of maintaining some flexibility. Geer's (1969) description of first days in the field illustrates this. She describes the qualitative researcher's immersion in the setting, beginning with some analytic concepts that were identified in previous research, guided by the theoretical framework and related research questions. These help the researcher determine what situations to observe, whom to interview, and what to ask. The researcher should establish the need and right to determine the precise focus of the research after these first days in the field when new insights begin to clarify patterns and focus the relevant themes.

One purpose of the research design section is to demonstrate that the researcher is capable of conducting qualitative research. Materials from courses in qualitative methodology or reading about it independently will provide a wealth of examples to draw on. The use of quotations and citations of other researchers' work demonstrates a knowledge of the ongoing methodological discourse about qualitative inquiry and the specific genre in which the study is situated. An increasing number of researchers have provided descriptions of the rationale and evolving research design; both classical and newer works are referenced at the end of this chapter.

Once the overall approach and a supporting rationale have been presented, the proposal outlines the setting or population of interest and plans for more specific sampling of people, places, and events. This outline provides the reader with a sense of the scope of the proposed inquiry and whether the intensity, amount, and richness of the data will encourage full responses to the research questions. The researcher may devise a chart depicting questions to explore, potential rich settings, and specific data collection strategies to display the logic of the design. In addition, the proposal should address issues of the researcher's role, including (a) entry, reciprocity, and ethics; (b) specific planned data collection techniques; (c) how the data will be recorded and managed; (d) preliminary strategies for data analysis; (e) design features for ensuring the trustworthiness of the study; and (f) a management plan with a timeline for the conduct and final reporting of the study.

The research design section should draw supporting evidence for the decisions by using relevant quotations from researchers who have written about these issues. For example, to explain researcher ethics relative to participants, the experience of Krieger (1985) studying a lesbian community is useful and compelling. Or the researcher can use Chaudhry's (1997) dilemmas as she studied Pakistani Muslim immigrants to illustrate that role issues are complex. Similarly, the researcher can use cites and concepts from her conceptual framework and literature review to suggest possible categories or themes for data analysis.

Finally, when possible, it is useful to include a list of preliminary or tentative interview questions and observation and coding categories. Many human subject review committees in universities require these; funding agencies will find them useful in assessing the quality of the proposal. These can be developed from a pilot study or from the literature review. Such an outline demonstrates that the researcher has an understanding of how to start gathering data as she begins the study and that she has an initial approach to analyzing the data. Table 3.2 presents an example of categories for observation in a qualitative study.

In the research design for *Power Language and Women's Access to Organizational Leadership,* Marshall (1986) took an interdisciplinary approach, using kinesics, proxemics, observation, and interviewing to examine the language and interactions of middle-management men and women. The study proposed a working hypothesis, based on sociolinguistic research, that women

**Table 3.2   Observations and Coding Categories for *Power Language and Women's Access to Organizational Leadership***

I. Verbal
  A. Tone
    1. Pitch
    2. Loudness
    3. Intonation
  B. Duration
    1. Length of sentence
    2. Conciseness
  C. Content
    1. Tag questions
    2. Phrases of tentativeness ("I believe," "I guess," "I think")
    3. Apologies
    4. Self-denigration
    5. Niceties
    6. Humor—dirty jokes/elaborate/quick asides
    7. Metaphors—sports
    8. Four-letter words
    9. Parts of speech: verbs, adjectives, pronouns ("royal 'we' ")
    10. Power language: aggressive, put-downs, patronizing, soft voice for dramatic purposes, references to experts
      a. Self (years of experience)
      b. Outside experts
    11. Political and value statements
    12. Exhibiting naïveté
  D. Silences
    1. Wait time
    2. Dramatization
II. Nonverbal
  A. Kinesics
    1. Face
      a. Eyes
      b. Rest of face
    2. Hands
    3. Stance
    4. Idiosyncratic
    5. Legs
  B. Proxemics
    1. Use of space
      a. Moving around room
      b. Moving from chair
    2. Desk—props
    3. Spread of territory
    4. Control of decor
  C. Appearance
    1. Dress
    2. Makeup
    3. Hair

**Table 3.2  Continued**

      4. Accessories
        a. Personal
        b. Work related
      5. Facial hair
III. Audience reaction
    A. Distraction
      1. Asides
      2. Paper shuffling
      3. Off-task behavior
      4. Humor
      5. Leaving group
      6. Body position changes
      7. Criticize speech
        a. Power language asides
        b. Ask to speak louder
    B. Engagement and feedback
      1. Head nodding
      2. Smiling
      3. Looking at speaker
      4. Eye contact
      5. Verbal agreements/critiques
      6. Asking questions
        a. On-task
        b. Clarification
      7. Body positioning
    C. Interruption
IV. Macro (global)
    A. Body positioning of groups
    B. Hand gestures
    C. Indications of agreement
    D. Use of objects
    E. Taking a break
    F. Side comments
    G. Amount of time women/men speak
    H. Arrangement of people map
    I. Formal/informal leader
    J. Amount of times women/men restructure agenda
    K. How women and men get recognized to speak
    L. Defying group norms
    M. Structured request for assistance
    N. Courtship behavior
    O. Proportion of meeting time used by men and women
    P. Female/male structured commands
    Q. Mirroring body movements
V. Combined verbal and nonverbal
    A. Greetings
      1. Touching
      2. Verbal salutations
    B. Eye pleading with groups

SOURCE: Marshall (1986, Appendix A). Reprinted by permission.

use less power-and-control language and therefore appear to have less leadership potential in settings that value power and control. For the reviewers who were deciding whether or not to fund such a nontraditional project, this outline was reassuring. It was developed from a mock pilot, in which Marshall and four doctoral students observed videotapes of meetings among middle managers and, using the framework from sociolinguistic literature, focused on key language and interaction variables. Reviewers are generally impressed by such concrete evidence of research direction.

## The Setting, Population, or Phenomenon

Unless a study is quite narrowly construed, researchers cannot study all relevant circumstances, events, or people intensively and in depth; they select samples. The first and most global decision, choosing the setting, population, or phenomenon of interest, is fundamental to the design of the study and serves as a guide for the researcher. This early, significant decision shapes all subsequent ones and should be described and justified clearly.

Some research is site specific. For example, research that asks, By what processes do women's studies programs become incorporated into universities? must focus on a setting where this takes place. In contrast, research that asks, By what processes do innovative units become incorporated into educational organizations? has a choice of many sites and many different substantive programs. Questions such as, By what processes have Peace Corps volunteers been able to effect long-term health improvements in communities? can be pursued in many sites throughout the world.

The decision to focus on a specific setting (e.g., the Women's Studies Program at the University of Massachusetts) is a fairly constrained choice; the study is defined by and intimately linked to that place. A choice to study a particular population (faculty in women's studies programs) is somewhat less constrained; the study can be conducted in more places than one. The decision to study a phenomenon (the socialization of new faculty) is even less constrained by either place or population. In these latter instances, the researcher determines a sampling strategy that is purposeful and representative.

If the study is of a specific program, organization, place, or region, some detail regarding the setting is crucial for the reader. A rationale should also be provided that outlines why this specific setting is more appropriate than others for the conduct of the study. What is unique? What characteristics of this setting are compelling and unusual? Justify this early and highly significant decision.

A realistic site is where (a) entry is possible; (b) there is a high probability that a rich mix of the processes, people, programs, interactions, and structures of interest are present; (c) the researcher is likely to be able to build trusting relations with the participants in the study; and (d) data quality and credibility of the study are reasonably assured. Although this ideal is seldom attained, the proposal nonetheless describes what makes the selection of this particular site especially sound. A site may be perfect for its representativeness, interest, and the range of examples of the phenomena under study, but if the researcher cannot gain access to the site and to a range of groups and activities within it, the study cannot succeed. Similarly, if the researcher is very uncomfortable or endangered in the site, the study will be hampered.

When the focus of the study is on a particular population, the researcher should present a strategy for sampling that population. For example, in a study of forced terminations of psychotherapy, Kahn's (1992) strategy was to post notices in local communities asking for participants. Much discussion ensued at her proposal hearing about the feasibility of this strategy. Given assurances about previous experiences of soliciting participants through this method, the committee agreed; the strategy was ultimately successful.

In the proposal, the researcher should anticipate questions about the credibility and trustworthiness of the findings; poor sampling decisions may threaten these findings. To justify a sample, one must know the universe and all of its relevant variables—an impossible task. Generally, the best compromise is to include a sample with reasonable variation in the phenomenon, settings, or people under study (Dobbert, 1982). Some sampling issues are described in Vignette 10, which may be helpful for researchers thinking through the sampling and site selection issues in any qualitative study.

\*     \*     \*     \*     \*

## Vignette 10

### Selecting Sites and Sampling

Issues of sampling can be illustrated with community studies. Although the famous Yankee City study seemed to demand a parallel study of the

Deep South, how were researchers to identify a city representative of the Deep South? After selecting several cities that fit the criteria of size and history, Warner (reported by Gardner in Whyte, 1984) met with leaders and established contacts in the communities, eventually selecting Natchez as the site for *Deep South: A Social Anthropological Study of Caste and Class* (Davis, Gardner, & Gardner, 1941).

Negotiations for entry and access to various levels of the "caste system" were aided by the involvement of two wife-husband teams, one black and one white. All four individuals were raised in the South and were familiar with appropriate behavior within the caste system, making it possible for them to observe, interview, and participate in activities, interactions, and sentiments representing all levels of the Natchez community, over a period of one year. They were able to record the overt and covert behavior and verbalization associated with significant social institutions and to do so across race, sex, and age groups, even in the most intimate cliques. According to Warner and Davis, "The methodological aim was to see every negro-white [sic] relationship from both sides of society, so as to avoid a limited 'white view' or a limited 'negro view' [sic]" (in Thompson, 1939, p. 235).

The reports demonstrated that Natchez, although not exactly like all other Southern communities, was *not atypical.* Setting abstract criteria, checking out sites in advance, and careful planning of entry ensured that (a) the research team could move throughout the community to gather data; and (b) Natchez was not an unrepresentative pocket of the research universe.

*     *     *     *     *

Vignette 10 provides an illustration of researchers' identifying the site that would maximize comparability and allow access to a wide range of behaviors and perspectives. Clearly, the selection of site and sample are critical decisions. Vignette 11 shows how site selection affects the viability of the whole study.

*     *     *     *     *

### *Vignette 11*

### *Selecting a Site to Maximize Access*

An actual town, described anonymously as "Elmtown," was selected by the Committee on Human Development of the University of Chicago as typical of Midwestern communities and therefore a suitable site for what the committee proposed in preliminary contacts with residents as a study of the "character development" of boys and girls (Hollingshead, 1975). One stimulus for the study was the paucity of research done by sociologists on the subject of adolescent behavior.

The researchers, a husband-and-wife team, made several preparatory visits to the community, establishing contacts with civic leaders and getting the lay of the land while locating housing for the ten months during which the study would be conducted. The specific focus of the study emerged from the prestudy visits and the first two months of the researchers' residence in Elmtown. The larger question—Is the social behavior of an adolescent a function of physiological changes in the maturing individual or of his or her experiences in society?—eventually led to the working hypothesis, "The social behavior of adolescents appears to be related to the positions that their families occupy in the status structure of the community" (Hollingshead, 1975, pp. 6-7).

To test the hypothesis, data were gathered by the research team in such a way as to disturb the setting as little as possible. They consulted school records and identified 752 boys and girls who either were enrolled in the local high school or should have been enrolled. Of these, 17 were dropped due either to a refusal to cooperate by religious academy officials (12 girls) or the unavailability of data about families' positions in the social structure (5 boys). Excluded were high school graduates and peers who had left school before graduating. The study group therefore consisted of 735 adolescents representing 535 families. Of these young people, 81% had been born in Elmtown, as had 62% of their parents.

The research team participated as full members of the community. They gained access to parents and institutional functionaries by their interest in adolescent "character development." This interest brought them invitations to speak before a variety of community organizations, resulting in additional contacts. They spent a considerable amount of time in informal settings with young people as well. They were at the high school before school, at noon, and after school; they attended most school activities, church affairs, Scout meetings, dances, and parties; and they skated, bowled, shot pool, played poker, and generally "hung out" where the youth were known to gather. "The observational technique of being with them as often as possible and not criticizing their activities, carrying tales, or interfering overcame the initial suspicion in a few weeks" (Hollingshead, 1975, p. 15).

\*     \*     \*     \*     \*

In Vignette 11, what the researchers did not say enabled virtually all of Elmtown to become part of the sample for their study. Their ability to gain access to a range of groups and activities was enhanced by their ability to blend in. Site and sample selection should be planned around practical issues, such as the researcher's comfort, ability to fit into some role during participant observation, and access to a range of subgroups and activities. In some proposals, particularly those for multisite studies conducted with several researchers or for studies of organizations, it is wise to make even finer decisions about sampling. This is discussed next.

## Selecting a Sample of People, Actions, Events, and/or Processes

Once the initial decision has been made to focus on a specific site, a population, or a phenomenon, waves of subsequent sampling decisions are made. The proposal describes the plan, as conceived before the research begins, that will guide sample selection, always mindful of the need to retain flexibility. Thus, the research questions focus site and sample selection; if they do not, the researcher, at the very least, makes explicit the procedures and criteria for decision making.

Well-developed sampling decisions are crucial for any study's soundness. Making logical judgments and presenting a rationale for these decisions go far in building the overall case for a proposed study. Decisions about sampling people and events develop concurrently with decisions about the specific data collection methods to be used and should be thought through in advance. When faced, for example, with the complexity of studying the meaning that women managers attach to computer-mediated communications, Alvarez (1993) had to decide what individuals and events would be most salient for her study.

\*   \*   \*   \*   \*

*Vignette 12*
_____

*Focusing on People and Events*

The general question guiding Alvarez's (1993) study was in what ways computer-mediated communications, specifically electronic mail, alter human communications within an organizational context. She was interested in the power equalization potential of e-mail communications among persons of unequal status within the organization and in the socioemotional content of messages sent and received in a medium of reduced social cues.

The sampling strategy began as a search for information-rich cases (Patton, 1990) to study individuals who manifested the phenomenon intensely. A related concern was to have both men and women participants in the study, given that the theoretical literature suggested that there are significant differences between men and women in ease of computer usage. Once she had identified participants and they had agreed to engage in the study with her, Alvarez had to make decisions about which specific events she wanted to observe or learn more about. She reasoned that observing the sending or receiving of a message would yield little; she therefore asked participants to share sets of correspondence with her and to participate in two in-depth interviews. The former request proved quite sensitive, because Alvarez was asking people to share their personal and professional mail with her. She reassured them of the confidentiality of the study and also showed them how to send copies of e-mail directly to her without revealing the direct recipient of the message. This reassured them sufficiently to result in a substantial set of messages that could then be content analyzed.

\*     \*     \*     \*     \*

In designing studies with multiple sites, with a team of researchers, or with both, plans for systematic sampling are crucial. Miles and Huberman (1994) provide excellent guidance for such planning. Vignette 13 illustrates the greater need for a sound sampling plan for a multisite, multiresearcher study. This plan is taken from the high school cultures study (Rossman, Corbett, & Firestone, 1984) and depicts the extensive thinking through of the places, circumstances, and people the researchers would have to learn about to respond thoughtfully and sensitively to the research questions.

\*     \*     \*     \*     \*

**Vignette 13**

*Sampling People and Behaviors*

To plan for the study, the researchers identified those events, settings, actors, and artifacts that would have the greatest potential to yield good data on each of five cultural domains: collegiality, community, goals and expectations, action orientation, and knowledge base for teaching. Items within each category provided parameters to frame data collection and represented the core data the researchers believed would be useful. See Table 3.3 for the framework in which the potential usefulness of each item for the five domains was assessed.

The researchers started with *settings* because these were the most concrete: After all, a synonym for settings is *places*. During the first few weeks in the field, they planned to collect data in the public places (main office, hallways, parking lot), the teachers' lounge or lunchroom, classrooms, meeting rooms, private offices, department offices or workrooms, the gymnasium or locker room. and the auditorium.

In each of these settings, certain *events* of interest would likely occur. For example, in the disciplinarian's office, there would be the handling of routine infractions, suspensions, or expulsions; in the counselor's office there might be crisis interventions. Both types of events would reveal beliefs about collegiality, community, and goals and expectations. In general, the researchers expected that the events of importance would include events during which professionals interacted: formal routines such as faculty and department meetings, evaluations, and union meetings; informal routines such as lunch or coffee breaks, preparation periods, recess, morning arrivals; and events during which professionals interacted with students, including teaching acts, extracurricular activities, suspensions and expulsions, roster changes, crisis counseling, postsecondary counseling, and assemblies and pep rallies.

The first category—events during which professionals interact—would provide major data on collegiality, goals and expectations, and the knowledge base for teaching. Faculty and department meetings would be crucial as teachers discussed the curriculum, testing, new state requirements, and homework policies as well as the more mundane aspects of high school life (announcements of schedule changes, field trips, general announcements). In these meetings, norms governing the local definition of teaching and norms regarding how teachers should relate to one another in a meeting setting would be evident. Morning routines and other informal encounters would also reveal these norms but in less structured settings. The brief encounters might contain requests for help, plans for meetings, supportive gestures, queries about how a particular concept or skill is best taught—any of these events would reflect notions of collegiality and definitions of teaching.

**Table 3.3  Data Collection: Sampling Plan**

| | Collegiality | Community | Goals and Expectations | Action Orientation | Knowledge Base |
|---|---|---|---|---|---|
| **SETTINGS** | | | | | |
| Public places (main offices, hallways) | X | X | X | X | X |
| Teachers' lounge or lunchroom | X | X | | | X |
| Classrooms | | X | X | X | X |
| Meeting rooms | X | | X | X | |
| Private offices | | | | | |
|   Counselor's | | X | X | | |
|   Disciplinarian's | | X | X | | |
|   Vice principal's for scheduling | | | X | | |
|   Coaches' | | X | X | | |
|   Principal's | | | X | | |
| Department office or workroom | X | | X | X | X |
| Gymnasium or locker room | | X | X | | |
| Auditorium | | X | X | | |
| **EVENTS** | | | | | |
| Events during which professionals interact | | | | | |
|   Faculty/department meetings | X | | X | | X |
|   Lunch/coffee break/recess | X | X | | | X |
|   In-service sessions | X | | | | X |
|   After school (local pub?) | X | X | | | |
| Events during which professionals and students interact | | | | | |
|   Teaching acts | | X | X | X | X |
|   Extracurricular activities | | X | X | X | |
|   Suspensions and expulsions | | X | X | X | |
|   Roster changes | | X | X | X | |
|   Crisis counseling | | X | X | X | |
|   Assemblies and pep rallies | | X | X | X | |
| **ACTORS** | | | | | |
| Administrators | | | | | |
|   Principal | | | X | X | X |

*(continued)*

**Table 3.3**  Continued

| | Collegiality | Community | Goals and Expectations | Action Orientation | Knowledge Base |
|---|---|---|---|---|---|
| Vice principal for discipline | | x | x | | |
| Vice principal for curriculum | x | | x | x | x |
| Vice principal for schedule/roster | | x | x | x | |
| Vice principal for activities | | | | | |
| Counselors | | x | x | x | |
| Coaches | | x | x | x | |
| Teachers | | | | | |
| Department heads | x | x | x | x | x |
| Different tenure in building | x | x | x | x | x |
| Different departments | x | x | x | x | x |
| Students | | | | | |
| Different ability levels | | x | x | x | |
| Different visibility | | x | x | x | |
| **ARTIFACTS** | | | | | |
| Documents | | | | | |
| Newspapers | | x | x | | x |
| Policy statements | | | x | x | x |
| Attendance records | | x | x | | |
| Disciplinary records | | x | x | | |
| Achievement test scores | | | x | | |
| Objects | | | | | |
| Logos | x | x | | | |
| Mascots | x | x | | | |
| Trophies | | | x | | |
| Decorations | | x | | | |
| Art work | | x | | | |
| Physical arrangements | x | x | | | |

SOURCE: Rossman, Corbett, and Firestone (1984, p. 54). Reprinted by permission.

The second category—events during which professionals and students interact—would provide data about community, goals and expectations, and action orientation. Both in the classroom and outside, when teachers and students interacted, they would reveal whether or not there was a sense of community, what their expectations were for one another regarding behavior and achievement, and whether teachers felt it was important to translate ideas and concepts into actions—lesson and courses.

As data collection progressed, the researchers wanted to be sure that they sampled the perceptions of the following *actors*: administrators, including the principal and the vice principals for discipline, instruction, and scheduling; counselors; coaches; teachers; department heads; students of different ability levels and different visibility within the school; and external actors, including superintendents, curriculum coordinators, board members, community members, and state education agency staff.

Finally, the researchers planned to collect or be able to describe certain *artifacts* that would provide data for each of the five domains. Included would be documents, school newspapers, policy statements, attendance records, disciplinary records, achievement test scores, objects, logos, mascots, trophies, decorations, and the physical arrangements of each school.

In the above plan, the emphasis was on observation, because many of the domains the researchers were trying to understand were implicit. Thus, they inferred norms and values from behavior patterns and from naturally occurring conversations. Interviews helped them understand the settings and reconstruct the history of change in the high schools.

*    *    *    *    *

The sampling plan shown in Vignette 13 tried to ensure that each site's events, rituals, resources, and interactions would be observed. Purposive and theoretical sampling, in which the theoretical framework and concepts guide sampling, are often built into qualitative designs. For example, previous research on professional cultures would suggest that the researcher should sample among individuals, events, and sentiments in the early stages of initiation into a profession. Often, however, researchers' site selection and sampling begins with accessible sites (convenience sampling) and builds on insights and connections from that early data collection (snowball sampling). Miles and Huberman (1994) usefully describe different approaches to sampling, as presented in Table 3.4. Although such plans are often subject to

**Table 3.4  Typology of Sampling Strategies in Qualitative Inquiry**

| Type of Sampling | Purpose |
| --- | --- |
| Maximum variation | Documents diverse variations and identifies important common patterns |
| Homogeneous | Focuses, reduces, simplifies, facilitates group interviewing |
| Critical case | Permits logical generalization and maximum application of information to other cases |
| Theory based | Finds examples of a theoretical construct and thereby elaborates and examines it |
| Confirming and disconfirming cases | Elaborates initial analysis, seeks exceptions, looks for variation |
| Snowball or chain | Identifies cases of interest from people who know people who know what cases are information rich |
| Extreme or deviant case | Learns from highly unusual manifestations of the phenomenon of interest |
| Typical case | Highlights what is normal or average |
| Intensity | Involves information-rich cases that manifest the phenomenon intensely, but not extremely |
| Politically important cases | Attracts desired attention or avoids attracting undesired attention |
| Random purposeful | Adds credibility to the sample when the potential purposeful sample is too large |
| Stratified purposeful | Illustrates subgroups, facilitates comparison |
| Criterion | Includes all cases that meet some criterion, useful for quality assurance |
| Opportunistic | Follows new leads, takes advantage of the unexpected |
| Combination or mixed | Involves triangulation and flexibility, meets multiple interests and needs |
| Convenience | Saves time, money, and effort but at the expense of information and credibility |

SOURCE: Miles and Huberman (1994, p. 28). Reprinted by permission.

change, given the realities of field research, at the proposal stage, they demonstrate that the researcher has thought through some of the complexities of the setting and has made some initial judgments about how to deploy her time. Such plans also indicate that the researcher has considered both the informational adequacy and efficiency of these methods. Related to these considerations, however, are the ethical issues of the researcher's role with participants. These issues are considered next.

## The Researcher's Role: Issues of Entry, Reciprocity, Personal Biography, and Ethics

In qualitative studies, the researcher is the instrument: Her presence in the lives of the participants invited to be part of the study is fundamental to the paradigm. Whether that presence is sustained and intensive, as in long-term ethnographies, or whether relatively brief but personal, as in in-depth interview studies, the researcher enters into the lives of the participants. This brings a range of strategic, ethical, and personal issues that do not attend quantitative approaches (Locke, Spirduso, & Silverman, 1993). The issues can be sorted into technical ones that address entry and efficiency in terms of role and interpersonal ones that capture the ethical and personal dilemmas that arise during the conduct of a study (Rossman, 1984). Clearly, the considerations overlap and have reciprocal implications; for clarity, however, each set of issues is addressed in turn.

### Technical Considerations

At the proposal stage, the technical considerations addressed include decisions about the deployment of the researcher's time and other resources and about negotiating access.

### Deploying the Self

Patton (1990) develops a series of continua for thinking about one's role in planning the conduct of qualitative research. This section relies on that work considerably. First, the researcher may plan a role that entails varying degrees of *participantness*—that is, the degree of actual participation in daily life. At one extreme is the full participant, who goes about ordinary life in a role or set of roles constructed in the setting. At the other is the complete observer, who engages not at all in social interaction and may even shun involvement in the world being studied. And, of course, all possible complementary mixes along the continuum are available to the researcher.

It is our experience that some sort of participation usually becomes necessary as the researcher helps out with small chores (or large ones), wants to learn more about a particular activity, or feels compelled to participate to meet the demands of reciprocity. Such interaction is usually highly informative while remaining informal.

Next, the researcher's role may vary as to its *revealedness* or the extent to which the fact that there is a study going on is known to the participants. Full disclosure lies at one end of this continuum; complete secrecy lies at the other. A raft of ethical issues surrounds covert research (see Taylor & Bogdan, 1984, chap. 3, for a provocative discussion) that winnow down to one fundamental question: Is the potential advancement of knowledge worth the deceit? Many researchers follow Taylor and Bogdan's (1984, p. 25) advice to be "truthful but vague" in the portrayal of the research purpose to participants. The researcher should discuss the issues around revealing or concealing the purpose of the study in the proposal.

Third, the researcher's role may vary in *intensiveness* and *extensiveness*— that is, the amount of time spent in the setting on a daily basis and the duration of the study over time. Various positions on both dimensions demand certain role considerations on the part of the researcher. For example, an intensive and extensive study requires the researcher to devote considerable time early on to developing trusting relations with the participants. Gathering pertinent data is secondary at that point. On the other hand, when the researcher will be minimally intrusive and present for a short period of time, building trusting relations must proceed in conjunction with gathering good data. In our view, this is difficult for novice researchers to accomplish.

Finally, the researcher's role may vary depending on the *focus of the study:* specific or diffuse. When the research questions are well developed beforehand and data appropriate to address those questions have been identified, the researcher's role can be managed efficiently and carefully to ensure good use of the available time (both the researcher's and the participants'). Even when well specified, however, sound qualitative design protects the researcher's right to follow the compelling question, the nagging puzzle that presents itself once in the setting. When the research questions are more diffuse and exploratory, the plan for deploying the self should ensure access to a number of events, people, and perspectives on the social phenomenon chosen for study.

Fortunately, some researchers who have used participant observation have provided extensive descriptions of their plans, rationales, and actual experiences. Notable among these are researchers who have engaged in significant reflection on the research endeavor and their lives as researchers. References to these works are listed at the end of this chapter.

### Negotiating Entry

The research design section of a proposal should contain plans for negotiating access to the site and/or participants through formal and informal gatekeepers in an organization, whether the organization is an urban gang or an Ivy League university. Instead of controlling and sanitizing their presence, qualitative researchers identify and present aspects of themselves that will be useful. The energy that comes from high personal interest (called bias in traditional research) is useful for gaining access. Access may be a continuous issue when the researcher moves around in various settings within an organization. The researcher should reveal a sensitivity for participants' testing of her and their reluctance to participate and should unquestionably respect their right not to participate in a study. Excellent discussions of issues of access can be found in general texts about qualitative research, referenced at the end of this chapter. Of particular interest is Anderson's (1976) experience in becoming accepted for an ethnographic study of an urban cultural group, detailed in Vignette 14.

*   *   *   *   *

### Vignette 14

### Negotiating Entry

A bleak corner of urban life. A bar and liquor store named Jelly's that also serves as a hangout for African American men in south Chicago. In such a place, an angry man pulls a knife on another, a wino sleeps off his last bottle, police cars cruise without stopping, all within the sight of children at play. Jelly's and its countless urban counterparts "provide settings for sociability and places where neighborhood residents can gain a sense of self-worth" (Anderson, 1976, p. 1).

Anderson determined that he was going to study this particular setting, but how was he to gain entry? His first observations indicated that "visitors" received special treatment, because the next person might prove to be "the police," "the baddest cat in Chicago," or someone waiting to follow another home and rip him off. In the words of the regular clientele at Jelly's, "unknown people bear watching" (Anderson, 1976, p. 5).

Anderson accepted visitor treatment for several weeks, being unobtrusive yet sociable, acquainting himself with the unwritten social rules. Being African American was insufficient justification for immediate acceptance by the "regulars." Enter Herman. Anderson cultivated a relationship with Herman that became a means for mutual protection of each other's "rep and rank" in the social status system at Jelly's. Anderson responded openly to Herman's persistent questioning, and several days later, Herman reciprocated by introducing Anderson to Sleepy, T J, and Jake: "He all right. Hey this is the study I been tellin' you about. This cat getting his doctor's degree." With this introduction to the regulars, Anderson's place in the social system had been defined. In short, it provided Anderson with a license to be around. Herman used Anderson to gain credibility at his on-the-job Christmas party, introducing Anderson as "cousin" and getting him to tell the regulars at Jelly's how well Herman got along with "decent folks and intelligent folks" (p. 20).

Anderson's role evolved naturally from the low-key, nonassertive role he initially assumed to prevent unwieldy challenges from those who might have felt threatened by a more aggressive demeanor, especially from a stranger. It is the kind of role any outsider must play—is forced into—if he is not to disrupt the "consensual definition of social order in this type of setting" (pp. 22-23).

*     *     *     *     *

Anderson's experience is typical of those proposing long-term ethnographic studies of particular groups. At times, the best entry is one, like this one, when there is an insider who provides sponsorship and helps the researcher seem nonthreatening. There are circumstances, however, when sponsorship can backfire, setting the researcher up for difficulties in accessing other groups within the organization. For those conducting studies of organizations, negotiating access may require perseverance and persistence with formal leaders within the organization, as Vignette 15 depicts.

*     *     *     *     *

### Vignette 15

*Politics and Persistence in Negotiating
and Maintaining Access*

Negotiating access for the conduct of the long-term study of culture and change in three American high schools (Rossman, Corbett, & Firestone, 1988) took more than 3 months for formal approval. A letter sent to the principal, briefly describing the study, then a follow-up telephone conversation led to a meeting with the principal and two of the researchers. This meeting was difficult because the principal questioned the concept of "culture" as being meaningful for schools and challenged whether one of the researchers was appropriate, since he had no professional experience in schools.

Then, in meetings with members of the teachers' union and with the entire faculty, the researchers were asked questions about their intentions, their credibility, their presentability, and their knowledge of schools and schooling. A somewhat suspicious faculty finally agreed to do the study. But getting over their defensiveness, establishing credibility, and winning over the power structure in the school were the first research tasks.

Given the challenges to her presence in the school, Rossman spent considerable time early on with the principal and his close associates, learning about their values and beliefs about the school and the children, building trust, and observing how power and influence were expressed through that small group of people. But to focus on specific departments would necessitate distancing herself from the principal and his close associates. Through contact with each department head, Rossman scheduled interviews and observations with several teachers representing the various subject matter specializations. As she spent more time with teachers in the lunchroom, in their classrooms, in the hallways, and after school, she found that the principal and his associates increasingly questioned her as to her whereabouts and what she was learning from the teachers.

The school had been through a series of traumatic events 4 years prior to the study and, some believed, was still reeling. During that time, teachers and administrators had formed two camps, each claiming that its views were true and proper. Rossman surmised that the principal was still concerned over those historic events and wanted to keep her from learning about those times or, barring that, at least to ensure that she heard a balanced presentation.

Rossman's dilemma was this: She could cater to the principal and his associates, being sure that they knew her activities each day and could keep track of her comings and goings. This continued close association with the power structure, however, might work against building trust with teachers, especially those who might have been involved in the earlier traumatic times. Would those teachers trust her after seeing her so closely associated with the principal? On the other hand, the principal controlled access to the high school: Without his permission, the study could end. Without his support and confidence in the researcher, the climate in which the study proceeded could become strained, at best.

Recognizing the dilemma, Rossman tried to balance the competing concerns. She made a point, each day, of telling the head secretary, one of the assistant principals, or another of the principal's close associates her general itinerary for the day. Having done that, she felt comfortable moving out into the school to uncover teachers' perspectives on the nature of the work and the social relations there. This single strategy helped protect the study from excessive scrutiny and ensured continued access to the remainder of the teachers.

*   *   *   *   *

Tensions do arise when researchers are involved over the long term, and researchers must plan strategies for easing those tensions. Researchers may also need to think about strategies to maintain the research instrument—that is, the self. Research designs should include strategies to protect the physical and emotional health and safety of the researcher by providing plans for quiet places in which he can write notes, reassess roles, retreat from the setting, or question the directions of the research. In some settings, the researcher's planning must go beyond comfort to planning to stay safe. Unfamiliar settings where strangers are unwelcome, where illegal activities may be observed, or where the researcher's race or gender makes her unwelcome require careful sensitivities (Lee, 1995). In anticipating such potential difficulties, proposals should cite the experiences of previous researchers and apply them to the current research to think through role strategies; some excellent sources are provided at the end of this chapter.

Gaining access to sites—receiving formal approval, like Jelly's sponsorship, a principal's approval, or the faculty's positive vote—requires time, patience, and sensitivity to the rhythms and norms of a group. At the proposal stage, the researcher should indicate that negotiations have begun and formal approval is likely or that she has knowledge about the nuances of entry and a healthy respect for participants' concerns.

### Efficiency

In qualitative studies, the researcher should think through how he will deploy the resources available for the study to ensure full responses to the research questions. Although this consideration overlaps directly with decisions about data gathering, issues of role also arise here. The researcher should think through carefully how he can deploy the self, as it were, to maximize the opportunities for gathering data. This consideration should be balanced against the resources available for the study, most notably time and energy. We would caution the novice, moreover, that once a study is begun, the tantalizing puzzles and intriguing questions mushroom. Even though the researcher reserves the right to pursue those, he should remain mindful of the goal of the project. Doctoral students often need to be gently prodded back into a structure for the completion of the work. Also, a priori but tentative statements about boundaries will help: A discussion of goals and limitations (e.g., five life histories; observations in one school for one year) and reminders of practical considerations (e.g., dwindling funds, the need to get a "real" job), serve as reminders that the research must be finite.

*Interpersonal Considerations*

One could argue that successful qualitative studies depend primarily on the interpersonal skills of the researcher. In general texts, this is often couched as building trust, maintaining good relations, respecting norms of reciprocity, and sensitively considering ethical issues. These entail an awareness of the politics of organizations as well as a sensitivity to human interaction. Because the conduct of the study often depends exclusively on the relationships the researcher builds with participants, interpersonal skills are paramount. We would go so far as to dissuade a would-be qualitative researcher from this approach if she does not possess the skills of easily conversing with others— being an active, patient, and thoughtful listener and having an empathetic understanding of and a profound respect for the perspectives of others. It is important to acknowledge that some people just cannot be good qualitative researchers.

Discussions of one's role in the setting and consideration of how this may affect participants' willingness to engage in thoughtful reflection help provide evidence that the researcher knows enough about the setting and the people, their routines, and their environments to anticipate how she will fit in. Researchers benefit from carefully thinking through their own roles, because most participants detect and reject insincere, unauthentic people.

In addition, researchers may have to teach the participants what the researcher's role is. They should describe their likely activities while in the setting, what they are interested in learning about, the possible uses of the information, and how the participants can engage in the research. Norms of reciprocity suggest that the researcher cannot be simply a spongelike observer, as Thorne (1983) describes in compelling detail in her reflections on studying war resistance in the 1960s, because many people will not respond to or trust someone who will not take a stand. Another vignette provides further illustration of these ideas: Vignette 16 describes how Rosalie Wax (1971) went about the complex task of building trust in her study of Native Americans.

*    *    *    *    *

### Vignette 16

### Building Trust

The extensive writing of anthropologist Rosalie Wax (1971) has emphasized the importance of the researcher's initial contacts with the members of the society or group chosen for study. The reciprocal relationship between host and field-worker enables the latter to avoid foolish, insulting, and potentially dangerous behavior; to make valuable contacts; and to understand the acceptance and repayment of obligations. "The most egregious error that a fieldworker can commit," according to Wax (1971, p. 47), is assuming that tolerance by hosts also implies their high regard and inclusion.

In her ethnographic community study of Native American reservation society, Wax found the women embarrassed and hesitant to open their poor, bare homes to the scrutiny of a researcher. Their trust and cooperation were essential to her study because Wax sought to understand the relationship between cultural patterns expressed in the home and poor school adjustment and underachievement of the children. In her account of the slow uncovering of answers, Wax reveals her method of making others comfortable with her presence. She permitted children to play with her typewriter. She employed some of the women as interviewers. Avoiding the social worker or Bureau of Indian Affairs do-gooder image, Wax interacted as woman to woman, always exploring but doing so with an interest in the welfare of the women's children.

*    *    *    *    *

Vignette 16 demonstrates that researchers should allow time and be sensitive to the need for time to pass, flexibility in their roles, and patience, because confidence and trust emerge over time through complex interactions. Roles and relationships do emerge in the field. At the proposal stage, however, the researcher should demonstrate a logical plan that respects the need for time to build relationships. It is not enough to state that trust and relationships are important. The researcher should also display the skills and sensitivities to deal with complexities in relationships that inevitably emerge during field-work. Moving on to another site is another way to manage—politically and ethically—a difficult situation: There are times when, even with the best planning, the researcher cannot gain entry to a site, as Vignette 17 shows.

*   *   *   *   *

### Vignette 17

### Moving On

Wanting to explore the interaction between community political demands and women and people of color's access to school district leadership, Marshall (1992) designed comparative case studies and identified two sites—two cities in the same region of the country with similar political cultures, demographic composition, and comparatively large numbers of women and people of color in leadership positions. The sites were chosen for comparability along those dimensions but with one significant differ-ence: "Change City" showed evidence of a political structure undergoing substantial change, whereas "Avondale" represented a more placid political climate. She crafted the following letter as a way of introducing herself and the study to important gatekeepers in the district:

Dear _____,

The purpose of this letter is to introduce myself and to ask you to please consider the possibility of allowing me to collect research data within your school system. I am enclosing my résumé. I am presently an Associate Professor in the Department of Educational Leadership at Vanderbilt Uni-versity. I have done extensive research on women and minorities within the field of educational administration.

This is a field research project in which I and two other researchers will visit administrators on-site to observe the activities of women or minority principals. All individuals and sites involved in this study will remain anonymous. I assure you that I will respect your need as superintendent to minimize politically sensitive issues. Consequently, the complete research will be published only in a professional journal.

I am conducting a long-term research project on school districts with large numbers of women and minority administrators. With your permission, I would like to conduct this research in [_____]. Enclosed you will find a copy of the entire research proposal, which I think you will find quite interesting.

Briefly, the focus of the study is the interaction of school district policy and successful incorporation of women and minorities within the administrative ranks, particularly within the principalship. [_____] was chosen because of the changes you are implementing at the administrative level. You stand out for taking strong action to rethink the principalship.

I would enjoy discussing this project with you on the telephone. I will contact your secretary during the week of April 23, 1990, to arrange a phone conversation with you at your convenience. Thank you for your time and consideration in this matter.

Sincerely,


At Avondale, Marshall encountered no more than the typical bureaucratic barriers to gaining access: letters to gatekeepers, meetings with district research directors, assurances of compliance with district monitoring of the research. Pleased with this response, she began the access process in Change City by subscribing to the local newspaper to learn about local politics and by placing phone calls to the superintendent, a newly hired African American man from another state. Weeks passed. Months passed. Her politely persistent calls resulted in a telephone relationship with the secretary! She devised other strategies: letters flattering to the superintendent, reassurances of the value of the research for the district, name-dropping, emphasizing the university letterhead and the study's connection to a national center on school leadership. Still no response.

Marshall found this puzzling, because superintendents are known to try to maintain at least diplomatic relationships with university faculty. It was also humiliating, because Marshall saw herself as somewhat expert at gaining access to policy settings, encouraging state officials to tell her insider stories, and getting past bureaucratic barriers (Marshall, 1984).

In conversations with a doctoral student with some connections to the new superintendent of Change City, Marshall searched for insights only to learn that this new superintendent was judicious with his time and extremely careful about controlling information as he dealt with an explosive dispute about resources, people of color in administrative positions, and political maneuvers to support incumbent white administrators. No wonder he was wary!

Intrigued with this turmoil and hungry to know more because it spoke so directly to the research topic, Marshall tried one last tactic: the chance meeting. With a little help from the superintendent's secretary, she learned of a small conference that the superintendent planned to attend, got herself invited, and was able to engage him in conversation during a coffee break. In the context of conference-related talk, she mentioned casually that she hoped to talk with him about doing research in the district. Gracious, interested, and promising to talk at length at the next break, the superintendent appeared open. One hour later, much to Marshall's chagrin, his assistant announced that the superintendent had been called back to the office to manage some emergency. Foiled again!

Marshall resumed the phone calls and letters with the added hint that the superintendent had promised a longer conversation. The silence from his office was deafening. It was time to let go of her pride and face facts. The political controversies about people of color in leadership positions—the very question that she wanted to study—was the tense and difficult issue that kept this superintendent from allowing the research to take place. It was clear that he was not about to risk the exposure of this political maelstrom through qualitative research. Marshall went back to the library to find another "Change City."

* * * * *

It is hard to admit when the original plan will not work. Sometimes, because the politics in a setting are so explosive, researchers must simply move on. At some point, they decide that the efforts to get around the barriers to entry are excessive, and they must respect the needs of key actors in the setting. With topics that are politicized and sensitive, the researcher should identify several potential sites so she can move to another site easily if one will not work. When one site will not work, the researcher can then move to an alternative with little delay.

## Reciprocity and Ethics

A thorough research proposal also demonstrates the researcher's awareness of reciprocity issues. Qualitative studies intrude into settings as people adjust to the researcher's presence. People may be giving their time to be interviewed or to help the researcher understand group norms; the researcher should plan to reciprocate. When people adjust their priorities and routines to help the researcher, or even just tolerate the researcher's presence, they are giving of themselves. The researcher is indebted and should be sensitive to this. Reciprocity may entail giving time to help out, providing informal feedback, making coffee, being a good listener, or tutoring. Of course, reciprocity should fit within the constraints of research and personal ethics and within the constraints of maintaining one's role as a researcher role.

## Ethics

The qualities that make a successful qualitative researcher are revealed through an exquisite sensitivity to the ethical issues present when we engage in any moral act. Ethical considerations are generic—informed consent and protecting participants' anonymity—as well as situation specific. Several authors discuss ethical considerations in the conduct of qualitative research, describing the dilemmas they have encountered. Role, reciprocity, and ethical issues must be thought through carefully in all settings but most particularly in sensitive and taboo areas. In developing the section of the proposal that addresses role and reciprocity issues, the qualitative researcher should draw on the advice and experience of previous researchers.

The competent research proposal, then, anticipates issues of negotiating entry, reciprocity, role maintenance, and receptivity and, at the same time, adheres to ethical principles. The researcher must demonstrate awareness of the complex ethical issues in qualitative research and show that the research is both feasible and ethical. If the researcher will be playing a deceptive role, she should demonstrate that this will not be harmful to the participants in the research. If the researcher will require people to change their routines or donate their time, it must be voluntary. What is routine and acceptable in one setting may be harmful in another; what is volunteered in one may be withheld in another. The researcher cannot anticipate everything, but she must reveal an awareness of, and an appreciation for and commitment to, ethical principles for research. Several authors have explored these issues in both general texts and articles, referenced at the end of this chapter, as well as in the studies described in the following vignettes.

\*     \*     \*     \*     \*

## Vignette 18

### Ethics and Ethnographic Fieldwork

Ethnographic research has traditionally been undertaken in fields that, by virtue of the contrast between them and the researcher's own culture, could be described as "exotic." The researcher's goal is to describe the symbols and values of such a culture without passing judgment based on his personal cultural context. Soloway and Walters (1977), however, point out that when a researcher studies those whose acts are considered criminal, profound ethical dilemmas arise: "When one decides to attempt to enter their world and to study it, the fieldworker arrives at a true moral, ethical, and legal existential crisis" (p. 161).

Although researchers are expected to suspend judgment even when investigating one of the dark fissures of their own culture, it is often very difficult to do so. Soloway and Walters (1977) assert that "the failure of urban anthropological studies of modern American culture is that this critical phenomenological judgment has not been substantially dealt with by urban anthropologists in any meaningful way" (p. 161).

One option is to carry out studies of criminal subcultures from within institutions, such as prisons or treatment centers. Critical of such a procedure, Soloway and Walters note that "if addicts are studied at Lexington [federal hospital], then the result is a study of patients. If addicts are studied in jail, the result is a study of prisoners" (p. 163).

To understand addiction, Soloway chose to enter the addicts' natural habitat. Entry was aided by his affiliation with a methadone treatment program and the fact that he was doing his research within the neighborhood where he had spent his childhood. One of his contacts during observation of the weekly distribution of methadone was Mario, an old neighborhood friend and a patient at the treatment center.

Mario saw this relationship as a source of status both within the program and on the street. He chose to test this relationship at one point, coming in high for his weekly dose. When he was refused the methadone because of his condition, he sought out his friend the ethnographer to intercede with the nurses. Not only did the researcher refuse to intercede, he rebuked Mario, saying, "I'm no lame social worker from the suburbs; you're high and everybody knows it. Now stop being such a c-!" (Soloway & Walters, 1977, p. 165). Even though he risked jeopardizing the researcher-informant relationship, the risk paid off. Mario eventually introduced Soloway to other addicts; this involvement with urban heroin addicts enabled him to observe them in the context of their total social milieu, where "junkie" was only part of their identity.

*     *     *     *     *

Was Soloway taking advantage of his friendship with Mario? Is the participant observer a friend to participants? Can the researcher be both observer and friend? How does one juggle the objectivity of the stranger and the friend's desires for the well-being of a friend? "The bind on the ethnographer's personal ethic is," according to Soloway and Walters, "that his total integrity cannot be maintained in either role" (p. 166). What represents a researcher's ethical response when observing or possibly becoming involved in criminal activity? Polsky (1969) insists that to study adult criminals in their natural settings, one must "make the moral decision that in some ways he will break the law himself" (pp. 133-134). On the other hand, Yablonsky (1965) asserts that participant observation among the criminally deviant merely serves, by way of the researcher's interest in the subject, to reinforce the criminal behavior.

In the exchange with Mario, the researcher attempted to strike a balance by employing the principle of relativism. According to this principle, ethnographers are not expected to renounce their own culturally formed consciences, nor are they to project those values on their subjects. "Relativism operationally guards against two dangers, the ethnographer's own ethnocentrism and an equally dangerous inverted ethnocentrism—that is, going native and personally identifying with the studied value system" (Soloway & Walters, 1977, p. 168). Not all qualitative studies present such extreme ethical dilemmas. It is, however, quite difficult to maintain the role of researcher when caught in the middle of events that seem to call for action, as the next vignette shows.

*     *     *     *     *

## Vignette 19

### Ensuring Ethical Behavior

Persons engaged in criminal acts are not likely to be open to completing a questionnaire about those activities. Because of this, qualitative approaches to research are often found in areas that extend beyond the parameters of either legality or morality. Doing observation and interviewing in such settings has presented and will continue to present field-workers with ethical dilemmas. What does the researcher do in the presence of illegal activities? Is the researcher's primary responsibility to the research task, to those being observed, to those assisting with the observation, or to society as a whole? When initiating entry into a field of research, can the researcher offer guarantees that her behavior will conform to specific ethical standards?

Manning's (1972) research into police work—primarily that of narcotics officers—demonstrates the ethical dilemmas faced by some field-workers. The researcher's role is limited—he may walk the beat with the police officer, ride in the patrol car with the police officer, even tag along when an arrest is about to be made. Yet the researcher cannot be a police officer, cannot wear the uniform, cannot take the risks, cannot make the arrests, cannot adopt the police officer's perspective. He also cannot be a criminal. What then?

Manning points out the contrast between the police officer and the researcher. The role of the former "seems to attract men who are apparently deeply ambivalent about the law, politically conservative, perhaps reactionary, and persons of lower- or lower-middle-class origins with a high school or less education" (p. 244). The social scientist, on the other hand, "tends to be politically liberal, of middle-class origins, highly educated, and intellectual" (p. 244). How do researchers go about courting the cooperation of individuals whose social ecology is so very different from their own? Must researchers assume identities other than their own? According to Westley (1967), a critical "norm" among law enforcement personnel is the maintenance of secrecy:

> It is carefully taught to every rookie policeman; it is observed by all the men, and there are powerful sanctions against its violation. The violator is cut off from vital sources of information and the protection of his colleagues in times of emergency. Secrecy means that policemen must not talk about police work to those outside the department. (p. 774)

Strike two. The researcher not only differs from the police officer in terms of social milieu but, along with anyone else asking lots of questions or appearing too curious, is simply not wanted. The seemingly innocent act of encouraging police officers to talk about their work may jeopardize their professional relationships as well as their safety. How ethical are such actions? What of the issue of the "watched cop" raised by Manning? Is it possible for police officers to be effective when they are aware of the fact that observation is taking place or when constrained by the need to keep in mind the safety of the researcher?

Manning (1972) extends the dilemma by referring to a researcher who observed a clear incidence of police brutality and who knew that the officer involved was aware of his observations. The researcher debated the pros and cons of complying with the law and turning the officer in, risking the destruction of the study, and remaining silent to gain the trust of those he was observing along with some leverage for later on. Manning contrasts this student—who opted for the benefits of silence—with another from the same project who, having observed a case of a police officer harassing blacks in an inner-city area, "indignantly reported the event [and] was banned from further observation" (pp. 251-252).

*    *    *    *    *

Although Vignette 19 describes quite dramatic dilemmas, researchers must anticipate more routine ethical issues and be prepared to make on-the-spot decisions that (one hopes) follow general ethical principles (see, especially, Punch, 1994; Spradley, 1980). Reading other researchers' discussions of ethical problems and dealing with hypothetical situations through case material can illuminate "standard" ethical considerations and refine the researcher's abilities to reason through moral argumentation. Vignette 20 draws from the work of a Chicana ethnographer as she struggled with the challenges in conducting research to fulfill her own goals while respecting those with whom she had conducted the study. The political and ethical dilemmas she confronted were acute, as she found herself co-opted by the dominant Anglo leaders in the community where she conducted her research.

*    *    *    *    *

## Vignette 20

### Ethics, Power, and Politics

In her work, Villenas (1996) describes being caught between her role as a Chicana ethnographer, the marginalized Latino community she studied, and the Anglo groups in power within the community. In her study, she examined the educational histories of Latina mothers who were recent immigrants in the small rural community of Hope City in North Carolina. She focused on telling the women's stories about how they created educational models for raising their children.

Villenas focused on how to overcome the Latino community's perception of her as a "privileged" ethnographer from an elite university. However, she missed the process by which she was co-opted by the dominant English-speaking community to legitimate their definitions of Latino family education and child-rearing practices as problematic and "lacking." By using the same language as the community leaders and not challenging it, she found herself complicitous in this negative representation.

Concerned about gaining access with community leaders, she censored herself when she spoke to the Anglo leaders and did not point out their racist language and demeaning depictions of the Latino community. In addition, the community leaders assumed that she shared their fear of poor persons and people of color and that she also saw the Latino community as a "problem." Because there were no Latino/as in the community in leadership positions with whom Villenas could align herself, she became the sole Latina accepted by community leaders. In this role, she was accepted as an insider in the Anglo community while, at the same time, seen as an outsider by the Latino community.

To counter this co-opted role, she started "to engage in small subversive strategies and acts of resistance" (p. 725). For example, when she was called on by community leaders to speak at meetings, she presented a positive depiction of the Latino community. Another time, she chose not to sit at a seat reserved for her at the head table with community leaders and instead chose to sit in the audience with friends she had made in the Latino community.

*     *     *     *     *

Vignette 20 shows that a researcher's role can be co-opted by people in positions of power. Although the intent of the research may be to show the positive aspects of a culture, it is easy for an inadequately self-reflective researcher to be appropriated by and become complicitous in the process by which marginalized groups are negatively depicted as a "problem." Continuing a discussion of ethical issues, Vignette 21 shows how potential dilemmas can be addressed at the proposal stage. The vignette offers excerpts from a discussion of ethical issues in a proposal for a study of gay, lesbian, and straight youth who participate in Gay/Straight Alliances in high schools. Designed to raise awareness of homophobia, these alliances are becoming an increasing part of the landscape of American secondary schools. In her proposal for a phenomenological study of the experiences of students, Doppler (1998) described the ethical issues inherent in her study in some detail. Because informed consent is critical to ensuring that a qualitative study has been ethically conducted, we include the forms she used with students and their parents (see Figures 3.2 and 3.3). Both the vignette and the figures are taken directly from her proposal.

*    *    *    *    *

### Vignette 21

#### Ethical Considerations for Gay and Lesbian Youth

##### Informed Consent

Because participants will be high school students, some of whom may be especially vulnerable because of being lesbian or gay or due to status as a heterosexual ally of lesbian and gay youth, it will be particularly important to protect them from any potential harm. Every possible avenue for protecting the anonymity of participants will be taken. Before agreeing to participate, potential interviewees will be given a verbal overview of the study along with the expectations for them and for myself. They will also be given an informed consent form for their parents to sign; their own consent will be asked for at the time of invitation to participate. They will be told they may withdraw from the study at any time. Participants will have the opportunity to read transcripts of each interview in which they share their reactions and will be asked to modify the transcript.

*Reciprocity*

Participants will receive acknowledgment of the importance of the work they are doing in their Gay/Straight Alliances (GSAs) around an emotionally charged issue with significant political and social implications for schools and for society. They will have an opportunity to voice their experiences and feelings in a safe setting with someone who will validate the importance of their participation in a GSA. Lesbian or gay students may receive the greatest benefit because they will have an opportunity to voice feelings and thoughts about which they may usually remain silent. Also, interacting with a lesbian educator who is happy and well-adjusted to life as a lesbian can provide a positive role model.

It is my hope that my research will enable me to be a more effective advocate for GSAs and for the students who participate in the alliances because I will understand more about the student perspective. Although the student perspective is actually the most important one, it is often unrecognized by adults who assume they know what students want and need.

On a cursory level, I will share power with participants by encouraging them to modify interview transcripts to make them fully accurate. Much more important is the power dispensed by providing opportunity for students to give voice to their experiences. In my own journey away from the silence of the closet, I have discovered that my personal power expands each time I voice my experience. I hope that the interview process provides such an opportunity for participants. I hope that I can model naming one's experience and then acting in ways that magnify helpful components while ending hurtful ones.

*Deception*

Deception will be avoided by conducting interviews with fully informed participants. The report of my findings will be as accurate and truthful as possible.

*Right to Privacy*

Pseudonyms will be used to protect the anonymity of participants. It is possible for this study, however, that some participants will want to have their names used as a rite of passage out of the closet. In that case, the implications of the use of actual names versus pseudonyms will be discussed with any participant who wants her or his name to be used. Participants will be promised every reasonable attempt to maintain confidentiality with the exception of self-reports of suicidality or abuse. . . .

### Advocacy/Intervention

I anticipate that ethical considerations around advocacy/intervention may create personal dilemmas during my fieldwork. During the course of interviews, it is likely that I will hear about harassment and discrimination. My impulse may be to intervene in the situation. At this point, I believe that it will be appropriate to be sure students know what avenues they can take to deal with harassment or discrimination. When that sort of situation arises, I will continue the interview to keep the flow going, but at the end of the interview session, I can offer to discuss channels of possible support within their individual schools or provide phone numbers for supports outside their schools. . . .

A situation involving illegal treatment of a GSA and its members arose when I was observing a workshop on improving GSAs. At the end of the workshop, I gave the students who described illegal treatment the phone number of Gay and Lesbian Advocates and Defenders (GLAD) and the name of a person to talk with there. They seemed genuinely pleased to receive the information. I was comfortable providing information that would allow students and their advisers to act on their own behalf. I plan to use this model for action during my data-gathering process.

It is possible that situations may arise in which I must intervene. For example, reports of suicidality or abuse would require intervention by going to the guidance department or appropriate youth protection agency.

It is unlikely that anything will arise that will make me feel compelled to stop my data collection. However, if that occurs, the focus of my project will be shifted to a description of what I learned, why I terminated data collection, and the implications of the situation that forced termination of data collection.

*     *     *     *     *

---

### Informed Consent for Dissertation Research Project Participation: Gay/Straight Alliance Participants in Public High Schools

Dear Gay/Straight Alliance Member:

I am a graduate student in the School of Education at the University of Massachusetts, Amherst. I would like to invite you to participate in a research project about the benefits and costs of participating in a Gay/Straight Alliance. I am interested in exploring the experiences of self-identified lesbian, gay, and heterosexual students who participate in GSAs.

Your participation will include being interviewed twice for forty-five minutes to an hour each time. A third interview of the same length may be added if it seems necessary after the first two interviews.

You may be vulnerable to someone's determining who you are and what you've said, but I will protect you from this possibility as much as possible by using a pseudonym for your name and for the school you attend. I will give you a hard copy of the transcript of each of your interviews. You will be able to make any changes you want. You have the right to withdraw from the study any time up until March 1, 1999. At that point, I will be in the final stages of the writing process and will not be able to remove quotations from the document.

This study will be shared with my dissertation committee and other appropriate members of the University of Massachusetts community. The dissertation that results from this work will be published in hard copy and microfiche, which will be housed at the W. E. B. DuBois Library on campus.

I appreciate your giving time to this study, which will help me learn more about the effect of participation in a GSA. If you have any questions, please feel free to call me at _____. You may also contact my committee chairperson, Professor _____ at _____.

Thank you,
Janice E. Doppler (signed)

---

Please sign below if you are willing to participate in the dissertation research project outlined above.

Signature _____

Print name_____

Date _____

**Figure 3.2. Informed Consent: Students**

**Informed Consent for Dissertation Research Project Participation:
Gay/Straight Alliance Participants in Public High Schools**

Dear Parent of a Gay/Straight Alliance Member:

I am a graduate student in the School of Education at the University of Massachusetts, Amherst. I would like to invite your daughter/son to participate in a research project about the benefits and costs of participating in a Gay/Straight Alliance. I am interested in exploring the experiences of self-identified lesbian, gay, and heterosexual students who participate in GSAs.

Her/his participation will include being interviewed twice for forty-five minutes to an hour each time. A third interview of the same length may be added if it seems necessary after the first two interviews.

She/he may be vulnerable to someone's determining who she/he is and what has been said, but I will protect her/him from this possibility as much as possible by using a pseudonym for each participant. I will give your child a hard copy of the transcript of each interview. She/he will be able to make any desired changes. Each participant has the right to withdraw from the study any time up until March 1, 1999. At that point, I will be in the final stages of the writing process and will not be able to remove quotations from the document.

This study will be shared with my dissertation committee and other appropriate members of the University of Massachusetts community. The dissertation that results from this work will be published in hard copy and microfiche, which will be housed at the W. E. B. DuBois Library on campus.

I appreciate your giving permission for your child to participate in this study, which will help me learn more about the effect of participation in a GSA. If you have any questions, please feel free to call me at _____. You may also contact my committee chairperson, Professor _____ at _____.

Thank you,
Janice E. Doppler (signed)

_____

Please sign below if you are willing to allow your daughter/son to participate in the dissertation research project outlined above.

Signature _____

Print name _____

Daughter/Son _____

Date _____

**Figure 3.3. Informed Consent: Parents**

Doppler's (1998) proposal continued with a carefully framed discussion, elaborated by examples, of how she would manage political independence, how she would protect her ownership of the data, and why potential benefits would outweigh any risks associated with conducting the study.

The preceding discussions have taken the reader through the recursive process of deciding on an overall approach to the study, building a rationale around it, discussing the site or participants, and thinking about their role and ethics in the conduct of the study. The next chapter describes an array of primary and supplementary data collection methods—the concrete answers to the "how will I do this study" question.

## Further Reading

### Rationale and Evolving Design

Becker, H. S., Geer, B., Hughes, E. G., & Strauss, A. L. (1961). *Boys in white: Student culture in medical school.* Chicago: University of Chicago Press.

Brantlinger, E. A. (1993). *The politics of social class in secondary schools* (1st ed.). New York: Teachers College Press.

Campbell, A. (1991). *The girls in the gang* (2nd ed.). Cambridge: Blackwell.

Chase, S. (1995). *Ambiguous empowerment: Women in the superintendency.* Amherst, MA: University of Massachusetts Press.

Janesick, V. J. (1994). The dance of qualitative research design. In N. K. Denzin & Y. S. Lincoln (Eds.), *Handbook of qualitative research* (pp. 209-219). Thousand Oaks, CA: Sage.

Lesko, N. (1988). *Symbolizing society: Stories, rites, and structure in a Catholic high school.* New York: Falmer.

Metz, M. H. (1978). *Classrooms and corridors: The crisis of authority in desegregated secondary schools.* Berkeley, CA: University of California Press.

Olesen, V. L., & Whittaker, E. W. (1967b). *The silent dialogue: A study in the social psychology of professional socialization.* San Francisco: Jossey-Bass.

Smith, L. (1971). *Anatomy of an educational innovation.* New York: John Wiley.

Valli, L. (1986). *Becoming clerical workers.* Boston: Routledge & Kegan Paul.

Whyte, W. F. (1981). *Street corner society: The social structure of an Italian slum* (3rd ed.). Chicago: University of Chicago Press.

### Personal Reflections

Eisner, E. W. (1991). *The enlightened eye: Qualitative inquiry and the enhancement of educational practice.* New York: Macmillan.

Geertz, C. (1988). *Works and lives: The anthropologist as author.* Palo Alto, CA: Stanford University Press.

Gitlin, A. (Ed.). (1994). *Power and method: Political activism and educational research.* New York: Routledge.

Glesne, C., & Peshkin, A. (1992). *Becoming qualitative researchers: An introduction.* White Plains, NY: Longman.

Golde, P. (1970). *Women in the field.* Chicago: Aldine.

Jorgensen, D. L. (1989). *Participant observation: A methodology for human studies.* Newbury Park, CA: Sage.

McLaughlin, D., & Tierney, W. G. (1993). *Naming silenced lives: Personal narratives and processes of educational change.* New York: Routledge.

Piotrkowski, C. S. (1979). *Work and the family system: A naturalistic study of working-class and lower-middle-class families.* New York: Free Press.

Van Maanen, J. (1988). *Tales of the field: On writing ethnography.* Chicago: University of Chicago Press.

Whyte, W. F. (1984). *Learning from the field: A guide from experience.* Beverly Hills, CA: Sage.

### Negotiating Entry and Access in General Texts

Bogdan, R. C., & Biklen, S. K. (1998). *Qualitative research for education: An introduction to theory and methods* (3rd ed.). Boston: Allyn & Bacon.

Eisner, E. W. (1991). *The enlightened eye: Qualitative inquiry and the enhancement of educational practice.* New York: Macmillan.

Patton, M. Q. (1990). *Qualitative research and evaluation methods* (2nd ed.). Newbury Park, CA: Sage.

Schwartz, H., & Jacobs, J. (1979). *Qualitative sociology: A method to the madness.* New York: Free Press.

Taylor, S. J., & Bogdan, R. (1984). *Introduction to qualitative research: The search for meanings* (2nd ed.). New York: John Wiley.

### Personal, Political, and Ethical Dilemmas

Bowen, E. S. (1964). *Return to laughter.* Garden City, NY: Doubleday.

Emerson, R. (1983). Introduction. In R. Emerson (Ed.), *Contemporary field research: A collection of readings* (pp. 255-268). Prospect Heights, IL: Waveland.

Everhart, R. B. (1977). Between stranger and friend: Some consequences of long-term fieldwork in schools. *American Educational Research Journal, 14,* 1-15.

Fine, M. (1994). Negotiating the hyphens: Reinventing self and other in qualitative research. In N. K. Denzin & Y. S. Lincoln (Eds.), *Handbook of qualitative research* (pp. 70-82). Thousand Oaks, CA: Sage.

Galliher, J. F. (1983). Social scientists' ethical responsibilities to superordinates: Looking up meekly. In R. Emerson (Ed.), *Contemporary field research: A collection of readings* (pp. 300-311). Prospect Heights, IL: Waveland.

Glesne, C. (1989). Rapport and friendship in ethnographic research. *International Journal of Qualitative Studies in Education, 2,* 43-54.

Krieger, S. (1985). Beyond subjectivity: The use of self in social science. *Qualitative Sociology, 8,* 309-324.

Lincoln, Y. S. (1997). Self, subject, audience, text: Living at the edge, writing in the margins. In W. G. Tierney & Y. S. Lincoln (Eds.), *Representation and the text: Re-framing the narrative voice.* Albany: State University of New York Press.

Olesen, V., & Whittaker, E. (1967a). Role-making in participant observation: Processes in the research-actor relationship. *Human Organization, 26,* 273-281.

Peshkin, A. (1988). In search of subjectivity: One's own. *Educational Researcher, 17,* 17-21.

Punch, M. (1986). *The politics and ethics of fieldwork.* Beverly Hills, CA: Sage.

Punch, M. (1994). Politics and ethics in qualitative research. In N. K. Denzin & Y. S. Lincoln (eds.), *Handbook of qualitative research* (pp. 83-97). Thousand Oaks, CA: Sage.

Rist, R. (1981, April). *Is there life after research? Ethical issues in the study of schools.* Paper presented at the annual meeting of the American Educational Research Association, Los Angeles.

Spradley, J. S. (1979). *The ethnographic interview.* New York: Holt, Rinehart & Winston.

Thorne, B. (1983). Political activist as participant observer: Conflicts of commitment in a study of the draft resistance movement of the 1960s. In R. Emerson (Ed.), *Contemporary field research: A collection of readings* (pp. 216-234). Prospect Heights, IL: Waveland.

Van Maanen, J. (1983). The moral fix: On the ethics of fieldwork. In R. Emerson (Ed.), *Contemporary field research: A collection of readings* (pp. 269-287). Prospect Heights, IL: Waveland.

Wax, M. L. (1983). On fieldworkers and those exposed to fieldwork: Federal regulations and moral issues. In R. Emerson (Ed.), *Contemporary field research: A collection of readings* (pp. 288-299). Prospect Heights, IL: Waveland.

# 4    Data Collection Methods

Qualitative researchers typically rely on four methods for gathering information: (a) participation in the setting, (b) direct observation, (c) in-depth interviewing, and (d) analyzing documents and material culture. These methods form the core of qualitative inquiry—the staples of the diet. Several specialized methods supplement these. This chapter provides a brief discussion of both the primary and secondary methods for consideration in designing a qualitative study. This discussion does not replace the many excellent, detailed references on specific data collection methods (we refer to several at the end of this chapter); its purpose is to guide the proposal writer in stipulating the methods of choice for his study and describing, for the reader, how the data generated will inform his research questions. How the researcher plans to use specific methods, however, depends on several considerations.

Extending the discussion in Chapter 1, Brantlinger's (1997) work provides a useful summary of seven categories of crucial assumptions. The first is how the researcher views the *nature of the research:* Is the inquiry technical and neutral, intending to conform to traditional research within her discipline, or is it controversial and critical with an explicit political agenda? Second, how does she construe her location, her *positioning relative to the participants:* Does she view herself as distant and objective or intimately involved in the lives of the participants? Third, what is the *"direction of her 'gaze' "* (p. 4): Is it outward toward "others"—externalizing the research problem—or does it include explicit inner contemplation? Fourth, what is the *purpose of the research:* Does she assume that the primary purpose of the study is professional and essentially private (e.g., promoting her career), or is it intended to be useful and informative to the participants or the site? Related to the fourth category is the fifth: Who is the *intended audience of the study*—the scholarly community or the participants themselves? Sixth, what is her *political positioning:* Does she view research as neutral, or does she claim a politically explicit agenda? Finally, the seventh arena is how she views the *exercise of agency:* Does she view herself and the participants as essentially passive or as "engaged in local praxis" (p. 4)? Assumptions made in these seven categories shape how the specific research methods are conceived and implemented throughout a study; explicit discussion of assumptions strengthens the overall logic and integrity of the proposal.

## Primary Methods

*Participation*

Developed primarily from the disciplines of cultural anthropology and qualitative sociology, participant observation (as this method is typically called) is both an overall approach to inquiry and a data-gathering method. Participant observation is to some degree an essential element of all qualitative studies. As its name suggests, participant observation demands firsthand involvement in the social world chosen for study. Immersion in the setting allows the researcher to hear, see, and begin to experience reality as the participants do. Ideally, the researcher spends a considerable amount of time in the setting, learning about daily life there. This immersion offers the researcher the opportunity to learn directly from his own experience of the setting. These personal reflections are integral to the emerging analysis of the cultural group of interest.

This method for gathering data is basic to all qualitative studies and forces consideration of the role or stance of the researcher as a participant observer. We have explored issues of role more fully in Chapter 3; we here reiterate that, at the proposal stage, it is helpful to elaborate on the planned extent of participation, what the nature of that involvement is likely to be, how much will be revealed about the study's purpose to the people in the setting, how intensively the researcher will be present, and how focused the participation will be. The researcher should stipulate how his participation will inform the research questions.

## Observation

Observation entails the systematic noting and recording of events, behaviors, and artifacts (objects) in the social setting chosen for study. The observational record is frequently referred to as *field notes*—detailed, nonjudgmental, concrete descriptions of what has been observed. For studies relying exclusively on observation, the researcher makes no special effort to have a particular role; often, to be tolerated as an unobtrusive observer is enough. Classroom observational studies are one example often found in education. Through observation, the researcher documents and describes complex actions and interactions. Without other sources of information, however, the meaning of these actions can only be inferred. This method assumes that behavior is purposeful and expressive of deeper values and beliefs. Observation can range from highly structured, detailed notation of behavior guided by checklists to more holistic description of events and behavior.

In the early stages of qualitative inquiry, the researcher typically enters the setting with broad areas of interest but without predetermined categories or strict observational checklists. The value here is that the researcher is able to discover the recurring patterns of behavior and relationships. After such patterns are identified and described through early analysis of field notes, checklists become more appropriate and context sensitive. Focused observation then is used at later stages of the study, usually to check analytic themes to see, for example, if they explain behavior and relationships over a long time or in a variety of settings.

Observation is a fundamental and highly important method in all qualitative inquiry: It is used to discover complex interactions in natural social settings. Even in in-depth interview studies, observation plays an important role as the researcher notes the interviewee's body language and affect in addition to her words. It is, however, a method that requires a great deal of the researcher. Discomfort, uncomfortable ethical dilemmas and even danger, the difficulty of managing a relatively unobtrusive role, and the challenge of identifying the "big picture" while finely observing huge amounts of fast-moving and complex behavior are just a few of the challenges. At the proposal stage, the researcher should describe the purpose of observing, in what phase of the study it is likely to be most fruitful, and how field notes will be used to respond to the research questions.

Figure 4.1 provides an example of field notes conducted for a study of kindergarten teachers. In these field notes, O'Hearn-Curran (1997) has formatted the descriptive notes in a column on the left while reserving a second column on the right for her observer's comments. These comments include her emerging analytic insights and comments about the actions. Observer's comments are often a quite fruitful source of analytic insights and clues to focus data collection more tightly. They may also provide important questions for subsequent interviews.

*In-Depth Interviewing*

Qualitative researchers rely quite extensively on in-depth interviewing. Kahn and Cannell (1957) describe interviewing as "a conversation with a purpose" (p. 149); it may be the overall strategy or one of several methods employed in a study. Interviewing varies in terms of a priori structure and in the latitude the interviewee has in responding to questions. Patton (1990, pp. 280-290) categorizes interviews into three general types: the informal conversational interview, the general interview guide approach, and the standardized open-ended interview.

Typically, qualitative in-depth interviews are much more like conversations than formal events with predetermined response categories. The researcher explores a few general topics to help uncover the participant's views but otherwise respects how the participant frames and structures the responses. This, in fact, is an assumption fundamental to qualitative research: The participant's perspective on the phenomenon of interest should unfold as the participant views it, not as the researcher views it. A degree of systematization in questioning may be necessary in, for example, a multisite case study or when many participants are interviewed. The most important aspect of the interviewer's approach concerns conveying the attitude that the participant's views are valuable and useful. This may, however, evoke ethical dilemmas for the interviewer; we discuss these more fully below.

Interviews have particular strengths. An interview is a useful way to get large amounts of data quickly. When more than one person participates (e.g.,

**SAMPLE FIELD NOTES**

Tuesday, November 13, 1997    12:40 p.m.
Observation                                      *Observer's Comments*

There are 17 children in the room. There are
3 adults: 1 teacher, 1 classroom assistant, and
1 student teacher (the student teacher is an
older woman).

The room is in the basement of the school.
The school is a brick building approximately 90
to 100 years old. The room is about 40 feet by
30 feet. The room is carpeted and is sectioned off
by furniture. There is an area with big books and          *The teacher seems to*
a chart in the left-hand back corner of the room.          *have done a great job*
Next to that is a shelf with a mixture of small            *of making the room*
books, tapes, and big books in baskets. Next to            *seem very inviting.*
that is a small area with toy kitchen furniture and        *The space itself is not*
dolls. There is an area with several tables in front       *optimal.*
of the kitchen area. There are many small chairs
pulled up to the table. In the front of the room is
an area with a sand table. There is a semicircle
table in the left-hand front corner of the room.
The walls are colorful with papers that have been
made by the children. One wall has papers with
apples on them. Another wall has pictures of
children with their names on the front of the
papers. There are several small windows in the
room and the fluorescent lighting seems to be the
major source of light.

The children have just come into the room.                 *Most of the children*
They have put their coats and backpacks onto               *appear to know*
their hooks in the hall outside.                           *the routine.*

**Figure 4.1. Sample Field Notes**

focus group interviews, discussed later), the interview process gathers a wide variety of information across a larger number of subjects than if there were fewer participants—the familiar trade-off between breadth and depth. Immediate follow-up and clarification are possible. Combined with observation, interviews allow the researcher to understand the meanings that people hold for their everyday activities.

Interviewing has limitations and weaknesses, however. Interviews involve personal interaction; cooperation is essential. Interviewees may be unwilling or may be uncomfortable sharing all that the interviewer hopes to explore, or they may be unaware of recurring patterns in their lives. The interviewer may not ask questions that evoke long narratives from participants either because of a lack of expertise or familiarity with local language or because of lack of skill. By the same token, she may not properly comprehend responses to the questions or various elements of the conversation. And at times, interviewees may have good reason not to be truthful (see Douglas, 1976, for a discussion).

Interviewers should have superb listening skills and be skillful at personal interaction, question framing, and gentle probing for elaboration. Volumes of data can be obtained through interviewing, but the data are time-consuming to analyze. Finally, there is the issue of the quality of the data. When the researcher is using in-depth interviews as the sole way of gathering data, she should have demonstrated through the conceptual framework that the purpose of the study is to uncover and describe the participants' perspectives on events—that is, that the subjective view is what matters. Studies making more objectivist assumptions would triangulate interview data with data gathered through other methods.

Figure 4.2 provides elaborated notes from an interview conducted for a study of students of color in a community college. Koski (1997) was particularly interested in how these students identified and defined effective teachers. She was intrigued with the notion of culturally relevant pedagogy and conducted several in-depth interviews with teachers identified by students as especially effective. She has formatted the notes from the interview to provide space for her comments, as did O'Hearn-Curran in the field notes presented in Figure 4.1.

In addition to generic in-depth interviewing are several more specialized forms of interviews, including ethnographic interviewing, phenomenological interviewing, elite interviewing, focus group interviewing, and interviewing children. We now describe each of these methods briefly.

---

**SAMPLE INTERVIEW NOTES**

---

Interview with DC
October 15, 1997
1:30-3:40

*DC is an advisor with an academic department. The interview was set up by the dean.*

---

Setting: DC's office in the academic department. It's bright and lively—colorful tapestry on one wall, posters on the other walls. A giant poster about "I am okay." Books and papers are everywhere. On the corner of the desk are some wood games: tic-tac-toe, pyramid, and others.

DC is a small, dark-colored woman with her hair in small but longish braids all over her head. She wears large glasses and a pinkish shade of lipstick that complements her coloring. She is lively, with a ready smile and a quick laugh. She comments on her height: "I'm smaller than all my advisees, so I'm not a threat to anyone."

I explain what I'm interested in and what my project is about. I tell her that I would like three things from her: One is an idea of what she as an adviser thinks are the attributes of a good teacher and what her students of color say, what teachers might possess those attributes, and what students I might talk to for the project.

*DC listens very intently here.*

*This is an awkward moment for me and for her. I wasn't sure what to do. This general question seems to surprise her.*

DC: "Okay. Good. Well, ask me a question."

KK: "Tell me a little bit about what you do."

DC: "I'm an adviser here. We get them in fresh off the street. I sit down with them and make out an educational plan. I like it when they know what's expected of them."

DC: "The educational plan lists not only courses to be taken but clubs and other student activities. It lists the advising events the student will attend."

*She hands me a form that she has worked on with a student. Just then someone comes in and tells her she has an important phone call that they can't transfer. She leaves for about ten minutes. I am able to look around.*

DC returns. KK: "How many students do you have?"

DC: "About 100."

KK: "100! Are you able to have a relationship with so many?"

*I don't remember her exact answer here. Something about keeping in touch.*

DC: "I feel I'm an advocate for students. I do whatever needs to be done to get them through this. I tell them not to overload, to relax about this. . . . I think being honest with students is important. If I don't know, I tell them. But we can always look it up on the Net!"

**Figure 4.2. Sample Interview Notes**

### Ethnographic Interviewing

Based on the discipline of cognitive anthropology, ethnographic interviewing elicits the cognitive structures guiding participants' worldviews. Described as "a particular kind of speech event" (Spradley, 1979, p. 18), ethnographic questions are used by the ethnographer to gather cultural data. Spradley (1979) identifies three main types of questions: descriptive, structural, and contrast. Descriptive questions allow the researcher to collect a sample of the participant's language. Structural questions discover the basic units in his cultural knowledge, and contrast questions provide the ethnographer with the meaning of various terms in the participant's language.

The value of the ethnographic interview lies in its focus on culture through the participant's perspective and through a firsthand encounter. This approach is especially useful for eliciting participants' meanings for events and behaviors and for generating a typology of cultural classification schemes. It also highlights the nuances of the culture. The method is flexible in formulating working hypotheses and avoids oversimplification in description and analysis because of its rich narrative descriptions.

There are weaknesses in this method, however. The ethnographer may impose her values through the phrasing of questions or interpretation of data. If the member of the cultural group chosen to participate does not represent that culture, the subsequent analysis will be impoverished. The success of this method, as in all interviewing, is highly dependent on the researcher's interpersonal skills.

### Phenomenological Interviewing

Phenomenological interviewing is a specific type of in-depth interviewing grounded in the tradition of phenomenology. Phenomenology is the study of lived experiences and the ways we understand those experiences to develop a worldview. It rests on an assumption that there is a structure and essence to shared experiences that can be narrated. The purpose of this type of interviewing is to describe the meaning of a concept or phenomenon that several individuals share.

As developed by Seidman (1998), three in-depth interviews compose phenomenological inquiry. The first focuses on past experience with the phenomenon of interest; the second focuses on present experience; and the third joins these two narratives to describe the individual's essential experience with the phenomenon. Prior to interviewing, however, the phenomenological researcher has written a full description of her own experience, thereby bracketing her experiences from those of the interviewees. This phase of the inquiry is referred to as *epoche.* The purpose of this self-examination is for the researcher to gain clarity from her own preconceptions, and it is part of the "ongoing process rather than a single fixed event" (Patton, 1990, p. 408).

The next phase is called *phenomenological reduction*; here, the researcher identifies the essence of the phenomenon (Patton 1990, p. 408). The researcher then clusters the data around themes that describe the "textures of the experience" (Creswell, 1998, p. 150). The final stage, *structural synthesis,* involves the imaginative exploration of "all possible meanings and divergent perspectives" (Creswell, 1998, p. 150) and culminates in a description of the essence of the phenomenon and its deep structure.

The primary advantage of phenomenological interviewing is that it permits an explicit focus on the researcher's personal experience combined with those of the interviewees. It focuses on the deep, lived meanings that events have for individuals, assuming that these meanings guide actions and interactions. It is, however, quite labor-intensive and requires a reflective turn of mind on the part of the researcher.

### "Elite" Interviewing

An elite interview is a specialized case of interviewing that focuses on a particular type of interviewee. "Elite" individuals are those considered to be influential, prominent, and/or well-informed people in an organization or community; they are selected for interviews on the basis of their expertise in areas relevant to the research.

Elite interviewing has many advantages. Valuable information can be gained from these participants because of the positions they hold in social, political, financial, or administrative realms. Elites can usually provide an overall view of an organization or its relationship to other organizations. They are more likely than other participants to be familiar with the legal and financial structures of the organization. Elites are also able to report on an organizations' policies, past histories, and future plans from a particular perspective.

Elite interviewing also presents disadvantages. It is often difficult to gain access to elites because they are usually somewhat elusive and busy people operating under demanding time constraints; they are also often difficult to contact initially. The interviewer may have to rely on sponsorship, recommendations, and introductions for assistance in making appointments with elite individuals.

Another disadvantage in interviewing elites is that the interviewer may have to adapt the planned-for structure of the interview, based on the wishes and predilections of the person interviewed. Although this is true with all in-depth interviewing, elite individuals are typically quite savvy and may resent the restrictions of narrow or ill-phrased questions. They may want an active interplay with the interviewer. Well practiced at meeting the public and being in control, an elite person may turn the interview around, thereby taking charge of it. Elites respond well to inquiries about broad areas of content and to a high proportion of intelligent, provocative, open-ended questions that allow them the freedom to use their knowledge and imagination.

Working with elites places great demands on the ability of the interviewer, who must establish competence by displaying a thorough knowledge of the topic or, lacking such knowledge, by projecting an accurate conceptualization of the problem through shrewd questioning. The interviewer's hard work usually pays off, however, in the quality of information obtained. Elites often contribute insight and meaning to the interview process because they are intelligent and quick-thinking people, at home in the realm of ideas, policies, and generalizations.

Focus Group Interviewing

The method of interviewing participants in focus groups comes largely from marketing research but has been widely adapted to social science and applied research. The groups are generally composed of 7 to 10 people (although they range from as small as 4 to as large as 12) who are unfamiliar to one another and have been selected because they share certain characteristics relevant to the study's questions. The interviewer creates a supportive environment, asking focused questions, to encourage discussion and the expression of differing opinions and points of view. These interviews may be conducted several times with different individuals so that the researcher can identify trends in the perceptions and opinions expressed, which are revealed through careful, systematic analysis (Krueger, 1988, p. 18).

This method assumes that an individual's attitudes and beliefs do not form in a vacuum: People often need to listen to others' opinions and understandings in order to form their own. One-to-one interviews may be impoverished because the participant had not reflected on the topic and feels unprepared to respond. Often, the questions in a focus group setting are deceptively simple; the trick is to promote the participants' expression of their views through the creation of a supportive environment.

The advantages of focus group interviews are that this method is socially oriented, studying participants in an atmosphere more natural than artificial experimental circumstances and more relaxed than the exposure of a one-to-one interview. When combined with participant observation, focus groups are especially useful for gaining access, focusing site selection and sampling, and even for checking tentative conclusions (Morgan, 1997). The format allows the facilitator the flexibility to explore unanticipated issues as they arise in the discussion. The results have high face validity: Because the method is readily understood, the findings appear believable. Furthermore, focus groups are relatively low cost, they provide quick results, and they can increase the sample size of qualitative studies by interviewing more people at one time (Krueger, 1988).

There are, however, certain disadvantages to this method as well: The interviewer has less control over a group interview than an individual one, which can result in lost time while dead-end or irrelevant issues are discussed; the data are difficult to analyze, because context is essential to understanding the participants' comments; the method requires the use of special room arrangements and highly trained observer moderators; the groups can vary a great deal and can be hard to assemble; and finally, there are logistical problems arising from the need to manage a conversation while getting good quality data.

### Interviewing Children

Children may be the primary focus of a study or one of many groups the researcher wants to interview. Their perspectives may be sought because they offer fresh insights. Increasingly, there are calls for including children's perspectives as relevant and insightful in learning more about aspects of their worlds. This is especially true in education where all too often those most affected by educational policy and programmatic decisions—the students—are absent from inquiry. There are special considerations, however, when the qualitative researcher proposes a study that involves children.

First are age considerations. Interviewing preschoolers, for example, is quite different from interviewing early adolescents. Both age groups have their unique challenges and rewards. Young children are often active; early adolescents are frequently very self-conscious. Three-year-olds, exploring their emerging language skills, can drive one to distraction with their incessant questions (often quite sophisticated ones!), whereas early adolescents may be taciturn. It is unrealistic to expect young children to sit still for long, but joining them in some activity can create a climate for focused "talk." Some adolescents may feel more comfortable with their peers in a focus group interview, whereas others may prefer the intimacy of one-to-one interviews. Decisions about how to gather data with various age groups requires sensitivity to their needs, their developmental issues, and flexibility.

Second are role considerations. Fine and Sandstrom (1988) note that the roles an adult researcher assumes when studying children vary along two dimensions: "(1) the extent of positive contact between adult and child, and (2) the extent to which the adult has direct authority over the child" (p. 14). They offer the roles of supervisor, leader, observer, and friend as appropriate roles. Of these, they find the role of friend the most fruitful, noting that the researcher then interacts with the children "in the most trusted way possible—without any explicit authority role" (p. 17). They caution, however, that age and power differences between adults and children are always salient.

### The Review of Documents

History and context surrounding a specific setting come, in part, from reviewing documents. Researchers supplement participant observation, interviewing, and observation with gathering and analyzing documents produced in the course of everyday events or constructed specifically for the research at hand. As such, the review of documents is an unobtrusive method, rich in portraying the values and beliefs of participants in the setting. Minutes of meetings, logs, announcements, formal policy statements, letters, and so on are all useful in developing an understanding of the setting or group studied. Similarly, research journals and samples of free writing about the topic can be quite informative.

Archival data are the routinely gathered records of a society, community, or organization, and may further supplement other qualitative methods. For example, marital patterns among a group of Mexicans, discovered through fieldwork in a community, could be tested through marriage records found in the offices of the county seat or state capitol. Descriptions of articulated funding priorities by policymakers could be corroborated (or not) through an analysis of budgetary allocations. As with other methodological decisions, the decision to gather and analyze documents or archival records should be linked to the research questions developed in the conceptual framework for the study. Furthermore, documents must be viewed with the skepticism that historians apply as they search for "truth" in old texts.

The use of documents often entails a specialized analytic approach called content analysis. The raw material for content analysis may be any form of communication, usually written materials (textbooks, novels, newspapers, e-mail messages); other forms of communication—such as music, pictures, or political speeches—may also be included. Historically, content analysis was viewed as an objective and neutral way of obtaining a quantitative description of the content of various forms of communications: Thus, counting the mention of specific items was important (Berelson, 1952, p. 18). As it has evolved, however, it is viewed more generously as a method for describing and interpreting the artifacts of a society or social group.

Probably the greatest strength of content analysis is that it is unobtrusive and nonreactive: It can be conducted without disturbing the setting in any way. The researcher determines where the greatest emphasis lies after the data have been gathered. Also, the procedure is relatively clear to the reader. Information can therefore be checked, as can the care with which the analysis has been applied. A potential weakness, however, is the span of inferential reasoning. That is, the analysis of the content of written materials or film, for example, entails interpretation by the researcher, just as in the analysis of interactively gathered data: Numbers do not speak for themselves. Care should be taken, therefore, in displaying the logic of interpretation used in inferring meaning from the artifacts.

Some combination of these primary research methods is typical for in-depth qualitative inquiry. In the following vignette, Shadduck-Hernandez (1997) articulates a complex design that incorporates several. Her proposal was for research about CIRCLE (Center for Immigrant and Refugee Leadership and Empowerment), a participatory project involving newcomer undergraduate students, graduate students, and members from refugee and immigrant communities.

\* \* \* \* \*

*Vignette 22*
_____

*Using Multiple Methods*

Imagine 12 university students, on a chilly Saturday morning, sprawled out on a classroom floor formulating their thoughts for a proposal on scattered sheets of newsprint. Laughter, silence, and intense discussion highlight the writing process of these authors who are first-generation refugee and immigrant (newcomer) students from China, Cambodia, Vietnam, Laos, and Korea participating in an undergraduate seminar on cross-cultural experiences in community development. After brainstorming various ideas, the students collectively decided on a proposal incorporating photography and art as the vehicle to portray the lived, and often misunderstood, experiences that they share with a group of 15 Vietnamese and Khmer youth they have been working with. This proposal has lead to a student-initiated and directed research project, A Collective Visual Portrayal, funded by the University of Massachusetts Chancellor's Counsel on Community, Diversity and Social Justice.

The organic and evolutionary educational process of CIRCLE over the past 3 years has allowed me to conduct different levels of preliminary research. This dissertation builds on this research, exploring how newcomer students view their educational experiences after having participated in a series of community development courses and outreach projects that validate their cross-cultural lives. Drawing on a range of qualitative data sources and informed by my comprehensive examination research, I also focus on how newcomer students and the facilitators working with them define themselves as leaders, activists, and educators through their academic course work and community involvement.

This research acknowledges the real tensions that exist in any qualitative research endeavor. Certain qualitative research models can be rigid, one-way streets if they seduce participants into a process of inquiry in which the researcher alone is the analyzer and interpreter of data. This study consciously tried to counter such situations by applying participatory research as the guide of the inquiry (Maguire, 1987; Reardon, Welsh, Kreiswirth, & Forester, 1993). Study participants have been involved in this inquiry as "researchers" and valued members of a learning team in order to produce knowledge that may help stimulate social change.

Stemming from a commitment to participatory processes, the research I am conducting is collaborative in nature, emerging from the students and the communities I work with. Collaboration and participation in developing critical learning environments produce pooled resources and shared expertise leading to integrated and collective activities. Collaboration, action, and reflection enhance the legitimacy of each participant's knowledge (Brice Heath & McLaughlin, 1993) and set the stage for the sources of multilevel data collection employed in this study. These six sources of data have evolved in complement with the development of CIRCLE courses and community outreach activities and support the concept of a pedagogy for affirmation, advocacy and action. They include the following:

1. Journal entries and self-reflection papers: These serve as the data for textual narrative analysis in this dissertation research.

2. A focus group interview with 8 undergraduate students at the end of a course where personal practice in community development is discussed and course content and process are reflected on.

3. In-depth interviews with 10 students: These contribute to the dissertation's oral narrative analysis data collection process.

4. Video and photography documentation have been collaboratively collected by study participants (students) and researchers around classroom and community events, evaluations, and student presentations: These form the dissertation's visual narrative analysis.

5. Oral history interviews conducted by students and youth with each other as part of A Collective Visual Portrayal project.

6. Research field notes, reflections, and academic papers for courses and conferences over the 4 years of my involvement with and participation in CIRCLE: These provide critical insights into my own theoretical development in relation to this research and my role as researcher in this study.

\* \* \* \* \*

Shadduck-Hernandez's (1997) discussion of the various sources of qualitative data—some generated as part of the CIRCLE project, others to be generated specifically for the dissertation—is eloquently congruent with her assumptions about the nature of this work, its purpose and audience, and her political stance. Note that she plans to rely on several methods: documents in the form of journals, self-reflective writing, and papers written for courses or conferences (both her own and those of the student participants); a focus group interview; in-depth interviews; and video and photography. The latter source of data—video and photography—are what we describe as secondary data collection methods, discussed next.

## Secondary Methods

In addition to the primary data-gathering methods outlined above, the researcher can choose to incorporate several secondary methods in the design of a study, as appropriate. Each of those described below is a full and complete method in and of itself and has a methodological literature explicating its nuances and subtleties. As in the preceding discussions, the ones that follow are necessarily simplified and brief, and the list is not exhaustive. The methods discussed are life histories and narrative inquiry; historical analysis; film, video, and photography; kinesics; proxemics; unobtrusive measures; surveys and questionnaires; and projective techniques and psychological testing.

### *Life Histories and Narrative Inquiry*

Life histories and narrative inquiry are methods that gather, analyze, and interpret the stories people tell about their lives. They assume that people live "storied lives" and that telling and retelling one's story helps one understand and create a sense of self. The researcher, working closely with the participant, explores a story and records that story. Life histories and narrative analysis are used across the social science disciplines and are particularly useful for giving the reader an insider's view of a culture or era in history (Edgerton & Langness, 1974).

#### Life Histories

Life histories seek to "examine and analyze the subjective experience of individuals and their constructions of the social world" (Jones, 1983, p. 147). They assume a complex interaction between the individual's understanding of his or her world and that world itself. They are, therefore, uniquely suited to depicting the socialization of a person into a cultural milieu and to make theoretical sense of it (Dollard, 1935). Thus, one understands a culture through the history of one person's development or life within it, told in ways that capture the person's own feelings, views, and perspectives. The life history is often an account of how an individual enters a group and becomes socialized into that group and therefore capable of meeting the normative expectations of that society for those of similar gender, social class, or age. Life histories emphasize the experience of the individual—how the person copes with society rather than how society copes with the stream of individuals (Mandelbaum, 1973).

Life histories are helpful in defining socialization and in studying aspects of certain professions. Their value goes beyond providing specific information about events and customs of the past—as a historical account might—by showing how the individual creates meaning within the culture. Life histories are valuable in studying cultural changes that have occurred over time, in learning about cultural norms and transgressions of those norms and in gaining an inside view of a culture. They also help capture the evolution of cultural patterns and how the patterns are linked to the life of an individual. Often, this point of view is missing from standard ethnographies (Edgerton & Langness, 1974).

One strength of life history methodology is that, because it pictures a substantial portion of a person's life, the reader enters into those same experiences. Second, the method provides a fertile source of hypotheses that might be tested by further study. Third, it depicts actions and perspectives across a social group that may be analyzed for comparative study. Life history methodology emphasizes the value of a person's own story and provides pieces in a mosaic that depicts a certain era or social group. Life histories are often used in feminist research as a way of understanding, relatively free of androcentric bias, how women's lives and careers evolve (Lawless, 1991).

Jones (1983) offers five criteria for life histories. First, the individual should be viewed as a member of a culture; the life history "describe[s] and interpret[s] the actor's account of his or her development in the common-sense world" (p. 153). Second, the method should capture the significant role that others play in "transmitting socially defined stocks of knowledge" (p. 153). Third, the taken-for-granted assumptions of the specific cultural world under study should be described and analyzed. These assumptions are revealed in rules and codes for conduct as well as in myths and rituals. Fourth, life histories should focus on the experience of an individual over time to capture the "processual development of the person" (p. 154). And fifth, the cultural world under study should be continuously related to the individual's unfolding life story.

The major criticisms of the life history are the difficulties of generalizing, limited principles for selecting participants, and few accepted concepts to guide analysis. Once the researcher is aware of the possible weaknesses in the method, he can circumvent them. Official records may provide corroborating information or may illuminate aspects of the culture absent from the individual's account. The researcher can substantiate the meanings presented in the history by interviewing others in the participant's life. For example, prior to publishing *The Professional Thief,* Sutherland and Conwell (1983) submitted the manuscript to four professional thieves and to two police detectives to assess possible bias and to ensure that their interpretations resonated with the understandings of other professional thieves and those who come in contact with them.

As with any qualitative genre, the abundance of data collected in a life history should be managed and reduced in some preliminary way before analytic headway can be made. Alternatives to the classical chronological order for presenting the interpretation include (a) critical dimensions or aspects of the person's life, (b) principal turning-points and the life conditions between them, and (c) the person's characteristic means of adaptation (Mandelbaum, 1973). A life history account can add depth and evocative illustration to any qualitative study.

### Narrative Inquiry

Closely related to the life history method is narrative inquiry, an interdisciplinary method that draws from traditions in literary theory, oral history, drama, psychology, folklore, and film philosophy and that views lives holistically (Connelly & Clandinin, 1990). The method assumes that people's realities are constructed through narrating their stories. The researcher explores a story told by a participant and records that story. Narrative analysis can be applied to any spoken or written account—for example, an in-depth interview.

Narrative inquiry requires a great deal of openness and trust between participant and researcher: The inquiry should be a mutual and sincere collaboration, a caring relationship akin to friendship that is established over time for full participation in the storytelling, retelling, and reliving of personal experiences. It demands intense active listening and giving the narrator full voice. Because it is a collaboration, however, both voices are heard.

This method is criticized for its focus on the individual rather than on the social context. Like life histories, however, it seeks to understand sociological questions about groups, communities, and contexts through individuals' lived experiences. Just as with any method that relies on participants' accounts, narrative may suffer from selective recall, a focus on subsets of experience, filling in memory gaps through inference, and reinterpretation of the past (Ross & Conway, 1986). Crites (1986, p. 168) cautions against "the illusion of causality"—the inference that the narrator's story sequencing has accurate cause-and-effect linkages. Narrative inquiry is also time-consuming and laborious and requires some specialized training (Viney & Bousefield, 1991). Over the past decade, researchers have articulated criteria for good narrative inquiry (see Connelly & Clandinin, 1990; Jones, 1983; Riessman, 1993).

Although narrative inquiry as a qualitative research method for the social sciences and applied fields is relatively new, it has a long tradition in the humanities because of its power to elicit "voice." Narrative analysis values the signs, symbols, and expression of feelings in language, validating how the narrator constructs meaning. It has been particularly useful in developing feminist and critical theory (Eisner, 1988; Grumet, 1988; Riessman, 1993).

Narrative inquiry may rely on journal records, photographs, letters, autobiographical writing, e-mail messages, and other data. Typically, field notes are shared with the narrator, and the construction of the written record may be done collaboratively. In the conduct of narrative inquiry, there is open recognition that the researcher is collaboratively constructing the narrator's reality, not just passively recording and reporting. Connelly and Clandinin (1990) assert that researchers need to "be prepared to follow their nose and, after the fact, reconstruct their narrative of inquiry" (p. 7). This becomes, in effect, the recounting of methodology.

### Historical Analysis

A history is an account of some past event or combination of events. Historical analysis is, therefore, a method of discovering, from records and accounts, what happened in the past. Historical analysis is particularly useful in qualitative studies for establishing a baseline or background prior to participant observation or interviewing. Sources of historical data are classified as either primary or secondary. Primary sources include the oral testimony of eyewitnesses, documents, records, and relics. Secondary sources include the reports of persons who relate the accounts of actual eyewitnesses and summaries, as in history books and encyclopedias.

The researcher should consider various sources of historical data: for example, (a) contemporary records, including instructions, stenographic records, business and legal papers, and personal notes and memos; (b) confidential reports, including military records, journals and diaries, and personal letters; (c) public reports, including newspaper reports and memoirs or autobiographies; (d) questionnaires; (e) government documents, including archives and regulations; (f) opinions, including editorials, speeches, pamphlets, letters to the editor, and public opinion polls; (g) fiction, songs, and poetry; and (h) folklore.

Historical analysis is particularly useful in obtaining knowledge of previously unexamined areas and in reexamining questions for which answers are not as definite as desired. It allows for systematic and direct classification of data. Historical research traditions demand procedures to verify the accuracy of statements about the past, to establish relationships, and to determine the direction of cause-and-effect relationships. In fact, many research studies have a historical base or context, so systematic historical analysis enhances the trustworthiness and credibility of a study.

There is a dialectic tension in historical analysis between contemporary social thought and that of the past; this dialectic may throw current thought into relief. Sensitivity should be given to the interpretation of the statements of others. Historical analysis cannot use a direct observation approach, and there is no way to test a historical hypothesis. There are also weaknesses in the classification of historical data. Documents may be falsified deliberately or may have been subject to incorrect interpretations on the part of the recorder. Words and phrases used in old records may now have different meanings. The meanings of artifacts are perceived and interpreted by the investigator. Errors in recording as well as frauds, hoaxes, and forgeries pose problems in dealing with the past. Thus, the researcher should retain a modest skepticism about the data.

### Films, Videos, and Photographs

Films and photographs have a long history in anthropology. Called *visual anthropology* or *film ethnography,* this tradition relies on films and photographs to capture the daily life of the group under study. Films provide visual records of passing natural events and may be used as permanent resources. The concept and method of the research film have emerged and are compatible with a variety of research methods and have been used to describe how people navigate in public places (Ryave & Schenkein, 1974) and the use of space (Whyte, 1980), to present findings (Jackson, 1978), and to empower partici- pants (Ziller & Lewis, 1981).

Research filming is a powerful tool for inquiry into past events. Film has the unique ability to capture visible phenomena seemingly objectively—yet always from the perspective of the filmmaker. Research film methodology requires the documentation of the time, place, and subject of the filming, as well as the photographer's intent and interests. Also, a great wealth of visual information emanates from all natural events: To attempt a "complete" record of even a small event would be a fruitless pursuit.

There are three kinds of sampling in films: opportunity, programmed, and digressive (Sorenson, 1968). Opportunity sampling documents unanticipated or poorly understood phenomena as they occur. Programmed sampling in- volves filming according to a predetermined plan—deciding in advance what, where, and when to film. Grounded in the research proposal's conceptual framework, this sampling strategy stipulates which events are likely to be significant. Such filming is guided by the research design rather than by intuition, as in opportunity sampling. Digressive sampling is deliberate searching beyond the obvious to the novel, to the places and events that are usually outside typical public recognition.

Researchers choose to use ethnographic film for its obvious strengths. The visual samples increase the value of any record. Film documents life crises and ceremonies, transmits cultural events to successive generations, and documents social conflicts (court, speakers, Senate sessions, and so on). The film researcher is limited only by what the mind can imagine and the camera can record. And, of course, events can be documented in the natural setting.

Film is particularly valuable for discovery and validation. It documents nonverbal behavior and communication, such as facial expressions, gestures, and emotions. Film preserves activity and change in its original form. It can be used in the future to take advantage of new methods of seeing, analyzing, and understanding the process of change. Film is an aid to the researcher when the nature of what is sought is known but the elements of it cannot be discovered because of the limitations of the human eye. Film allows for the preservation and study of data from nonrecurring, disappearing, or rare events. With films, interpretation of information can be validated by another researcher or by participants. The researcher can obtain feedback on the authenticity of interpretation, and the film can be reshot to be more authentic. Two excellent examples of ethnographic film are *Educating Peter* (Home Box Office Project Knowledge, 1992), the story of the experiences of a boy with severe cognitive challenges in a regular classroom, and *High School,* a depiction of life in a comprehensive high school in the early 1970s (Wiseman, 1969).

Film has certain weaknesses and limitations. There are always fundamental questions: For example, What is the nature of truth? Does the film manipulate reality? Concern exists about professional bias and the interests of the film-maker. On the practical side, film is expensive and most research budgets are minimal. Production can be problematic. The researcher needs technical expertise. And filming can be very intrusive, affecting settings and events. Film cannot be published as a part of a book, journal, or dissertation. Finally, serious consideration must be given to the ethics of ethnographic filming.

*Kinesics*

Learning about society can be enhanced if we study not only what people say with their lips but also what their body movements reveal. The study of body motion and its accompanying messages is a technique known as *kinesics.* Specifically, kinesics is the study of body motion communication. Motion is analyzed systematically in a way that allows the researcher to see and measure significant patterns in the communication process.

Birdwhistell (1970) asserts that nonverbal body behaviors function like significant sounds that combine into single or relatively complex units, like words. Body movements ranging from a single nod to a series of hand and leg gestures can attach additional meaning to spoken words. All kinesics research rests on the assumption that, without being aware of it, individuals are engaged constantly in adjustments to the presence and activities of other persons. People modify and react verbally and nonverbally; their nonverbal behavior is influenced by culture, gender, age, and other factors associated with psychological and social development.

Birdwhistell labels four channels in the communicative process: vocal, visual, olfactory, and tactile. It is important for the researcher to be aware of these channels, because the interaction between researcher and subject consists of a steady flow of nonverbal communication clues. Behind the words are messages that both parties are communicating. Armed with a knowledge of nonverbal clues, the researcher can monitor subjects' behaviors, discovering their attitudes and giving their actions additional meaning. Body language can express unconscious thoughts that may be essential for observers to decode if they are to analyze situations accurately.

In the interpretation of body language lies one of the weaknesses of kinesics. Novice "body readers" who have a "pop psych" understanding of the science of kinesics may make incorrect, perhaps damaging, interpretations of behavior. Related closely to this possibility of misinterpretation is that the body language concept can be trivialized. For example, many studies focus on frequency counts of isolated units of behavior that alone convey little meaning. Knowing that a person blinked 100 times during a 15-minute interview is not significant unless the context of the situation is also apparent.

The strengths of kinesic analysis are that it provides a view into unconscious thoughts and provides a means for triangulation of verbal data. A researcher can be more confident about the accuracy of information provided by a participant if the speaker's body language is congruent with his words. Also, the researcher can monitor her own nonverbal behavior to clarify messages sent to the subject and to stay in touch with her own feelings during data collection.

Kinesic analysis is limited because body language is not universal, and researchers must be aware of cultural differences. Many gestures signal different meanings in different cultures; for example, in some countries, an up-and-down head nod signifies no and side-to-side movement of the head means yes. Body movements must be interpreted in context, and only experts can make fine-tuned kinesic interpretations. Body language such as movements of tiny jaw or neck muscles or amount of pupil dilation should be interpreted cautiously.

## Proxemics

*Proxemics* is the study of people's use of space and its relationship to culture. The term was coined by Hall (1966), although he did not perform the original work in this area. Many studies have been conducted on the activities that take place in bars, airports, subways, and other public places where individuals have to deal with one another in limited space. Using proxemics, the researcher focuses on space, ranging from interpersonal distance to the arrangement of furniture and architecture. Anthropologists have used proxemics to determine the territorial customs of particular cultures. Proxemics have been useful in the study of the behavior of students in the classroom and of marital partners undergoing counseling.

There are several advantages to the use of proxemics. It is unobtrusive, and usually it is difficult for a subject to mislead the observer deliberately. Because proxemics is concerned with nonverbal behavior, subjects would have to be skillful to "lie" about their feelings. Proxemics is useful for studying the way individuals react to others regarding space and the invasion of their territory. Likewise, proxemics can be used in cross-cultural studies because people's use of personal space varies greatly from one culture to the next. Finally, proxemic analysis is useful for studies in areas such as the effect of seating arrangements on student behavior or the effect of crowding on workplace productivity.

The greatest disadvantage of proxemics as a data collection method is that to gain accurate information the researcher must be skilled in the interpretation of the observed behaviors. If the researcher is observing a conference or a business meeting, the manner in which the subjects take their seats can be of vital importance, but the data must be interpreted carefully. Exclusive reliance on proxemics could be misleading because it might suggest relationships that do not exist. Because of the relative youth of proxemics as a data collection method, few space measurement instruments are available in the field of research, further limiting its diverse use. The use of proxemics is increasing throughout research arenas. It provides a revealing and interesting method of gathering information about individual social behavior.

*Unobtrusive Measures*

Unobtrusive measures are methods for collection of data that do not require the cooperation of the subjects and, in fact, may be "invisible" to them. Webb, Campbell, Schwartz, and Sechrest (1966) describe these measures as "nonreactive research," because the researcher is expected to observe or gather data without interfering in the ongoing flow of everyday events. Data collected in this manner are categorized as documents, archival records, and physical evidence. Of the three, documents and archival records are the most frequently used in qualitative studies and were discussed earlier.

Physical evidence not produced specifically for the purpose of research often constitutes data; the following example provides an illustration. During the 1960s, the floor tile around the hatching-chick exhibit at the Chicago

Museum of Science and Industry had to be replaced every 6 weeks. The tile in other parts of the museum did not require replacement for years. The selective erosion of the tiles, indexed by the replacement rate, provided a measure of the relative popularity of exhibits (Webb et al., 1966).

Unobtrusive measures are particularly useful for triangulation. As a supplement to interviews, nonreactive research provides another perspective on the phenomenon, elaborating its complexity. These methods can be used without arousing notice from subjects, and data collection is relatively easy because it often involves using data (e.g., bills, archival records, sales records) already collected by someone else.

When used in isolation, however, unobtrusive measures may distort the picture. Erosion and survival may be affected by activities unknown to the researcher. For example, tiles near the hatching-chick exhibit may wear out because the exhibit is close to the candy machine, not because of the exhibit's popularity. Some researchers consider the use of unobtrusive methods (e.g., monitoring exchanges on newsgroups or searching through garbage to be unethical: They feel that those studied should be informed of the nature of the research.

When the researcher needs information on measures of frequency or attendance, when direct observation would be impossible or would bias the data, this method is useful. Unobtrusive data collection is often aided by hardware such as audiotapes, hidden cameras, one-way mirrors, gauges, and infrared photos.

### Questionnaires and Surveys

Researchers administer questionnaires to some sample of a population to learn about the distribution of characteristics, attitudes, or beliefs. In deciding to survey the group of people chosen for study, researchers make one critical assumption—that the characteristic or belief can be described or measured accurately through self-report. In using questionnaires, researchers rely totally on the honesty and accuracy of participants' responses. Although this limits the usefulness of questionnaires in delving into tacit beliefs and deeply held values, there are still many occasions when surveying the group under study can be useful.

Questionnaires typically entail several questions that have structured response categories and may include some that are open-ended. The questions are examined (sometimes quite vigorously) for bias, sequence, clarity, and face validity. Questionnaires are usually tested through administration to small groups to determine their usefulness and, perhaps, reliability.

Sample surveys consist of the collection of data in a standardized format, usually from a probability sample of the population. The survey is the preferred method if the researcher wishes to obtain a small amount of information from a large number of subjects.

Survey research is the appropriate mode of inquiry for making inferences about a large group of people from data drawn on a relatively small number of individuals from that group. The basic aim of survey research is to describe and explain statistically the variability of certain features of a population. The general logic of survey research gives a distinctive style to the research process; the type of survey instrument is determined by the information needed. There are three types of surveys: mail, telephone, and personal interview. Any method of data collection, however, from observation to content analysis, can be and has been used in survey research.

Most survey studies involve cross-sectional measurements made at a single point in time or longitudinal measurements taken at several different times. Other forms of survey research include trend studies examining a population by studying separate samples at different points in time, cohort studies examining a bounded population, and panel studies examining a single sample of individuals at several points in time. Analysis of survey data takes the form of quantitative analysis that relies mainly on either descriptive or inferential statistics.

The relative advantages and disadvantages of survey research are highlighted through the following criteria: (a) appropriateness of the method to the problem studied, (b) accuracy of measurement, (c) generalizability of the findings, (d) administrative convenience, and (e) avoidance of ethical or political difficulties in the research process.

There are some definite advantages of surveys when the goals of research require obtaining quantitative data on a certain problem or population. Surveys facilitate research in politically or ethically sensitive areas. They are used in programs for public welfare or economic development. Large surveys often focus on sensitive or controversial topics within the public domain.

Strengths of surveys include their accuracy, generalizability, and convenience. Accuracy in measurement is enhanced by quantification, replicability, and control over observer effects. Survey results can be generalized to a larger population within known limits of error. Surveys are amenable to rapid statistical analysis and are comparatively easy to administer and manage.

Surveys have weaknesses, however. For example, they are of little value for examining complex social relationships or intricate patterns of interaction. The strengths of surveys can also be weaknesses. Although controlling accuracy, a survey cannot assure without further evidence that the sample represents a broader universe. Thus, the method of drawing the sample and the sample size is critical to the accuracy of the study and its potential for generalizability. Also, even though surveys are convenient, they are generally a relatively expensive method of data collection. Finally, surveys may result in an invasion of privacy or produce questionable effects in the respondent or the community. Some research projects may enhance the position or resources of a particular group, and conflicts frequently arise between sponsors and research teams concerning how problems are defined.

*Projective Techniques and*
*Psychological Testing*

Some types of interpretive psychological strategies were developed many years ago by clinical psychologists to obtain personality data. These strategies have been used fairly extensively in comparative studies about culture and for analysis of personality dynamics. Based on an internal, perceptual frame of reference, the techniques assume that one can get a valid picture of a person by assessing the way the individual projects his personality onto some standard, ambiguous stimuli.

Standardization and ambiguity are common elements in tests of this nature, although "clinical" judgments are the primary interpretation bases of responses to these stimuli. Results are typically expressed in the form of a verbal report assessing the subject's dominant needs and ambitions, tolerance of frustrations, attitudes toward authority, major internal conflicts, and so on. The reputation and qualifications of the tester sometimes play a role in how the report is received and how much credibility is attached to the interpretation.

Two of the most well-known and frequently used psychological strategies of this notion are the Rorschach inkblot test and the Thematic Apperception Test (TAT). The original idea behind both includes the assumption that the stimuli are ambiguous so that the subject has to be imaginative and "projective" in response to those stimuli. The Rorschach test uses pictures (symmetrical inkblots), usually presented in a predetermined order, with the subject's reporting what each picture resembles or suggests. The number, quality, and variety of the subject's responses are compared with specific personality types and with prior experiences with the responses of other people to the same stimuli. In the TAT, the subject is asked to tell stories about a set of picture scenes. Test results are used to assess personality traits such as aggressiveness, dependence, and sexual conflicts.

Although projective instruments have been the object of considerable criticism for many years, they are still commonly employed in clinical contexts by psychologists. Yet questions remain as to their validity and reliability; environmental and cultural factors may also affect results. Today, concern focuses on more concrete aspects of personality traits, such as self-esteem and styles of interpersonal behavior, rather than on the vague generalizations that characterized earlier interpretive schemes.

Recently a number of other psychological tests and measurements have been developed for use in qualitative and anthropological research. Examples include the study of (a) the perception of illusions, which uses optical and auditory illusions to examine differences in perception related to differences in types of environments; (b) judgments of aesthetic qualities, which rely on pictures of art objects or musical stimuli to elicit opinions concerning aesthetic excellence; (c) psychomotor skills, which use physical activity measures to indicate personality qualities such as introversion and extroversion; (d) games people engage in, to provide significant information about community and social behavior; and (e) games as a laboratory device, which uses a specific game involving family members to determine a relationship between communication patterns and socioeconomic differences. Various other qualitative methods have been devised for studying entire communities, group living patterns, and social integration of individuals in different residential contexts; these are referenced at the end of this chapter.

## Combining Data Collection Methods

Many qualitative studies combine several data collection methods over the course of the study, as seen in Shadduck-Hernandez's (1997) proposal discussed in Vignette 22. The researcher can assess the strengths and limitations of each method, then decide if that method will work with the particular questions and in the particular setting for a given study. Tables 4.1 and 4.2 display the strengths and limitations of each data collection method, based on how it is generally used in qualitative studies. The tables should help researchers to select the best combination of methods: Limitations in one method can be compensated for by the strengths of a complementary one.

In drafting the proposal, the researcher should consider whether the method will provide adequate information, be cost-effective, and be feasible in terms of the subtleties of the setting and the resources available for the study. The relative emphasis on participation in many qualitative studies, for example, suggests certain methods over others. Lutz and Iannaccone (1969) provide guidelines for method selection based on role, as shown in Table 4.3. These choices should be logically linked to the conceptual framework and research questions, the overall strategy of the study, and early decisions about role.

Vignette 23 describes how a researcher selected specific data collection methods to elicit information about a long-term health care facility.

*     *     *     *     *

### Vignette 23

### Choosing Data Collection Methods

How might one's view of life be shaped by residence in a long-term health care facility? A doctoral student in health care management (Kalnins, 1986) wanted to examine—in depth and detail—the contexts, processes, and interactions that shaped patients' perspectives. She reasoned that a qualitative approach would be most fruitful in picking up everyday actions and interactions about complex social structures.

Kalnins's major purpose in the study was to understand the meanings given to events by participants. She referred to the work of Schatzman and Strauss (1973) by noting the following:

> The researcher *must* get close to the people whom he [sic] studies; he understands that their actions are best comprehended when observed on the spot—in the natural, ongoing environment where they live and work. The researcher himself [sic] must be at the location, not only to watch but also to listen to the symbolic sounds that characterize this world. A dialogue with persons in their natural situations will reveal the nuances of meaning from which their perspectives and definitions are continually forged. (Kalnins, 1986, pp. 5-6)

*(continued p. 136)*

**Table 4.1  Strengths of Data Collection Methods**

| Strength | PO | O | I | FGI | DR | N | HA | F | Q | P | K | PT | UM |
|---|---|---|---|---|---|---|---|---|---|---|---|---|---|
| Fosters face-to-face interactions with participants | x | | x | x | | x | | | | | | D | |
| Useful for uncovering participants' perspectives | x | | x | | | x | | | | | | D | |
| Data collected in natural setting | x | x | x | x | D | x | | x | | x | x | | x |
| Facilitates immediate follow-up for clarification | x | | x | x | | x | | | | D | D | | |
| Good for documenting major events, crises, social conflicts | x | x | | x | x | x | x | x | | | | | |
| Collects data on unconscious thoughts and actions | x | | | | D | D | | x | | x | x | x | x |
| Useful for describing complex interactions | x | x | x | x | | x | x | x | | x | x | D | |
| Good for obtaining data on nonverbal behavior and communication | x | x | D | D | | D | | x | | x | x | D | x |
| Facilitates discovery of nuances in culture | x | x | x | x | D | x | x | x | | x | x | x | x |
| Provides for flexibility in formulating hypotheses | x | x | x | x | D | x | x | x | | x | x | x | x |
| Provides context information | x | x | x | x | x | | x | x | | | | | |
| Facilitates analysis, validity checks, and triangulation | x | x | x | x | x | | | x | x | x | x | x | x |
| Facilitates cooperation | x | D | D | x | | x | | | | | | x | |
| Data easy to manipulate and categorize for analysis | | | | | x | | | | x | x | x | | D |
| Obtains large amounts of data quickly | x | x | | x | | | x | x | | | | x | |
| Allows wide range of types of data and participants | x | | | D | D | | | | | D | D | | x |
| Easy and efficient to administer and manage | | | | | x | | x | | x | x | x | | x |
| Easily quantifiable and amenable to statistical analysis | | | | | x | | | | x | x | x | x | x |
| Easy to establish generalizability | | | | | D | | D | | x | x | x | x | x |
| May draw on established instruments | | | | | x | | | | x | x | x | x | x |

NOTE: x = strength exists; D = depends on use. PO = participant observation; O = observation; I = interview; FGI = focus group interviewing; DR = document review; N = narratives, life and oral histories; HA = historical analysis; F = film; Q = questionnaire; P = proxemics; K = kinesics; PT = psychological techniques; UM = unobtrusive measures.

**Table 4.2  Weaknesses of Data Collection Methods**

| Weakness | PO | O | I | FGI | DR | N | HA | F | Q | P | K | PT | UM |
|---|---|---|---|---|---|---|---|---|---|---|---|---|---|
| Can lead researcher to "miss the forest while observing the trees" | x | x | x | D | x | x |  | x | x | x | x | x | x |
| Data are open to multiple interpretations due to cultural differences | x | x | x | x | x | x | x | x | x | x | x | x | x |
| Requires specialized training |  |  |  | x |  |  |  | x | x | x | x | x |  |
| Dependent on cooperation of small group of key individuals | x |  | x |  |  | x |  |  |  |  |  | x |  |
| Fraught with ethical dilemmas | x | x | x | x |  | x |  | x |  |  |  | x | D |
| Difficult to replicate | x | x | x | x |  | x | D | x |  |  |  | x |  |
| Data often subject to observer effects | x | x |  | x |  |  |  |  |  |  |  | D |  |
| Expensive materials and equipment | x |  |  |  |  |  |  | x |  |  |  |  | x |
| Can cause discomfort or even danger to researcher | x |  |  |  |  |  |  |  |  |  |  | x |  |
| Especially dependent on openness and honesty of participants | x |  | x | x |  | x |  |  |  |  |  |  |  |
| Overly artistic or literary style can obscure the research | x | x | x | x |  | x | x | x |  |  |  | x |  |
| Highly dependent on the "goodness" of research question | x | x | x | x | D | x | x | x | x | x | x |  | x |
| Highly dependent on the ability of the researcher to be resourceful, systematic, and honest | x | x | x | x | x | x | x |  | x |  |  | x |  |

NOTE: x = weakness exists; D = depends on use. PO = participant observation; O = observation; I = interview; FGI = focus group interviewing; DR = document review; N = narratives, life and oral histories; HA = historical analysis; F = film; Q = questionnaire; P = proxemics; K = kinesics; PT = psychological techniques; UM = unobtrusive measures.

**Table 4.3  Data Collection Methods Related to Observation Role**

| Method | Role | | | Comment |
|---|---|---|---|---|
| | I—Participant as Observer | II—Observer as Participant | III—Observer as Nonparticipant | |
| Observation and recording of descriptive data | + | + | + | Particularly useful to Role I in areas of guarded interaction and sentiment |
| Recording direct quotations of sentiment | + | + | + | Same as above |
| Unstructured interview | + | + | * | If the researcher is skillful, a structure emerges |
| Structured interview guides | − | * | + | Most useful in survey work (e.g., census) |
| Detailed interaction guides | − | − | * | Most useful in small-group work |
| Interaction frequency tallies | + | + | + | Meaningful in leadership studies |
| Paper-and-pencil tests | | | | Very helpful in certain circumstances for |
|   Questionnaires | − | − | + | certain purposes |
|   Scales | − | − | + | |
|   Achievement or ability | − | − | * | |
| Written records | | | | Very important to |
|   Newspaper | + | + | * | Role I in checking |
|   Official minutes | + | + | * | reliability of observed |
|   Letters | + | + | * | data |
|   Speeches | + | + | * | |
| Radio and television reports | + | + | * | Same as above |

SOURCE: Lutz and Iannaccone (1969, p. 113). Reprinted with permission.
NOTE: + = likely to be used; * = may occasionally be used; − = difficult or impossible to use.

From the variety of data collection strategies, she proposed a combination of direct observation, participant observation, and semistructured interviewing. Her beginning point would be direct observation of residents and staff in various areas of the facility, "witnessing events which particularly preoccupied the hosts, or indicated special symbolic importance to them" (Schatzman & Strauss, 1973, p. 59). This would allow her to get a holistic view and to gather data that would inform the interview process.

Kalnins's plan as participant observer would be to observe the residents and staff in the natural setting of the long-term health care facility, requiring her "commitment to adopt the perspective of those studied by sharing in their day-to-day experiences" (Denzin, 1970, p. 185). In her proposal, Kalnins anticipated that participant observation and interviewing would run concurrently, allowing data from each to be used to substantiate events, explore emerging hypotheses, and make further decisions about the conduct of the research. She referred to Becker and Geer (1969), arguing that participant observation allows the researcher to (a) check definitions of terms the participants use in the interview in a more natural setting (i.e., casual conversations with others); (b) observe events the participants cannot report because they do not want to, feeling that to speak of some particular subject would be impolitic, impolite, or insensitive; and (c) observe situations described in interviews and thus become aware of differing perspectives presented by the participants (p. 326).

Her role as participant observer would mean that Kalnins would become immersed in the lives and activities of those she was studying. She understood the interactive-adaptive nature of participant observation, reflecting the complex relationship between field observation and emerging theory, and the impact of this relationship on decisions about further data collection. Her decisions about the data to be collected and methods for collecting those data would be guided by Wilson's (1977, p. 255) list of five relevant types of data employed to get at meaning structures: (a) the form and content of verbal interaction between participants, (b) the form and content of verbal interaction with researcher, (c) nonverbal behavior, (d) patterns of actions and nonaction, and (e) traces, archival records, artifacts, and documents.

To generate facts, opinions, and insights (Yin, 1984), Kalnins planned for open-ended structured interviews (using questionnaires) that would enable the exploration of many topics but that could focus on cultural nuances, firsthand encounters, and the perceptions, meanings, and interpretations of others. Information would also be gathered from various documents and archives, lending a historical perspective to the study.

\*   \*   \*   \*   \*

Vignette 23 illustrates how a researcher chose an array of data collection methods, knowing that each method had particular strengths and how each would help elicit certain desired information. Participant observation would immerse her in the lives of the patients, giving her a personal perspective on life in a long-term health care facility. Observation would provide focused data about specific settings and events within the facility. In-depth, semistructured interviews would explore the meaning of events and actions held by participants and allow her to test her emerging interpretations. One advantage of using multiple qualitative methods is the potential to evoke unexpected data. Another is the fundamental flexibility of qualitative methods: She could modify her data collection strategy based on what she learned in the field. This vignette shows that data collection strategies and methods cannot be chosen in a vacuum. Intensive examination of the possible methods, trying them out, examining their potentials, and fitting them to the research question, site, and sample are important design considerations. In addition, researchers must consider their *own* personal abilities in carrying out any particular overall approach or method.

## General Principles for Designing
## Data Collection Strategies

In the proposal, the methods planned for data collection should be related to the type of information sought. Zelditch's (1962) chart, reproduced in Table 4.4, provides guidelines for three large categories of methods: enumerating, participant observation, and in-depth interviewing. Each broad category best yields a particular type of information. In determining which method to use, the researcher should carefully examine the questions guiding the study: Many questions that appear to be "how" questions are really "how many" questions in disguise. For example, the selection of participant observation to help uncover how a program developed will not adequately respond to the "how many" questions that might be embedded in it.

The researcher should determine the most practical, efficient, feasible, and ethical methods for collecting data as the research progresses. He might start with participant observation as he seeks to identify questions, patterns, and domains. This strategy may change as the research becomes more focused and progresses toward more specific questions and clearer concepts that suggest

**Table 4.4  Information Types and Methods of Obtaining Information**

| | Method of Obtaining Information | | |
| Information Type | Enumerations and Samples | Participant Observation | Interviewing Informants |
|---|---|---|---|
| Frequency distributions | Prototype and best form | Usually inadequate and inefficient | Often, but not always, adequate; if adequate, efficient |
| Incidents, histories | Not adequate by itself; not efficient | Prototype and best form | Adequate, with precautions, and efficient |
| Institutionalized norms and statuses | Adequate but inefficient | Adequate but inefficient, except for unverbalized norms | Most efficient and hence best form |

SOURCE: Zelditch (1962, p. 575). Reprinted by permission.

the use of representative samples. Then the researcher could develop surveys and enumerate the findings. On the other hand, the findings might be descriptions, not numbers. If the research goal is description of processes, concepts, categories, and typologies, sampling and counting are merely tools of analysis, not necessarily part of the research findings. The proposal should demonstrate that the researcher is capable of designing and selecting data collection methods that are appropriate, well thought-out, and thorough. Because the research question may change as the research progresses, the methods may change and the researcher must ensure this flexibility. Vignette 24 provides an example.

*             *             *             *             *

### Vignette 24

### Design Flexibility[1]

A graduate student wanted to explore the implementation of a state mandate for local school councils. Rodriguez first proposed participant observation of meetings and in-depth interviews with board members. The data collection plan showed a schedule for observing the meetings, goals for interviewing, and a time allowance for analysis of data and for follow-up data collection. But in the process of initial data collection and preliminary analysis, he discovered that teacher resentment of the councils was creating a pattern of unintended negative consequences. This discovery could have important implications for policy development. Did Rodriguez have to stay with the original question and data collection plan? Wouldn't a design alteration offer important insights?

Rodriguez reasoned that if he could describe the processes whereby well-intended policy is thwarted, policymakers could gain insight that might help them make timely alterations in policy development or implementation. Given this possible benefit to the study, he could choose to focus subsequent data collection on the conflicts between teacher needs and the mandate to school boards that they implement councils. This would require him to turn to additional literatures on, for example, teacher needs, teacher participation in decision making, or teacher unions. He might also need to employ additional data collection methods (such as surveying teacher needs, observing teacher union meetings, and doing historical research on the reactions of teacher lobbies to mandates for school councils), or he might need to sample additional settings or people. As the research question became more focused, his initial research design and data collection strategy would most likely undergo some changes.

*     *     *     *     *

In the example in Vignette 24, the research proposal probably did not include a plan for analysis of lobbying efforts or observation of collective bargaining sessions. It would, however, be entirely appropriate—indeed recommended—for the researcher to modify the research proposal if an exciting and significant focus emerges from early data collection. In fact, the primary strength of the qualitative approach is this very flexibility that allows, even encourages, exploration, discovery, and creativity.

Along with choosing appropriate strategies for data collection, the researcher must address the complex processes of managing, recording, and analyzing data. Rather than discrete, sequential events, these processes occur dialectically throughout the conduct of a qualitative study: Analysis occurs as themes are identified, as the deeper structures of the social setting become clear, and as consequent modifications are made in the initial design. At the proposal stage, however, the researcher should present some initial ideas about how the data will be managed and stored, and provide some preliminary discussion of the processes for analyzing those data. We discuss these issues in the next chapter.

## Note

1. This vignette is fictitious.

## Further Reading

### *Participant Observation*
Bogdan, R. C., & Biklen, S. K. (1998). *Qualitative research in education: An introduction to theory and methods* (3rd ed.). Boston: Allyn & Bacon.
Delamont, S. (1992). *Fieldwork in educational settings: Methods, pitfalls, and perspectives.* London: Falmer.
Jorgensen, D. L. (1989). *Participant observation: A methodology for human studies.* Newbury Park, CA: Sage.
Pelto, P., & Pelto, G. H. (1978). *Anthropological research: The structure of inquiry* (2nd ed.). New York: Cambridge University Press.
Spradley, J. S. (1980). *Participant observation.* New York: Holt, Rinehart & Winston.
Wolcott, H. F. (1995). *The art of fieldwork.* Walnut Creek, CA: AltaMira.

### *Observation*
Adler, P. A., & Adler, P. (1994). Observational techniques. In N. K. Denzin & Y. S. Lincoln (Eds.), *Handbook of qualitative research* (pp. 377-392). Thousand Oaks, CA: Sage.
Evertson, C., & Green, J. (1985). Observation as inquiry and method. In M. C. Wittrock (Ed.), *Handbook of research on teaching* (pp. 162-213). New York: Macmillan.
Lofland, J., & Lofland, L. H. (1995). *Analyzing social settings: A guide to qualitative observation and analysis* (3rd ed.). Belmont, CA: Wadsworth.
Smith, C. D., & Kornblum, W. (Eds.). (1996). *In the field: Readings on the field research experience.* Westport, CT: Praeger.

### *Generic In-Depth Interviewing*
Fontana, A., & Frey, J. H. (1994). Interviewing: The art of science. In N. K. Denzin & Y. S. Lincoln (Eds.), *Handbook of qualitative research* (pp. 361-376). Thousand Oaks, CA: Sage.
Holstein, J. A., & Gubrium, J. F. (1995). *The active interview.* Thousand Oaks, CA: Sage.
McCracken, G. (1988). *The long interview.* Newbury Park, CA: Sage.
Patton, M. Q. (1990). *Qualitative research and evaluation methods* (2nd ed.). Newbury Park, CA: Sage.
Rubin, H. J., & Rubin, I. S. (1995). *Qualitative interviewing: The art of hearing data.* Thousand Oaks, CA: Sage.
Tripp, D. H. (1983). Co-authorship and negotiation: The interview as act of creation. *Interchange, 14,* 32-45.
Weiss, R. S. (1994). *Learning from strangers: The art and method of qualitative interview studies.* New York: Free Press.

### Ethnographic Interviewing

Filstead, W. (Ed.). (1970). *Qualitative methodology.* Chicago: Markham.

Spradley, J. S. (1979). *The ethnographic interview.* New York: Holt, Rinehart & Winston.

Wolcott, H. F. (1985). On ethnographic intent. *Educational Administration Quarterly, 3,* 187-203.

### Phenomenologic Interviewing

Bogdan, R. C., & Taylor, S. (1975). *Introduction to qualitative research methods: A phenomenological approach to the social sciences.* New York: John Wiley.

Denzin, N. K. (1970). *The research act: A theoretical introduction to sociological methods.* New York: McGraw-Hill.

Denzin, N. K. (1978). *The research act: A theoretical introduction to sociological methods* (2nd ed.). New York: McGraw-Hill.

Holstein, J. A., & Gubrium, J. F. (1995). *The active interview.* Thousand Oaks, CA: Sage.

Kvale, S. (1996). *InterViews: An introduction to qualitative research interviewing.* Thousand Oaks, CA: Sage.

Seidman, I. E. (1998). *Interviewing as qualitative research: A guide for researchers in education and the social sciences* (2nd ed.). New York: Teachers College Press.

Taylor, S. J., & Bogdan, R. (1984). *Introduction to qualitative research: The search for meanings* (2nd ed.). New York: John Wiley.

Van Manen, M. (1990). *Researching lived experience: Human science for an action sensitive pedagogy.* Buffalo: State University of New York Press.

### Interviewing "Elites"

Becker, T. M., & Meyers, P. R. (1974-1975). Empathy and bravado: Interviewing reluctant bureaucrats. *Public Opinion Quarterly, 38,* 605-613.

Hertz, R., & Imber, J. B. (1995). *Studying elites using qualitative methods.* Thousand Oaks, CA: Sage.

Marshall, C. (1984). Elites, bureaucrats, ostriches, and pussycats: Managing research in policy settings. *Anthropology and Education Quarterly, 15,* 235-251.

Platt, J. (1981). On interviewing one's peers. *British Journal of Sociology, 32,* 75-85.

Thomas, R. (1993). Interviewing important people in big companies. *Journal of Contemporary Ethnography, 22*(1), 80-96.

Webb, E., & Salancik, J. (1966). The interviewer or the only wheel in town. *Journalism Monograph, 2.*

Zuckerman, H. (1972). Interviewing an ultra-elite. *Public Opinion Quarterly, 36*(5), 159-175.

### Focus Group Interviewing

Birn, R., Hague, P., & Vangelder, P. (1990). *A handbook of market research.* London: Routledge & Kegan Paul.

Krueger, R. A. (1988). *Focus groups: A practical guide for applied research.* Newbury Park, CA: Sage.

Morgan, D. L. (1997). *Focus groups as qualitative research* (2nd ed.). Thousand Oaks, CA: Sage.

Stewart, D. W., & Shamdasani, P. N. (1990). *Focus groups: Theory and practice.* Newbury Park, CA: Sage.

### Interviewing Children

Fine, G. A., & Sandstrom, K. L. (1988). *Knowing children: Participant observation with minors.* Newbury Park, CA: Sage.

Pollard, A. (1987). Studying children's perspectives: A collaborative approach. In G. Walford (Ed.), *Doing sociology of education* (pp. 95-118). London: Falmer.

### Content Analysis

Cohen, S. L., & Fredler, J. E. (1974). Content analysis of multiple messages in suicide notes. *Life-Threatening Behavior, 4,* 75-95.

Funkhouser, G. R. (1973). The issues of the sixties: An exploratory study. *Public Opinion Quarterly, 37,* 62-75.

Weber, R. P. (1985). *Basic content analysis.* Beverly Hills, CA: Sage.

### Life Histories and Narrative Inquiry

Chessman, C. (1954). *Cell 2455 death row.* Englewood Cliffs: NJ: Prentice Hall.

Connelly, F. M., & Clandinin, D. J. (1990). Stories of experience and narrative inquiry. *Educational Researcher, 19,* 2-14.

Dollard, J. (1935). *Criteria for the life history.* New Haven, CT: Yale University Press.

Edgerton, R. T., & Langness, L. L. (1974). *Methods and styles in the study of culture.* San Francisco: Chandler & Sharp.

Etter-Lewis, G., & Foster, M. (1996). *Unrelated kin: Race and gender in women's personal narratives.* New York: Routledge.

Gluck, S. B., & Patai, P. (Eds.). (1991). *Women's words: The feminist practice of oral history.* New York: Routledge.

Hollingsworth, S. (1991). *Narrative analysis on literacy education: A story of changing classrooms* (Research Series 202). East Lansing, MI: Institute for Research on Teaching.

Josselson, R. (Ed.). (1996). *Ethics and process in the narrative study of lives.* Thousand Oaks, CA: Sage.

Josselson, R., & Lieblich, A. (Eds.). (1993). *The narrative study of lives.* Newbury Park, CA: Sage.

Keiser, R. L. (1969). Cupid's story. In R. L. Keiser, *The vice lords: Warriors of the street.* New York: Holt, Rinehart & Winston.

Mandelbaum, D. G. (1973). The study of life history: Gandhi. *Current Anthropology, 14,* 177-207.

Martin, R. R. (1995). *Oral history in social work: Research, assessment, and intervention.* Thousand Oaks, CA: Sage.

Mercier, L., & Buckendorf, M. (1992). *Using oral history in community history projects.* Rock Springs, WY: Oral History Association.

Minister, K. (1991). A feminist frame for the oral history interview. In S. B. Gluck & D. Patai (Eds.), *Women's words: The feminist practice of oral history* (pp. 27-41). New York: Routledge & Kegan Paul.

Mitchell, W. J. (Ed.). (1981). *On narrative.* Chicago: University of Chicago Press.

Neuenschwander, J. A. (1995). *Oral history and the law.* Denton, TX: Oral History Association.

Polkinghorne, D. E. (1988). *Narrative knowing and the human sciences.* Albany: State University of New York Press.

Riessman, C. K. (1993). *Narrative analysis.* Newbury Park, CA: Sage.

Sarbin, T. R. (Ed.). (1986). *Narrative psychology: The storied nature of human conduct.* New York: Praeger.

Slim, H., & Thompson, P. (1995). *Listening for a change: Oral testimony and community development.* Philadelphia: New Society Publishers.

Thompson, P. (1988). *The voice of the past.* Oxford, UK: Oxford University Press.

Viney, L. L., & Bousefield, L. (1991). Narrative analysis: A method of psychosocial research for AIDS-affected people. *Social Science and Medicine, 23,* 757-765.

Webb, M. B. (1990). Listen and learn from narratives that tell a story. *Religious Education, 85,* 617-630.

Yow, V. R. (1994). *Recording oral history: A practical guide for social scientists.* Thousand Oaks, CA: Sage.

### Historical Analysis

Barzun, J., & Graff, H. F. (1970). *The modern researcher.* New York: Harcourt, Brace & World.

Brooks, P. C. (1969). *The use of unpublished primary sources.* Chicago: University of Chicago Press.

Fischer, D. H. (1970). *Historians' fallacies: Toward a logic of historical thought.* New York: Harper & Row.

Gottschalk, L. A. (1969). *Understanding history.* New York: Knopf.

Schatzman, L., & Strauss, A. (1973). *Field research: Strategies for a natural sociology.* Englewood Cliffs, NJ: Prentice Hall.

Tuchman, G. (1994). Historical social science. In N. K. Denzin & Y. S. Lincoln (Eds.), *Handbook of qualitative research* (pp. 306-323). Thousand Oaks, CA: Sage.

### Film, Video, and Photography

Asch, T. (Producer). (1970). *The feast* [Film]. Washington, DC: U.S. National Audiovisual Center.

Collier, J., & Collier, M. (1986). *Visual anthropology: Photography as a research method.* Albuquerque: University of New Mexico Press.

Dowrick, P. W. (1991). *Practical guide to using video in the behavioral sciences.* New York: John Wiley.

Fagot, B., & Hagan, R. (1988). Is what we see what we get? Comparisons of taped and live observations. *Behavioral Assessment, 10,* 367-374.

Gardner, R. (1974). *Rivers of sand* [Film]. New York: Phoenix Films.

Greenberg, B. S. (1980). *Life on television: Content analysis of U.S. TV drama.* Norwood, NJ: Ablex.

Harper, D. (1994). On the authority of the image. In N. K. Denzin & Y. S. Lincoln (Eds.), *Handbook of qualitative research* (pp. 403-412). Thousand Oaks, CA: Sage.

Hockings, P. (Ed.). (1995). *Principles of visual anthropology.* New York: Mouton de Gruyter.

Luckenbill, D. F. (1981). Researching murder transactions. In T. C. Wagenaar (Ed.), *Readings for social research.* Belmont, CA: Wadsworth.

Pepler, D. J., & Craig, W. M. (1995). A peek behind the fence: Naturalistic observations of aggressive children with remote audiovisual recording. *Developmental Psychology, 31*(4), 548-553.

Rollwagen, J. (Ed.). (1988). *Anthropological filmmaking.* New York: Harwood Academic.

Walker, R., & Weidel, J. (1985). Using photographs in a discipline of words. In R. G. Burgess (Ed.), *Field methods in the study of education.* Lewes, UK: Falmer.

Wiseman, F. (1969). *High school* [Film]. Boston: Zippora Films.

### Kinesics

Birdwhistell, R. L. (1970). *Kinesics and content: Essays on body motion communication.* Philadelphia: University of Pennsylvania Press.

Bull, P. (1983). *Body movement and interpersonal communication.* New York: John Wiley.

Rutter, D. R. (1984). *Aspects of nonverbal communication.* Amsterdam, The Netherlands: Swets & Zeitlinger.

Scherer, K. R., & Ekman, R. (Eds.). (1982). *Handbook of methods in nonverbal behavior research.* New York: Cambridge University Press.

Siegman, A. W., & Feldstein, S. (Eds.). (1987). *Nonverbal behavior and communication* (2nd ed.). Hillsdale, NJ: Lawrence Erlbaum.

### Proxemics

Berman, P. W., & Smith, V. L. (1984). Gender and situational differences in children's smiles, touches, and proxemics. *Sex Roles, 10,* 347-356.

Crane, D. R., & Griffin, W. (1983). Personal space: An objective measure of marital quality. *Journal of Mental and Family Therapy, 9,* 325-327.

Edgerton, B. (1979). *Alone together.* Berkeley: University of California Press.

Freedman, J. (1975). *Crowding and behavior.* New York: Viking.

Hall, E. T. (1966). *The hidden dimension.* Garden City, NY: Doubleday.

Hall, E. T., & Hall, M. R. (1977). Nonverbal communication for educators. *Theory Into Practice, 16,* 141-144.

Hinton, B. E. (1985). Selected nonverbal communication factors influencing adult behavior and learning. *Lifelong Learning, 8,* 23-26.

Loughlin, C. F., & Suina, J. H. (1983). Reflecting the child's community in the classroom environment. *Childhood Education, 60,* 18-21.

Scheflen, A. E. (1976). *Human territories: How we behave in space-time.* Englewood Cliffs, NJ: Prentice Hall.

### Unobtrusive Measures

Bouchard, T. J. (1976). Unobtrusive methods and inventory of uses. *Sociological Methods and Research, 4,* 267-300.

Christensen, H. T. (1960). Cultural relativism and premarital sex norms. *American Sociological Review, 25,* 31-39.

Maddock, R., Kenny, C. T., Lupfer, M. B., & Rosen, C. V. (1977). A nonreactive measure of lost time among employees. *Journal of Psychology, 92,* 199-203.

Sechrest, L. (Ed.). (1979). *Unobtrusive measurement today.* San Francisco: Jossey-Bass.

Webb, E., Campbell, D. T., Schwartz, R. D., & Sechrest, L. (1966). *Unobtrusive measures: Nonreactive research in the social sciences.* Chicago: Rand McNally.

Webb, E., & Weick, K. E. (1979). Unobtrusive measures in organizational theory: A reminder. *Administrative Science Quarterly, 24,* 650-659. '

### Survey Methods

Alwin, D. (1978). *Survey design and analysis.* Beverly Hills, CA: Sage.

Belson, W. A. (1982). *The design and understanding of survey questions.* Hants, UK: Gower.

Benson, D. K., & Benson, J. L. (1975). *A guide to survey research teams.* Columbus, OH: Benchmark.

Cox, J. (1996). *Your opinion, please: How to build the best questionnaires in the field of education.* Thousand Oaks, CA: Corwin.

Czaja, R., & Blair, J. (1996). *Designing surveys: A guide to decisions and procedures.* Thousand Oaks, CA: Pine Forge.

Jick, T. D. (1979). Mixing qualitative and quantitative methods: Triangulation in action. *Administrative Science Quarterly, 24,* 602-661.

Sudman, S., & Bradburn, N. M. (1982). *Asking questions.* San Francisco: Jossey-Bass.

### *Projective Techniques and Psychological Testing*

Coles, R. (1971). *Children of crisis: 2. Migrants, sharecroppers, mountaineers.* Boston: Little, Brown.

Coles, R. (1977). *Privileged ones: The well-off and the rich in America.* Boston: Little, Brown.

Edgerton, R. (1973). Method in psychological anthropology. In R. Naroll & R. Cohen (Eds.), *A handbook of method in cultural anthropology* (2nd ed., pp. 338-353). New York: Columbia University Press.

Naroll, R., & Cohen, R. (Eds.). (1970). *A handbook of method in cultural anthropology.* New York: Columbia University Press.

Pelto, P., & Pelto, G. H. (1978). *Anthropological research: The structure of inquiry* (2nd ed.). New York: Cambridge University Press.

Rizzuto, A. (1979). *The birth of a living God: A psychoanalytic study.* Chicago: University of Chicago Press.

# 5 Recording, Managing, and Analyzing Data

Once the overall strategy, site and sample selection, and data collection methods have been determined, the researcher should discuss how these voluminous data will be recorded, managed, and analyzed. At the proposal stage, this discussion can be brief, but it should provide the reader with a sense that the data will be recorded efficiently and managed in ways that allow for easy retrieval. In addition, the proposal should present initial strategies for analysis. The writer should be prepared to provide examples of ways data collection and analysis might proceed; pilot studies or previous research are excellent sources for such examples.

## Recording and Managing Data

The proposal section on research design should include plans for recording data in a systematic manner that is appropriate for the setting, participants, or both and that will facilitate analysis. The researcher should demonstrate an awareness that techniques for recording observations, interactions, and interviews will not intrude excessively in the ongoing flow of daily events. In some situations, even taking notes interferes with, inhibits, or in some way acts on the setting and the participants. Plans to use tape recorders, cameras, and other mechanical devices should be delineated in the proposal, demonstrating that the researcher will use data-recording strategies that fit the setting and the participants' sensitivities and that these will only be used with participants' consent.

In action and participatory research approaches, the researcher's intrusiveness in the setting is not an issue. Because these approaches are fundamentally interactive and include participants quite fully in framing questions and gathering data, the researcher's presence is considered an integral part of the setting. Whatever the qualitative approach, however, researchers should practice and build habits for labeling audiotapes, carrying extra batteries, and finding quiet places for taking notes; such practices will pay off by keeping data intact, complete, organized, and accessible.

In addition, the researcher should plan a system to ease retrieval for analysis. In more "objectivist" proposals, researchers may have lists of predetermined categories for data coding. Relying on such categories facilitates retrieval and analysis, but to remain true to qualitative research assumptions, the researcher must plan decision rules for altering those categories during focused analysis. Furthermore, planning ahead for the color coding of notes to keep track of dates, names, titles, attendance at events, chronologies, descriptions of settings, maps, sociograms, and so on is invaluable for piecing together patterns, defining categories for data analysis, planning further data collection, and especially for writing the final product of the research. Vignette 25 provides descriptive detail of one such effort.

*    *    *    *    *

### Vignette 25

*Data Management*

In her dissertation research on women's socialization in school administration, Marshall (1979) developed a process by which data transcription, organization, and analysis were combined in a single operation. Her entry into the field and interviewing were directed by a conceptual framework and a set of guiding hypotheses.

She conducted data analysis by trying out conceptual levers such as Goode's (1960) role strain theory, identified in the course of the literature review. Goode's theory guided the analysis of data pertaining to conflicts experienced by women entering male sex-typed careers while continuing to live with the stereotypical expectations of mother, wife, and community member. Building on Goode's work, Marshall devised a career-role strain theory that included feminine identity and sexuality crises prompted by the demands of working in a male-normed profession.

Employing constant comparative data analysis, she developed a grounded theory of women's socialization in male sex-typed careers that explained the socialization period of transition. During this period, women resist the pull of aspiration, resent the exclusion, are angry at the double demands, and yet simultaneously create new ways to fill the roles. Observational notes and prefieldwork mapping of sites or subjects were recorded on legal-sized, hard-backed notebooks that could be held in the lap or used on the run. Following each interview, Marshall added semitranscribed field notes of audiotaped conversations, selecting conceptually intriguing phrases that either connected with previous literature or suggested patterns emerging from the analysis of previous data.

The process of preserving the data and meanings on tape and the combined transcription and preliminary analysis greatly increased the efficiency of data analysis. The researcher's transcription, done with the literature review, previous data, and earlier analytic memos in mind, became a useful part of data analysis and not mere clerical duty.

This is not to suggest a reprieve from the transfer of data to index cards, coding of data, sorting of cards to identify overlapping categories, organization of codes into more inclusive and abstract domains, methodological notes, analytic memos, theoretical notes, case summaries, charts, and dummy tables, all representing further steps in analysis. Combining the initial transcription with analysis, however, moved the study forward efficiently and did so without threat to the exploratory value of qualitative research or to data quality.

*    *    *    *    *

Vignette 25 is just one researcher's way of managing complex and thick data. Over the years, researchers have developed a variety of data management strategies ranging from color and number codings on index cards to computer programs; these techniques are often shared as part of the "folklore of fieldwork." Schatzman and Strauss's (1973) classic suggestions on observational notes, methodological notes, theoretical notes, and analytic memos are quite useful, as is Maxwell's (1996) discussion of analytic memos. Whatever method is devised, it must enable the researcher to organize data while making them easily retrievable and manipulable. Most general introductory texts on qualitative methods provide extended discussions of processes of analyzing data; we reference several at the end of this chapter. Below we offer a process of generic data analysis; the researcher should discuss her preliminary strategies at the proposal stage.

## Generic Data Analysis Strategies

Data analysis is the process of bringing order, structure, and interpretation to the mass of collected data. It is a messy, ambiguous, time-consuming, creative, and fascinating process. It does not proceed in a linear fashion; it is not neat. Qualitative data analysis is a search for general statements about relationships among categories of data; it builds grounded theory (Strauss & Corbin, 1997). It is the search among data to identify content for ethnographies and for participants' "truths."

This section of the research proposal should describe to the reader initial decisions about data analysis and should convince the reader that the researcher is sufficiently knowledgeable about qualitative analysis to consider data organization, theme development and interpretation, and report writing. Although none of these can be given exhaustive consideration in the proposal, the researcher should convince the reader that thought and awareness have gone into planning the analysis phase of the study. What follows is a discussion of some considerations the researcher should bring to this section.

Whether the researcher prefigures the analysis before data collection, begins the process during data collection, or waits until all data have been gathered is related to the qualitative genre and assumptions of the study. Generating categories of data to collect, or cells in a matrix, can be an important focusing device for the study (see Table 3.3). Tightly structured, highly organized data-gathering and data-analyzing schemes, however, often

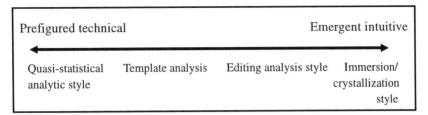

**Figure 5.1. A Continuum of Analysis Strategies**
SOURCE: Adapted from Crabtree and Miller (1992, pp. 17-20).

filter out the unusual, the serendipitous—the puzzle that if attended to and pursued would provide a recasting of the entire research endeavor. Thus, a balance must be struck between efficiency considerations and design flexibility.

Crabtree and Miller (1992) offer a continuum of ideal-type analysis strategies (see Figure 5.1), although they note that "nearly as many analysis strategies exist as qualitative researchers" (p. 17). At the extreme objectivist end of the continuum are technical, scientific, and standardized strategies. At this end, the researcher has assumed an objectivist stance relative to the inquiry and has stipulated the categories in advance. At the other end are the "immersion strategies" (pp. 17-18), which do not prefigure categories and which rely heavily on the researcher's intuitive and interpretive capacities. "Template" and "editing" (pp. 17-18) analysis strategies reside along the continuum, with the template process more prefigured and stipulative than the editing processes. Template strategies rely on sets of codes to apply to the data; these may undergo revision as the analysis proceeds. Editing strategies are less prefigured: "The interpreter engages the text naively, without a template" (p. 20), searching for segments of text to generate and illustrate categories of meaning.

In qualitative studies, data collection and analysis typically go hand in hand to build a coherent interpretation of the data. The researcher is guided by initial concepts and developing understandings but shifts or modifies them as she collects and analyzes the data. Her overall strategy, thus, rests more toward the interpretive/subjectivist end of the continuum than the technical/objectivist end. Schatzman and Strauss (1973) succinctly portray the process of qualitative data collection and analysis:

> Qualitative data are exceedingly complex and not readily convertible into standard measurable units of objects seen and heard; they vary in level of abstraction, in frequency of occurrence, in relevance to central

questions in the research. Also, they vary in the source or ground from which they are experienced. Our model researcher starts analyzing very early in the research process. For him, the option represents an *analytic* strategy: he needs to analyze as he goes along both to adjust his observation strategies, shifting some emphasis towards those experiences which bear upon the development of his understanding, and generally, to exercise control over his emerging ideas by virtually simultaneous checking or testing of these ideas. . . . Probably the most fundamental operation in the analysis of qualitative data is that of discovering significant *classes* of things, persons and events and the *properties* which characterize them. In this process, which continues throughout the research, the analyst gradually comes to reveal his own "is's" and "because's": he names classes and links one with another, at first with "simple" statements (propositions) that express the linkages, and continues this process until his propositions fall into *sets,* in an ever-increasing density of linkages. (pp. 108-110)

The researcher should use the preliminary research questions and the related literature developed earlier in the proposal to provide guidelines for data analysis. This earlier grounding and planning can be used to suggest several categories that can serve to code the data initially for subsequent analysis.

As a coherent interpretation with related concepts emerges from analysis, negative instances will lead to new data collecting and analysis that serve to strengthen the interpretation. This interpretation solidifies as major modifications occur less often and concepts fall into established categories. Finally, analysis will be sufficient when the critical categories are defined, the relationships between them are established, and they are integrated into an elegant, credible interpretation.

## Analytic Procedures

Typical analytic procedures fall into six phases: (a) organizing the data; (b) generating categories, themes, and patterns; (c) coding the data; (d) testing the emergent understandings; (e) searching for alternative explanations; and (f) writing the report. Each phase of data analysis entails data reduction as the reams of collected data are brought into manageable chunks and interpretation as the researcher brings meaning and insight to the words and acts of the participants in the study. At the proposal stage, the researcher should project what this process will entail, in preliminary ways. The procedures to be followed, initial guides for categories, and potential coding schemes all indicate to the reader that this crucial phase of the research will be managed competently.

The interpretive act remains mysterious in both qualitative and quantitative data analysis. It is a process of bringing meaning to raw, inexpressive data that is necessary whether the researcher's language is standard deviations and means or rich description of ordinary events. Raw data have no inherent meaning; the interpretive act brings meaning to those data and displays that meaning to the reader through the written report.

## Organizing the Data

Reading, reading, and reading once more through the data forces the researcher to become familiar with those data in intimate ways. People, events, and quotations sift constantly through the researcher's mind. During the reading process, the researcher can list on note cards the data available, perform the minor editing necessary to make field notes retrievable, and generally "clean up" (Pearsol, 1985) what seems overwhelming and unmanageable. At this time, the researcher could also enter the data into one of several software programs for the management or analysis of qualitative data or both (see Tesch, 1990, for an extended treatment of software for qualitative data analysis). As Patton (1990) notes,

> The data generated by qualitative methods are voluminous. I have found no way of preparing students for the sheer massive volumes of information with which they will find themselves confronted when data collection has ended. Sitting down to make sense out of pages of interviews and whole files of field notes can be overwhelming. Dealing with all those pieces of paper seems like an impossible task. (p. 379)

He then underscores how much of qualitative reporting consists of descriptive data, the purpose of which is to display the daily events of the phenomenon under study. Careful attention to how data are being reduced is necessary throughout the research endeavor. In some instances, direct transfer onto predeveloped data recording charts is appropriate, as with the template strategies. Miles and Huberman (1994) suggest several schema for recording qualitative data. Such techniques streamline data management, help ensure reliability across several researchers, and are highly recommended. In using graphics and schema, however, the researcher should guard against losing the serendipitous finding.

### Generating Categories, Themes, and Patterns

For researchers relying on editing or immersion strategies, this phase of data analysis is the most difficult, complex, ambiguous, creative, and fun. Although there are few descriptions of this process in the literature, it remains the most amenable to display through example. The analytic process demands a heightened awareness of the data, a focused attention to those data, and an openness to the subtle, tacit undercurrents of social life. Identifying salient themes, recurring ideas or language, and patterns of belief that link people and settings together is the most intellectually challenging phase of data analysis and one that can integrate the entire endeavor. Through questioning the data and reflecting on the conceptual framework, the researcher engages the ideas and the data in significant intellectual work. For editing and immersion strategies, the categories are generated through prolonged engagement with the data—the text. These categories then become buckets or baskets into which segments of text are placed.

The process of category generation involves noting patterns evident in the setting and expressed by participants. As categories of meaning emerge, the researcher searches for those that have internal convergence and external divergence (Guba, 1978). That is, the categories should be internally consistent but distinct from one another. Here, the researcher does not search for the exhaustive and mutually exclusive categories of the statistician but, instead, identifies the salient, grounded categories of meaning held by participants in the setting.

Patton (1990) describes the processes of inductive analysis where the salient categories emerge from the data. The researcher may use "indigenous typologies" (p. 306) or "analyst-constructed typologies" (pp. 393-400) to reflect the understandings expressed by the participants. Indigenous typologies are those created and expressed by participants and are generated through analyses of the local use of language.

Analyst-constructed typologies are those created by the researcher that are grounded in the data but not necessarily used explicitly by participants. In this case, the researcher applies a typology to the data. As with all analysis, this process entails uncovering patterns, themes, and categories and may well be subject to the "legitimate charge of imposing a world of meaning on the participants that better reflects the observer's world than the world under study" (Patton, 1990, p. 398). In a related strategy, through logical reasoning, classification schemes are crossed with one another to generate new insights or typologies for further exploration in the data. Usually presented in matrix format, these cross-classifications suggest "holes" in the already-analyzed data, suggesting areas where data might be *logically* uncovered. Patton, however, cautions the researcher not to allow these matrices to lead the analysis but instead to generate sensitizing concepts to guide further explorations: "It is easy for a matrix to begin to manipulate the data as the analyst is tempted to force the data into categories created by the cross-classification to fill out the matrix and make it work" (p. 412). Examples of two logically constructed matrices are presented in Figures 5.2 and 5.3.

## Coding the Data

Coding data is the formal representation of analytic thinking. The tough intellectual work of analysis is generating categories and themes. The researcher then applies some coding scheme to those categories and themes and diligently and thoroughly marks passages in the data using the codes. Codes may take several forms: abbreviations of key words, colored dots, numbers— the choice is up to the researcher. Computer software programs for data analysis (see Tesch, 1990; Weitzman & Miles, 1995) typically rely on abbreviations of key words. For example, in a dissertation proposal, Tucker (1996) discussed how she might use the following codes for her data:

| | |
|---|---|
| TCARE.LIS | Teacher's caring as demonstrated through listening |
| TCARE.Q'S | Teacher's caring as demonstrated through honoring questions |
| TDIS.RACISMO | Teacher's disrespect as demonstrated through overt racism |

Were she not using software, she might have planned to use different colored dots to place on the interview transcripts and field notes or to underline passages with different colored highlighting pens. Whatever system the

## behaviors towards dropouts

|  |  | taking responsibility ↔ shifting responsibility to others |  |
|---|---|---|---|
| teachers' beliefs about how to intervene with dropouts | rehabilitation ↕ | counselor/friend: help kids directly | referral agent: refer them to other helping agencies |
| | maintenance (caretaking) | traffic cop: just keep them moving through the system | ostrich: ignore the situation and hope someone else does something |
| | ↕ punishment | old-fashioned school master: make them feel the consequences | complainer: somebody should remove the problem kids |

**Figure 5.2. An Empirical Typology of Teacher Roles in Dealing With High School Dropouts**
SOURCE: Patton (1990, p. 413). Reprinted by permission.

## outreach

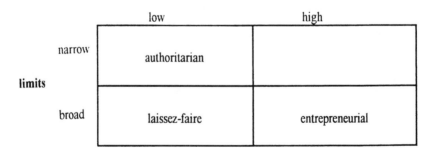

**Figure 5.3. Three Ideal-Typical Approaches to Training and Dissemination**
SOURCE: Firestone and Rossman (1986, p. 308). Reprinted by permission.

researcher plans to use, she should know that the scheme will undergo changes—coding is not a merely technical task. As the researcher codes the data, new understandings may well emerge, necessitating changes in the original plan.

## Testing Emergent Understandings

As categories and themes are developed and coding is well under way, the researcher begins the process of evaluating the plausibility of his developing understandings and exploring them through the data. This entails a search through the data during which the researcher challenges the understanding, searches for negative instances of the patterns, and incorporates these into larger constructs, as necessary.

Part of this phase is to evaluate the data for their usefulness and centrality. The researcher should determine how useful the data are in illuminating the questions being explored and how they are central to the story that is unfolding about the social phenomenon.

## Searching for Alternative Explanations

As the researcher discovers categories and patterns in the data, she should engage in critically challenging the very patterns that seem so apparent. The researcher should search for other, plausible explanations for these data and the linkages among them. Alternative explanations *always* exist; the researcher must search for, identify, and describe them, and then demonstrate how the explanation offered is the most plausible of all. This recalls the discussion in Chapter 1 concerning *the proposal as an argument* that offers assertions about the data, provides substantial evidence for those assertions, builds a logical interrelationship among them, and presents a summation of how the assertions relate to previous and future research.

## Writing the Report

Writing about qualitative data cannot be separated from the analytic process. In fact, it is central to that process, for in the choice of particular words to summarize and reflect the complexity of the data, the researcher is engaging in the interpretive act, lending shape and form—meaning—to massive amounts of raw data. We suggest that, at the proposal stage, the researcher consider what modalities she will use for final reporting. For dissertations, this is typically done by outlining the chapters to be included in the final document. For funded research proposals, reporting may entail periodic written reports as well as other forms of dissemination. These may include conferences, newsletters, documentary films, or exhibitions. Despite interest in alternative dissemination strategies and reporting formats, the written report remains the primary mode for reporting the results of research.

Several models for report writing exist. Taylor and Bogdan (1984, chaps. 8-12) suggest five different approaches. First is the purely descriptive life history. Here, the author presents one person's account of his or her own life, framing that description with analytic points about the social significance of that life. Second is the presentation of data gathered through in-depth interviews and participant observation, where the participants' perspectives are presented and their worldviews form the structural framework for the report. The third approach attempts to relate practice (the reality of social phenomena) to theory. Here, descriptive data are summarized, then linked to more general theoretical constructs. Taylor and Bogdan's fourth approach is the most theoretical. To illustrate it, they provide an example using a study of institutions for individuals with severe cognitive challenges; the report addresses sociological theory about institutionalization and the symbolic management of conditions in total institutions. Their final approach is an attempt to build theory by drawing on data gathered from several types of institutions and under various research conditions. The report they use as an example addresses issues of the presentation of self under various difficult circumstances and attempts to draw theoretical conclusions across types of institutions, types of persons, and types of circumstances.

Van Maanen (1988) identifies three different genres in qualitative writing. *Realist tales* are the most recognized genre, displaying a realist account of the culture under study and published in articles or scholarly monographs in a third-person voice with clear separation between the researcher and the researched. Established by "grandparents" of ethnography such as Margaret Mead, William Foote Whyte, Howard Becker, and Branislaw Malinowski, this tradition set the standards and criteria for credibility, quality, and respectability in qualitative work. Van Maanen (1988) views these as frequently "flat, dry and sometimes unbearably dull" (p. 48).

*Confessional tales* are highly personalized accounts with "mini-melodramas of hardships endured in fieldwork" (Van Maanen, 1988, p. 73). This genre aims to display the author's powers of observation and the discipline of good field habits to call attention to the ways building cultural description is part of social science. Powdermaker (1966) is a classic example of this genre.

In *impressionist tales* the field-worker displays her own experiences in the field—a sort of autoethnography. Bowen's work (1964) provides a classic example; more current ones include Krieger (1985) and Thorne (1983). The separation of the researcher from the researched is blurred in this genre, and the tale is told through the chronology of fieldwork events, drawing attention to the culture under study but also to the fieldwork experiences that were integral to the cultural description and interpretation.

Considerations of role, ethics, and political stance affect report writing. One may choose to present many truths or multiple perspectives or presume to have identified one truth. Choosing to say "I interpreted this event" rather than "the data revealed" must be a clear decision. Postmodern and feminist discussions help researchers clarify such decisions. Writing *your* truth about others' lives is an assertion of power and can violate earlier assertions about working ethically and sensitively with participants (Tierney & Lincoln, 1997; Lather, 1991).

Two approaches to qualitative research and their attendant reporting are worthy of special mention—case studies and action research. Both begin with the assumption that research must begin in natural settings and incorporate historical and organizational contexts; they may use the full array of data collection strategies; and their typical reporting formats are of note.

Case Study Reports

Reports of research on a specific organization, program, or process (or some set of these) are often called case studies (Yin, 1984). Case studies rely on historical and document analysis, interviewing, and typically, some forms of observation as data collection. A rich tradition of community studies, organizational research, and program evaluations documents the illustrative power when research focuses in depth and in detail on specific instances of the phenomenon of interest. Case studies take the reader into the setting with a vividness and detail not typically present in more analytic reporting formats.

Action Research Reporting

Research with practitioners, and often *by* practitioners, who want to improve their own situation and discover and solve problems is called action research. Research questions are defined collaboratively with participants; the researcher's role is often that of facilitator who expands the questions through consultation, problem posing, and knowledge of existing literature. Although systematic inquiry traditions are followed, innovative and evolving data collection strategies may shift as the inquiry proceeds (McKernan, 1991). Reporting from action research may take several forms. A written report may be collaboratively produced; this would depend on the interests and needs of participants. Frequently, short oral reports or displays of "lessons learned" in photo montages, exhibitions, or documentary films are preferred.

Because action research is fundamentally determined by participants—for their own uses—rather than by the scholarly needs of the researcher, reporting should be true to that guiding principle. Reporting, whatever form it takes, has built-in relevance. Usefulness to participants may be more important than methodological rigor (Argyris & Schön, 1991). The researcher, as participant, may become a trusted insider with access seldom possible in more traditional observer roles (Cole, 1991). Often, action researchers take an activist, critical, and emancipatory stance, using the research process as an empowering process in an organization or a community (Cancian & Armstead, 1992; Fals-Borda & Rahman, 1991; Reason, 1994).

Researchers hope their reports will contribute to societal improvement, either directly in action and participatory approaches or indirectly by enhancing policy or programmatic decisions. Recall the discussion of a study's potential significance in Chapter 2. Choosing participatory action research, however, can be an ideological stance, a determination to try to change the world in direct ways, as Vignette 26 illustrates.

*     *     *     *     *

### Vignette 26

*Planning Reporting for Qualitative*
*Participatory Evaluation*

Research design and data collection strategies can be structured to facilitate the active participation of the individuals being researched. An example of this is the work of Paul Castelloe, a graduate student in social work who designed a participatory evaluation study of the Learning Together program in North Carolina (Castelloe & Legerton, 1998). The program is designed to serve two purposes: (a) increase the school preparation of children, ages 3 to 5, with no other preschool experience and (b) strengthen their caregivers' capacity to provide education and developmental support.

Drawing on the work of Fraser (1997) and Mouffe and LeClau (1985), Castelloe designed his research project with a *radical* democratic philosophy to create an evaluation process committed to sharing power with research participants. Although traditional research designs place the researcher(s) in the sole position of determining research design and creating research questions, participatory action research brings the individuals being studied into the research process. With his interest in grassroots change and democratic processes, Castelloe *democratically* structured his study to collect data in a way that would include participants. This approach led to data collection techniques designed to include individuals at all levels (including those traditionally silenced in a study—the individuals that a policy is supposed to "help,"—e.g., caregivers and students).

Castelloe designed his study to teach the program staff and community members the skills required to conduct an evaluation. In this role, he decided to serve as facilitator and "co-laborer" in the collaborative evaluation process. The direction, plan, questions, and goals of the evaluation were designed to be a cocreation between Castelloe and the program staff, program participants, and the community in which the program is located.

The primary data collection techniques selected were in-depth interviews, observational methods, and focus group interviews. He created several strategies to include participants in the research decision-making process. For example, he developed interview questions in collaboration with program administrators, program staff, and community members and asked them to provide feedback on data transcripts.

His philosophy and rationale concerning democratic process served to guide his overall approach to include participants in the research process and examine whether the Learning Together program was democratic, participatory, and inclusive. Collectively, Castelloe and the participants determined how and when reporting would take place. These deliberations strengthened the democratic principles of their work together.

*     *     *     *     *

The following two vignettes depict challenges and considerations that researchers brought to writing up their reports. Vignette 27 shows how analysis and writing are interwoven throughout a study, and Vignette 28 comes from a study of incest in which the challenges of writing were substantial.

*   *   *   *   *

### Vignette 27

### Interspersing Reporting and Analysis

Often, data analysis and writing up the research are thought of and portrayed as two discrete processes. Increasingly, however, researchers are using the writing up of research as an opportunity to display, in the body of the report, how data analysis evolved. Gerstl-Pepin (1998) accomplished this quite elegantly in her study of educational reform.

Gerstl-Pepin constructed a theoretical framework to critically examine whether an arts-based educational reform movement in North Carolina functioned as a counterpublic sphere (Fraser, 1997) and led to democratically structured educational policy and reform. Although interested in examining theoretical issues concerning the prospects for democratically structured reform, she was also interested in telling the story of the reform movement.

To balance these two interests, Gerstl-Pepin decided to take an approach similar to Lather and Smithies (1997) and weave her shifts in thinking about research questions into the body of the text. Her interest in including the researcher's evolving thought processes arose out of an awareness of shifting research paradigms that highlight the subjectivity of the researcher. While analyzing the data, Gerstl-Pepin encountered "teachable moments" in the research process in which her conceptualization and understanding of the research developed and shifted. She included these pieces within the narrative story about the reform movement as separate boxes of text and titled these pieces "Interludes: Reflections on the Research." They were included at various points in the narrative, depicting shifts in her thinking process and research focus. These pieces served as stories within the story and were intended to allow the reader to participate not only in the story of the reform process but also in the discovery process for the researcher.

*   *   *   *   *

Philosophical inquiry and shifting paradigms highlight the subjectivity of the researcher and her relationship to the research process. Placing analytic memos, methodological notes, or "interludes" in the report makes these processes transparent. Our last vignette for this chapter, Vignette 28, presents the ethical dilemmas of reporting about taboo topics.

\* \* \* \* \*

*Vignette 28*

---

*"Talking Taboo": Continuing the*
*Research Relationship*

During analysis and reporting data, Kiegelmann (1997) was inventive with methods to protect her research participants. This is always important, but for her research on brother-sister incest she was particularly attuned to how participants had trusted her with emotion-laden and highly sensitive aspects of their lives. One had even shared her childhood journal in which she wrote just minutes after the incest occurred. Kiegelmann and the participants had become a support group, continuing to meet after the research was finished.

As data analysis proceeded, Kiegelmann identified themes and noted the range of nuances in the study participants' talk. Previous literatures guided her, especially writings about girls' views of femininity, of "good girls," and girls' ways of knowing. Three voice clusters emerged: silent voices, embodied voices, and naming voices. Anticipating the need to report, to have validity checks, and to regain permission for using their words, Kiegelmann created biographies of each woman and sent them to the women, inviting their comments. She received feedback and commentary from them, which she incorporated into her writing. As she neared completion, she sent a draft of the full study to all of them. Each participant used this opportunity to offer more details but not to change the interpretations. Furthermore, she invited the participants to write statements directly to the readers of the research, giving the women the final word. Thus, the trusting relationships were maintained beyond the time of the study, the study's "truthfulness" was increased, and she avoided taking away power and control over the representation of their lives from the participants.

\* \* \* \* \*

This vignette reveals a highly ethical sensitivity to the participants in the study. Kiegelmann honored their life stories and voices throughout the process. This involved several iterations: writing biographies, sending them to the participants for commentary, incorporating their feedback, sending the full draft for further commentary, and incorporating the women's final comments in the final document. Although this process was time-consuming, it expressed Kiegelmann's deep commitment to the women and to the ethical conduct of her study.

Into the various phases of data analysis and report writing are woven considerations of the soundness, usefulness, and ethical conduct of the qualitative research study. Some consideration should be given to issues of the value, truthfulness, and soundness of the study throughout the design of the proposal. Considerations of role, for example, should address the personal biography of the researcher and how that might shape events and meanings. In what ways is the research, whether participatory or more objectivist, altering the flow of daily life? Similarly, selection of the setting and sampling of people and behaviors within that setting should consider the soundness of those decisions and present a clear rationale that has guided those choices. Chapter 7 continues this discussion of considerations of the soundness and ethical conduct of the study.

Chapters 3, 4, and 5 have brought the reader through the complex, sometimes tedious process of building a design and choosing research methods for the research study. This section of the proposal should demonstrate that the researcher is competent to conduct the research; knowledgeable about the issues, dilemmas, choices, and decisions to be made in the design and conduct of the research; and immersed in the literature that provides guidance for the qualitative researcher. The research design should be well written and should reveal a sensitivity to various issues, the capacity to be reflective about the nature of inquiry and the substantive questions at hand, and a willingness to tolerate some ambiguity during the conduct of the study. These qualities will stand the researcher in good stead over the course of the research. In addition, however, the researcher should demonstrate some knowledge of the management of resources in the design of a qualitative study. This is the focus of the next chapter.

# Further Reading

## On Data Analysis

Emerson, R. M., Fretz, R. I., & Shaw, L. L. (1995). *Writing ethnographic fieldnotes*. Chicago: University of Chicago Press.

Kelle, E. (Ed.). (1995). *Computer-aided qualitative data analysis*. Thousand Oaks, CA: Sage.

Miles, M. B., & Huberman, A. M. (1994). *Qualitative data analysis: An expanded sourcebook* (2nd ed.). Thousand Oaks, CA: Sage.

Mills, G. E. (1993). Levels of abstraction in a case study of educational change. In D. J. Flinders & G. E. Mills (Eds.), *Theory and concepts in qualitative research: Perspectives from the field* (pp. 103-116). New York: Teachers College Press.

Patton, M. Q. (1990). *Qualitative research and evaluation methods* (2nd ed.). Newbury Park, CA: Sage.

Silverman, D. (1993). *Interpreting qualitative data: Methods for analyzing talk, text and interaction*. Newbury Park, CA: Sage.

Tanaka, G. (1997). Pico College. In W. G. Tierney & Y. S. Lincoln (Eds.), *Representation and the text: Re-framing the narrative voice* (pp. 259-304). Albany: State University of New York Press.

Thornton, S. J. (1993). The quest for emergent meaning: A personal account. In D. J. Flinders & G. E. Mills (Eds.), *Theory and concepts in qualitative research: Perspectives from the field* (pp. 68-82). New York: Teachers College Press.

Weitzman, E. A., & Miles, M. B. (1995). *Computer programs for qualitative data analysis*. Thousand Oaks, CA: Sage.

## On Writing

Ellis, C., & Bochner, A. P. (Eds.). (1996). *Composing ethnography: Alternative forms of qualitative writing*. Walnut Creek, CA: AltaMira.

Gitlin, A. (Ed.). (1994). *Power and method: Political activism and educational research*. New York: Routledge.

Meloy, J. M. (1994). *Writing the qualitative dissertation: Understanding by doing*. Hillsdale, NJ: Lawrence Erlbaum.

Richardson, L. (1990). *Writing strategies: Reaching diverse audiences*. Newbury Park, CA: Sage.

Richardson, L. (1994). Writing: A method of inquiry. In N. K. Denzin & Y. S. Lincoln (Eds.), *Handbook of qualitative research* (pp. 516-529). Thousand Oaks, CA: Sage.

Stake, R. (1995). *The art of case study research*. Thousand Oaks, CA: Sage.

Tierney, W. G., & Lincoln, Y. S. (Eds.). (1997). *Representation and the text: Re-framing the narrative voice*. Albany: State University New York Press.

Van Maanen, J. (1988). *Tales of the field: On writing ethnography*. Chicago: University of Chicago Press.

Van Maanen, J. (Ed.). (1995). *Representation in ethnography*. Thousand Oaks, CA: Sage.

Zinsser, W. (1990). *On writing well: An informal guide to writing nonfiction* (4th ed.). New York: Harper.

# 6 Planning Time and Resources

The process of planning and projecting the resource needs for a qualitative study is an integral aspect of proposal development. The resources most critical to the successful completion of the study are time, personnel, and financial support. The last of these is not always readily available, especially in dissertation research; serious consideration, however, must be given to time and personnel. There are also many hidden costs associated with qualitative research that may become apparent only after the researcher has carefully analyzed and reflected about the study's demands. Convincing funding agencies that the expenses are worthwhile may be a challenge.

This chapter provides the researcher with detailed analyses and projections of the resource demands of qualitative research. Using four vignettes as illustrations, we provide general guidelines for consideration in the development and projection of resource needs. Vignette 29 shows the process of planning resource needs for large-scale research; it is adapted from Anthony and Rossman's (1990) proposal to evaluate a Commonwealth of Massachusetts restructuring initiative. This multiperson, multisite, multiyear proposal was developed with ample financial resources and a long time frame for completion of the project. In contrast, Vignette 30 reveals the planning process of a doctoral student proposing a study of recidivism among criminal offenders. This study was a solo venture, with few financial supports to back it up. The contrast between Vignettes 29 and 30 is intended to display how each proposal must address difficult resource questions. Vignette 31 demonstrates the need to teach reviewers about the intense resource demands of qualitative research. Finally, Vignette 32 shows how researchers tried to convince a funding agent of the need for financial resources for secondary analyses of qualitative data.

Careful, detailed consideration of the resource demands of a study is critical in demonstrating that the researcher is knowledgeable about qualitative research, understands that the inherent flexibility will create resource difficulties at some point in the study, and has thought through the resource issues and recognizes the demands that will be made.

Some resource decisions cannot be made until basic design issues have been resolved. The researcher, however, should consider resources as she struggles with the conceptual framework and design issues of the study. For example, a researcher cannot decide to conduct a multisite, multiperson project with no prospect of financial resources in sight, nor can she prudently plan to conduct a long-term, intensive participant observation study when she knows she must continue to work full-time and cannot possibly devote the necessary time to the study. Thus, general resource considerations and design decisions proceed in parallel fashion and are major criteria for the do-ability of the study.

In the narrative structure of the proposal, after discussion of the design of the study, the researcher should address resource needs specifically. These include time demands and management, personnel needs and staffing, and financial support for the entire endeavor. Two vignettes are presented below, followed by a discussion of the major resource needs of each. The vignettes are intended to display the strategies for resource allocation decisions given two quite different studies.

## Planning Resources for a Large Study

Although the resource needs for a long-term, complex study are substantially more elaborate than those for dissertation research, the processes of projecting those resources remain very similar. Vignette 29 details how resource decisions were made in planning for a large-scale evaluation of a state restructuring initiative. Titled Restructuring for the Integration of All Students, this discretionary grants program funded seven school districts in the Commonwealth of Massachusetts to encourage experimentation with the fuller inclusion of students with disabilities and those receiving bilingual and compensatory education services in the regular classroom. Each district was awarded grants varying from $25,000 to $125,000 per year for 5 years for this initiative. The request for proposals (RFP) for an evaluation of this effort stipulated certain design features (e.g., qualitative and quantitative methods) and targeted the overall budget at $350,000, although this would be renegotiated each year of the contract.

In designing a proposal to evaluate this restructuring initiative, Anthony and Rossman (1991) had to make careful decisions regarding resource allocations. Several critical resource decisions flowed from the overall design of the study, which had two major components: (a) multisite, multiresearcher, multiyear case studies of implementation in the seven school districts and (b) a cost-benefit analysis of this new, inclusive model of providing categorical services. A study of this scope demanded adequate resources in time (sufficient to document implementation at the district and school levels), in personnel (capable of thoroughly and efficiently gathering the needed data), and in financial support for personnel, travel, data analysis, and report writing.

The first task in projecting resource needs was to organize the study's activities into manageable tasks. These were identified as (a) meetings with Department of Education project staff, (b) meetings of the evaluation team, (c) meetings with district coordinators for feedback, (d) site visits for data gathering, (e) data analysis, and (f) report writing. Initial projections of necessary time were made and then substantially refined, as the associated cost projections were made. That is, the research team first planned the ideal study, one in which resources were virtually infinite. At first go-around, this plan called for initial site visits to each district, followed by several site visits during each of the 5 years of the study. Refinements were made when realistic costs in terms of time, personnel, and travel were estimated. Table 6.1 (following Vignette 29) shows the final allocation of staff days to tasks.

This recursive process characterized all the resource planning activities. As the principal investigators (PIs) identified important aspects of the study that would require time and effort (i.e., more data), the study grew and grew. These ideal projections then had to be grounded in real considerations of the total budget allocated for the study. By making projections based on the study's conceptual framework and the requirements of the RFP, the researchers ensured sound adherence to the initial research questions. The following is paraphrased from the evaluation proposal (Anthony & Rossman, 1991) and details the final allocation of resources to each research task.

*    *    *    *    *

*Vignette 29*
────────────

*Projecting Resources for a*
*Large-Scale Study*

The evaluation of Restructuring for the Integration of All Students requires an approach that will be responsive to the uniqueness of each district and will also provide data useful in formulating policy for all districts. Because it is so difficult to generalize from single cases (Kennedy, 1979), the evaluation will focus on cross-site analyses that will identify major patterns (Herriott & Firestone, 1983). This approach recognizes the need to inform policymakers about the importance of local variation (Corbett, Dawson, & Firestone, 1984; Rossman, Corbett, & Firestone, 1988) that cannot be explored unless the cases are compared. The evaluation, moreover, hopes to provide policymakers with clear descriptions of implementation at the many levels involved in such efforts: district, school, and classroom. The evaluation approach relies on nested contexts, an approach that gathers data from the multiple levels pertinent to a full understanding of the educational and policy implementation issues of restructuring for integration.

Finally, because the phenomenon to be evaluated is complex, multiple evaluation methods are required to provide a multifaceted description of restructuring in the seven districts. The use of both qualitative and quantitative data in a mixed-methods design (Greene, Caracelli, & Graham, 1989) will enhance the pragmatic usefulness of the evaluation to policymakers (Rossman & Wilson, 1985).

There are two major elements of the evaluation: case studies of the seven districts and the development of a cost-benefit model and initial analyses of each district and selected individual students. Each element is detailed below.

## Case Studies

The case studies are designed to document the issues and outcomes of implementing comprehensive integration and to focus on the local district as the primary unit of analysis. Because each district's history, culture, capacity and will, resources, and parallel efforts are so different, a district focus will permit full elaboration of those contextual variations that shape policy implementation in important ways. The evaluation team, therefore, plans to concentrate its efforts on each district through four annual site visits to district offices and the sample schools, supplemented by ongoing data collection at the district level. The assumption here is that local variability profoundly effects the issues addressed and shapes local capacity to respond to state policy initiatives (Rossman, Corbett, & Dawson, 1986; Rossman et al., 1988).

## District-Level Data Gathering

District-level data gathering will include interviewing central office administrators, gathering district-wide statistical data (for the cost-benefit analyses), and documenting ongoing implementation of the district's initiative over the 5 years of funding. This will entail gathering documents such as teacher minigrant proposals, proposal awards, newsletters, minutes of planning team meetings, documentation of staff development activities, and so on.

This district-level data gathering will provide evidence for the policy formulation and planning processes each district undertakes, as well as descriptions of the implementation strategies employed. It will also permit assessments of coordination of services at the district level, as well as organizational strengths and challenges.

## School-Level Data Gathering

The school-level analyses are planned to rely on multiple sources of data: in-depth interviews, observations, surveys, and document analysis. At the four annual site visits to each district, the evaluators plan to conduct interviews, observe meetings and classrooms, and gather documents. In-depth interviews will be conducted with building administrators, teachers, students (both regular and those receiving special services), and parents.

Attendance at relevant planning meetings will provide additional insight into implementation issues. Observations of classrooms will be made, focusing on the developing opportunities for interaction between regular education children and children with disabilities. These qualitative data will be supplemented with surveys of all teachers in the sample schools and a randomly selected sample of parents from each school to provide breadth of understanding of various role groups' perspectives. Finally, school-level documents (financial, minutes of meetings, memoranda, program description, for example) will be gathered to elaborate further an understanding of local implementation. An assessment of the technical assistance needed from the Department of Education (DOE) will also be made, as required by the RFP, based on the resource analysis and survey results described above.

*School selection strategy.* Selection of schools within districts will follow each district's implementation plan, focusing on the levels selected by each. Sampling of schools, of classrooms, and of individual teachers, counselors, and students within schools for interviewing and observation will be purposeful (Patton, 1980). Generally, the proposal design includes one high school, one middle/junior high school, and two or three elementary schools. This selection strategy recognizes the benefits accruing to studying a small number of schools in depth; the associated loss is of broader data across a number of schools. An in-depth assessment of three or four schools per district is most consistent with the philosophy of the restructuring initiative.

### Refinement of Research Design

Regular refinement of the research design is built into the proposed research schedule. The primary purpose of this activity is to create structured opportunities to communicate with important audiences for feedback about the research, notably the DOE and the districts involved. The underlying premise for formally building opportunities for refinement into the schedule is simply that a project of this scope requires the regular rethinking and adjustment of efforts consistent with a formative evaluation.

### Data Management

The fieldwork will generate a considerable amount of data that demands a management system. First, original field notes will be stored by site and by round of fieldwork. Second, after each trip, field notes will be reorganized around a set of categories deriving from the research questions. These categories will be revised to reflect additional data that does not fit initial questions. This process will serve as a crude but effective coding system. These documents will be typed to facilitate use by all members of the research team. Third, two sets of memoranda files will be kept. One will be for substantive issues. In this file, researchers will maintain a running dialogue of issues to consider and interesting events to note. The second will be for methodological issues. These memoranda will focus on the progress and problems of the fieldwork, providing important information relevant to the research reports.

## Data Analysis

Data analysis will rely on three mechanisms to ensure rich and authentic descriptions of the schools and districts as inclusion initiatives are implemented. The first is regularly scheduled meetings of the research team. The purposes of these meetings are (a) to keep the team members aware of the fieldwork at all the sites; (b) to discuss emerging issues, concerns, hypotheses, or data collection problems; and (c) to ensure, through feedback among the team, that comparable data collection activity goes on at all the sites.

The second mechanism is analytic memoranda. These memoranda will be drafted by team members and will serve as guides for further exploration of categories in the field, as checks on the site-specific data collected, and as verification of emerging hypotheses. They will also serve as the basis for discussion at the team meetings.

Finally, the evaluation will result in several case studies and cross-site reports. The case studies will offer rich detail about specific school and district implementation activities. They will be shared with participants in the study to sharpen the analysis by incorporating participants' views as validity checks and to engage participants in the study. The primary analytic focus, however, will be on cross-site reports. These will be organized around the important dimensions described in the conceptual portion of the proposal as shaping substantial change: the political, technical, and cultural.

The processes of data analysis will entail three activities: data reduction, data display, and conclusion drawing/verification. These activities will proceed concurrently during the research project, although any one may take precedence over the others at various times.

Data reduction will begin as soon as the important topics or themes are identified and will continue throughout data collection and report writing. Each choice or research decision (whether of topic, site, person to interview, or what to record as field notes) will involve data reduction because it will be a narrowing, a selecting from all possible choices (Miles & Huberman, 1994). Other instances of data reduction will occur during the coding of data and report writing. Each reduction act will help to bring the masses of data into more manageable proportion, thereby making them easier to comprehend and work with. It will be important, however, to remain open to the novel or unexpected insight that may emerge.

The plan describes data display as one process for presenting the data. For qualitative data, display usually takes a narrative form. They also will be displayed in graphic formats such as matrices, charts, graphs, and tables. Displaying data in these formats forces the evaluation team to consider what is known and not known about the phenomenon in question and may suggest new relationships, propositions, and explanations for further analysis. Thus, data, display will promote analysis by disciplining the evaluation team to identify what is known and not known about the districts and will also summarize the results of analysis. The study will include classical narrative displays of ideal types but may also entail the use of charts and graphs as suggested by Miles and Huberman (1994); the exact form will depend on the data.

Drawing conclusions and verifying them will also take place before, during, and after data collection. Before data collection, the evaluation team will have vague and unformed hunches that might lead to conclusions. As analysis proceeds, however, these conclusions will be tested out and elaborated systematically for their soundness and sturdiness. The conclusions will become more explicit as they are verified by the data in increasingly grounded analyses.

The proposal describes data reduction, data display, and conclusion drawing/verification as the activities of data analysis occurring recursively throughout the study. Rather than suggesting that each type of activity will occur at a specific phase of the research process, the proposal highlights how the activities interrelate and build on one another. Data display may spur conclusions that then will require verification; data reduction through coding may suggest a particular format that will make the data more comprehensible. Thus, each set of activities build on the others recursively; all three will coalesce to present a comprehensive and robust explanation of the successes and challenges of implementing inclusion initiatives.

*Reports*

The RFP requires regular reporting to the Department of Education: regular meetings followed by memoranda of understanding, a baseline report, annual reports, and a final, summative report. The annual reports are envisioned as comprehensive, book-length documents summarizing initiatives in each district, profiling certain statistical information and providing cross-case analyses in the form of an executive summary. In addition, the evaluators plan to ensure that, with award of the contract, independent publication will be pursued in both academic and practitioner-oriented journals. In addition, dissemination is planned to include presentations at professional meetings (e.g., the meetings of the American Educational Research Association) and to staff at the sites under study. The final product is proposed as a book-length document describing the entire project.

The entire scope of evaluation activities, deliverables (written memoranda and reports), and their attendant costs are projected through four tables. The first projects the assignment of staff and staff time to specific tasks and activities and is reproduced as Table 6.1. This table presents the person-days necessary for the completion of the various activities of the evaluation. The second table reorganizes this information and presents it by year, thereby projecting the personnel and time necessary for each year's activities; it is reproduced as Table 6.2. The proposal includes a time line that projects the flow of activities over the course of the evaluation and is presented as Table 6.3. Finally, the budget summary for the evaluation is presented in Table 6.4.

*       *       *       *       *

*Time*

As Vignette 29 illustrates, projecting sufficient time to undertake a full and richly detailed study that also remains doable is a difficult task but one that can be rewarding. Thinking through the time necessary for various research activities can be sobering even for experienced researchers; the novice learns a great deal by going through this discipline. For example, each of the research tasks described in this vignette required a certain number of days for its successful completion. The first step in projecting time demands was to determine the optimal number of days for each site visit. Although this depended on the year of the study, the evaluation team was able to estimate

**Table 6.1  Assignment of Staff and Staff Time to Tasks and Activities**

| Tasks and Activities | Time Line | | Staff and Staff Time (days) | | |
| | | PI | Co-PI | Evaluators (7) |
|---|---|---|---|---|
| 1. Data gathering | Y1 Mar-Jn 91 | 10 | 10 | 12 |
| Data analysis | Y2 Sep-May 92 | | | 16 |
| Report preparation | Dec-Jan 92 | 10 | 10 | |
| | Feb-Mar 92 | 10 | | |
| | | | | |
| 2. Preparation for | Y1 | 4 | 4 | |
| meetings, meetings, | Y2 | 10 | 10 | |
| follow-up memo | Y3 | 10 | 10 | |
| preparation | Y4 | 10 | 10 | |
| | Y5 | 10 | 10 | |
| | | | | |
| 3. Preparation for | Y1 | 2 | 2 | |
| meetings, meetings, | Y2 | 8 | 8 | |
| follow-up report | Y3 | 8 | 8 | |
| preparation | Y4 | 8 | 8 | |
| | Y5 | 8 | 8 | |
| | | | | |
| 4. Data gathering | Y1 Mar-May 91 | | | 6 |
| | Y2 Sep-Apr 92 | | | 10 |
| Data analysis | Mar-Apr 92 | | 4 | 5 |
| Cost-benefit design | Jly-Jn 92 | 20 | | |
| Report preparation | May-Jn 92 | 10 | 10 | |
| | | | | |
| 5. Data gathering | Y2 Sep-May 92 | | | 10 |
| | Y3 Sep-Apr 93 | | | 24 |
| | Y4 Sep-Apr 94 | | | 24 |
| Data analysis | Y2 Jn-Apr 92 | 3 | 5 | 5 |
| | Y3 Jn-Apr 93 | 40 | 30 | 30 |
| | Y4 Jn-Apr 94 | 40 | 30 | 30 |
| Report preparation | Y3 May-Jn 93 | 10 | 10 | |
| | Y4 May-Jn 94 | 10 | 10 | |
| | | | | |
| 6. Data gathering | Y5 Sep-Dec 94 | | | 15 |
| Data analysis | Jly-Dec 94 | 28 | 28 | 10 |
| Report preparation | Jan-May 95 | 45 | 43 | |
| Ongoing adminis- | Y1 | 8 | 8 | |
| tration and super- | Y2 | 28 | 28 | |
| vision of grant | Y3 | 28 | 28 | |
| | Y4 | 28 | 28 | |
| | Y5 | 20 | 20 | |

SOURCE: Anthony and Rossman (1990, pp. 23-1, 2). Reprinted with permission.
NOTE: PI = principal investigator.

**Table 6.2  Staff and Staff Time, by Year and Task**

|  | *PI* | *Co-PI* | *Evaluators (7)* |
|---|---|---|---|
| Year 1, March-June 1991 | | | |
| Task 1 | 10 | 10 | 12 |
| Task 2 | 4 | 4 | — |
| Task 3 | 2 | 2 | — |
| Task 4 | — | — | 6 |
| Oversight and administration | 2 | 2 | — |
| Totals | 18 | 18 | 18 |
| Year 2, July-June 1992 | | | |
| Task 1 | 20 | 10 | 16 |
| Task 2 | 10 | 10 | — |
| Task 3 | 8 | 8 | — |
| Task 4 | 30 | 14 | 15 |
| Task 5 | 3 | 5 | 15 |
| Oversight and administration | 10 | 10 | — |
| Totals | 81 | 57 | 46 |
| Year 3, July-June 1993 | | | |
| Task 2 | 10 | 10 | — |
| Task 3 | 8 | 8 | — |
| Task 5 | 50 | 30 | 54 |
| Oversight and administration | 10 | 10 | — |
| Totals | 78 | 58 | 54 |
| Year 4, July-June 1994 | | | |
| Task 2 | 10 | 10 | — |
| Task 3 | 8 | 8 | — |
| Task 5 | 50 | 30 | 54 |
| Oversight and administration | 10 | 10 | — |
| Totals | 78 | 58 | 54 |
| Year 5, July-June 1995 | | | |
| Task 2 | 10 | 10 | — |
| Task 3 | 8 | 8 | — |
| Task 6 | 55 | 42 | 25 |
| Oversight and administration | 10 | 10 | — |
| Totals | 83 | 70 | 25 |

SOURCE: Anthony and Rossman (1990, pp. 23-3, 4). Reprinted with permission.
NOTE: PI = principal investigator.

days by deciding on the number of interviews possible in each school, the hours to allocate for observations, the amount of time necessary to talk with the central office staff, and the amount of time needed to gather documents and other archival data.

In qualitative proposals, the number of days allocated to data gathering becomes a metric for estimating the time required for other tasks, such as data

**Table 6.3  Time Line for Completion of Tasks and Deliverables**

| Month | July | Aug | Sep | Oct | Nov | Dec | Jan | Feb | Mar | Apr | May | June |
|---|---|---|---|---|---|---|---|---|---|---|---|---|
| **Task** | | | | | | | | | | | | |
| **Year 1** | | | | | | | | | | | | |
| DOE meetings | | | | | | | | X | | X | | |
| Evaluators' meetings | | | | | | | | | | X | | |
| RAs' meetings | | | | | | | X | | X | | | |
| Data gathering | | | | | | | | | | | ——— | ——→ |
| Data analysis | | | | | | | | | | | | |
| **Year 2** | | | | | | | | | | | | |
| DOE meetings | | X | | X | | X | | X | | X | | X |
| Evaluators' meetings | | | | | X | | | | | | X | |
| RAs' meetings | | | X | | X | | | X | | X | | |
| Data gathering | ——— | —— | —— | —— | —— | ——→ | | | | | | |
| Data analysis | ——— | —— | —— | —— | —— | —— | —— | ——→ | | | | |
| Report preparation | ——→ | | | | | | — | D | ——— | —— | —— | D |
| **Years 3 & 4** | | | | | | | | | | | | |
| DOE meetings | | X | | X | | X | | X | | X | | X |
| Evaluators' meetings | | X | | | X | | | X | | | X | |
| RAs' meetings | | | X | | X | | | X | | X | | |
| Data gathering | | | ——— | —— | —— | —— | —— | —— | —— | ——→ | | |
| Data analysis | ——— | —— | —— | —— | —— | —— | —— | —— | —— | ——→ | | |
| Report preparation | ——→ | | | | | | ——— | —— | —— | —— | —— | D |
| **Year 5** | | | | | | | | | | | | |
| DOE meetings | X | X | | X | | X | | X | | X | X | X |
| Evaluators' meetings | | X | | | X | | | X | | | X | |
| RAs' meetings | | | X | | X | X | | | | | | |
| Data gathering | | | ——— | —— | —— | ——→ | | | | | | |
| Data analysis | ——— | —— | —— | —— | —— | ——→ | | | | | | |
| Report preparation | | | | | | | ——— | —— | —— | —— | —— | D |

SOURCE: Anthony and Rossman (1990, pp. 23-25). Reprinted with permission.
NOTE: D = deliverable; DOE = Department of Education; RA = research assistant.

management, analysis, and report writing. That is, the amount of data gathered dictates the amount of time needed to manage and analyze those data. Once the researcher has projected time for fieldwork, a management plan can be developed. The projections developed for Table 6.1 helped construct a framework for estimating costs, discussed below.

The researcher should also use this kind of framework to address practical concerns. A time management chart, research agenda, calendar of research events, description of research phases, or some other concrete plan shows a funding agency or dissertation committee that the researcher has thought

**Table 6.4 Budget Summary (in dollars)**

| Item | Yr 1 | Yr 2 | Yr 3 | Yr 4 | Yr 5 |
|------|------|------|------|------|------|
| Personnel | 15,442.0 | 56,424.0 | 56,116.0 | 55,726.0 | 47,140.0 |
| Travel | 1,819.4 | 4,516.6 | 4,675.0 | 4,675.0 | 2,200.0 |
| Telephone and consumables | 540.0 | 1,975.0 | 1,964.0 | 1,950.0 | 1,650.0 |
| Photocopying | 463.0 | 2,821.0 | 1,683.0 | 1,672.0 | 2,357.0 |
| Postage | 49.5 | 1,650.0 | 49.5 | 49.5 | 49.5 |
| Equipment | 5,000.0 | — | — | — | — |
| **Totals** | 21,683.9 | 67,386.6 | 64,487.5 | 64,072.5 | 53,396.5 |
| **Total request** | 271,027.0 | | | | |

SOURCE: Anthony and Rossman (1990, p. 27-1). Adapted by permission.

through the specific people, settings, events, and data involved in conducting the research. This demonstrates that the research is feasible. But the researcher should remind the reader that this plan is a *guide;* it is a tentative road map that will most likely undergo some modifications as data are collected and analyzed and as new patterns for more focused data collection become apparent. The chart serves as a guide for initial contacts and reminds the reader of the inherently flexible nature of qualitative research.

## Personnel

The allocation of time to tasks also shapes decisions about personnel needs. In Vignette 29, as the scope of the study developed (number of sites, single- or multiple-person research teams), personnel decisions could be made. The principal investigators, by university contract, could allocate the equivalent of the summer months and one day per week to the effort. Their time would be supplemented by a cadre of graduate students who would be awarded research assistantships to work on the project for no more than 20 hours per week for the academic year, with additional summer funding budgeted into the proposal. These person loadings are seen in the budget for the evaluation, presented as Table 6.4.

## Financial Resources

For dissertation research or sole-investigator studies, analyzing tasks can help the researcher decide to purchase certain services—for example, audiotape transcription or data processing. This analysis can also introduce the novice to the variety of tasks associated with the project. Determination of the resources necessary for the conduct of the study must often wait until fundamental design decisions have been made. Those design choices, however, must be made with some knowledge about the finances available to support the study. In the preceding vignette, the evaluators knew that they were constrained by a total budget (direct costs) of approximately $100,000 per year but that this would extend over 5 years. Because the contract was renegotiated each year, moreover, there was the possibility of increasing that amount (or of having it reduced!).

Although this may seem a considerable sum to the novice proposal writer, planning a multisite, multiyear study with intensive data gathering as a primary design goal became quite difficult within this budget. Travel and personnel costs would increase with inflation and rising salaries. Direct personnel and travel costs represented a substantial proportion of the total budget.

The other major costs associated with the evaluation activities included (a) equipment (computers, fax machine); (b) office supplies, telephones, and postage; (c) books and subscriptions; (d) printing and duplicating; and (e) contracted services (tape transcription, data analysis, consultants). Because the costs of data analysis specialists vary considerably, the proposal writer should consult local costs and time allocations in developing that portion of a qualitative proposal. The time required for thorough transcription also varies: Each hour of tape requires from 3 or 4 hours to 7 or 8 hours for transcription. Thus, the cost of tape transcription could vary enormously; whether 3 or 8 hours, however, it is very expensive.

## Planning Dissertation Research

Many of the same issues confronted in the large-scale evaluation project are apparent in Vignette 30, a proposal for dissertation research. Although the scope is considerably smaller, similar resource challenges emerged in planning the study.

\*    \*    \*    \*    \*

## *Vignette 30*

## *Feasibility and Planning for Dissertation Research*

"Should I do a study that is clean, relatively quick, limited, and do-able so as to finish and get on with my professional life, or should I do something I really want to do that may be messy and unclear but would be challenging and new enough to sustain my interest?" (Hammonds-White, personal communication, August 5, 1987)

A doctoral student, finding any number of stumbling blocks standing between her and the completion of her dissertation project, was asked to reflect on the process through which the research plan had been developed. Her response indicated that, as with one who prepares to make any kind of major investment, a preliminary notion of how to proceed should be tempered by a comparison of anticipated costs and available resources. In this student's case, she had to weigh energy (the researcher's physical and emotional stamina), time, and finances.

The demands of the student's chosen research methods were many. Seeking to explore a process, she chose naturalistic inquiry, which would encourage her to search for multiple views of reality and the ways such views were constructed. Her training, experience, and interest in counseling psychology, coupled with a positive assessment of her knowledge and competence in this field, constituted excellent sources of personal energy. This was an area of particular interest (the want-to-do-ability); methods were elegantly suited to that substantive focus. The researcher realized, however, that personal energy and a deep commitment to the topic were not going to be sufficient.

She looked to the university for two types of support that she described as "risk-taking support" and "learning support." The first type of support would offer encouragement to someone attempting to go beyond the conventional in his or her research. The second type was offered by faculty members who possessed the interests and the skills necessary to advise her.

In addition to personal energy and commitment and faculty support, a third source of energy was a support group made up of others who were engaged in dissertation research. Of that group she wrote, "We meet every other week, set short-term goals for ourselves, and help each other with the emotional highs and lows of the process."

The commitment of time required of an individual doing qualitative research is substantial. This particular researcher was quick to advise that those following similar research plans would do well to build into their proposals more time than they thought would be required, to make allowances for the unexpected. In her case, a change in her family situation necessitated a return to full-time employment, thus suspending her research when it was only two-thirds complete.

In addition, financial resources need to be equal to the financial demands of a study. When it appeared unlikely that grant monies would be available to finance her research, the student opted for a smaller-scale study that she could finance personally.

*     *     *     *     *

Vignette 30 illustrates the importance of being practical and realistic. Although it is impossible to anticipate all the potential stumbling blocks, a thoughtful and thorough research proposal will address the issue of feasibility by making an honest assessment of available energy, time, and financial resources and requirements.

During the planning for and conduct of the above study, several resource issues became apparent. First, the commitment to a research project that is a graduate student's dissertation research is different from the commitment required of the researchers in Vignette 29. A dissertation, often the first major independent scholarly work, carries both professional and personal significance that few subsequent research projects will. Furthermore, the project described in Vignette 29 had built-in supports for the researchers. As a team project funded by an external agent, commitments to colleagues and professional responsibilities to the funding agent were adequate to sustain commitment and rebuild interest when it began to wane. A dissertation demands different kinds of supports; the most important are those of mentors and peers.

### Mentors and Peers

In planning qualitative dissertation research, support from university faculty to make judgments about the adequacy of the proposal is crucial. At least one committee member, preferably the chair, should have had experience conducting qualitative studies. Such experience enables the faculty to help in making decisions about how to allocate time realistically to various tasks, given that all-important idea that qualitative research often takes much more time than one might predict. Faculty support and encouragement are critical for developing research proposals that are substantial, elegant, and doable and for advocacy in the larger university community to legitimize this particular study and qualitative research generally.

The experiences of our graduate students suggest that the support of peers is crucial for the personal and emotional sustenance that students find so valuable in negotiating among faculty whose requests and demands may be in conflict with one another. Graduate seminars or advanced courses in qualitative methods provide excellent structures for formal discussions as students deal with issues arising from role management to building grounded theory in their dissertations. Student support groups also build in a commitment to others not unlike that found in the team project described in Vignette 29. By establishing deadlines and commitments to one another, students become more efficient and productive. These groups bridge the existential aloneness of the conduct of dissertation research. Finally, rereading literature on qualitative inquiry is both a support and a reminder of the traditions and challenges faced by all of us. It helps to know that William Foote Whyte managed ethical dilemmas in the field, too.

### Time on a Small Scale

Developing a qualitative dissertation proposal demands sensitivity to the time necessary for the thorough completion of the project. This is where the experience of mentors on the university faculty becomes crucial. Complying with institutional review board requirements for proceeding ethically requires time for their review and approval. Gaining access to a setting can take 6 months or more and may require the skills of a diplomat. As in Vignette 30, personal circumstances may intervene to alter dramatically the student's available time and energy to conduct the study. Thus, even though not all critical events can be anticipated, planning for more time than initially appears necessary is prudent.

### Financing

In some fields (notably, mental health, urban planning, anthropology, and international education), financial support may be available through federal agencies or private foundations for dissertation research. Unfortunately, this is not typically the case in most social science fields, in education, or in other applied fields. Opportunities sometimes become available, however, to work on a university professor's funded grant as a research assistant. Such was the case in Vignette 29, which supported four graduate students annually, several of whom dovetailed their research interests with those of the project.

Much more common, especially in education, is the case in Vignette 30, where the student had to modify the proposed research to conform to the personal financial resources she was able to devote to the project. Recall that this same process occurred in the funded research described in Vignette 29. The researchers planned the ideal study based on design considerations and the purposes of the study and then had to modify that ideal design based on the real budgetary constraints under which they operated.

In the conduct of dissertation research, many costs, some obvious and some hidden, will arise over the course of the study. Planning ahead for these makes them less surprising and therefore a bit more manageable. These costs cluster into three categories: materials, services, and personal.

*Materials.* The materials necessary for the completion of a dissertation may include word-processing equipment and materials, computer software for data analysis, computer disks, note cards and filing systems, tape recorders and tapes, video equipment and cameras, books, articles, and copies of completed dissertations. The student should project the costs in each category, being sure to include photocopying costs for journal articles, drafts of the work as it proceeds, and copies of the final document.

*Services.* The services necessary for the completion of the dissertation vary depending on the skills of the student. Typical services, however, might include tape transcribing, word processing, statistical data analysis consulting, and professional proofreading and editing. At the end of the work, the student often wants to have copies of the work professionally bound; this is an additional service that might be important for the student to consider in projecting overall costs.

*Personal costs.* Personal costs are the most difficult to specify but may also be the most important in terms of perceived costs to the individual student. Dissertation work is unlike any the student has ever undertaken. It is not like a large course; it is not like reading for exams: It is of quite a different magnitude than either of those. The sustained effort necessary to complete the project takes time away from all the other commitments in the student's life, whether these are work, family, friends, or professional associations and volunteer groups. Students who are the most successful in moving through the phases are those who build support networks for themselves within their families or through friends and colleagues. Even though not all the costs associated with personal sacrifice can be anticipated, knowledge that the undertaking is not trivial and will require sacrifices on the part of the student can make the entire process more manageable.

Sometimes, researchers seek new funds to continue a project that uncovered interesting data. It is difficult to convince funding agency reviewers that a reworking of data analysis is a worthwhile venture. Vignette 31 describes a researcher trying to convince funding agency reviewers that a secondary analysis of qualitative data was worthy of financial support.

*   *   *   *   *

### Vignette 31

*Walking the Reviewers Through*
*Qualitative Analysis*

The data collected were voluminous comparative qualitative and quantitative data from key state education policymakers in six states. From a study funded by the National Institute of Education, Mitchell, Wirt, and Marshall (1986) developed a taxonomy of state mechanisms for influencing school programs and practices and showed the effect of political culture and the relative power of education policymakers to affect the choices made in state capitals. Captivated by the richness of the interview data, Marshall began to develop a grounded theory of assumptive worlds—understandings that policymakers have about the way things are done, as demonstrated in their stories. Although this theory had been published (Marshall, Mitchell, & Wirt, 1985, 1986), Marshall knew it needed further development and refinement. She sought funding from the National Science Foundation's Political Science Program, promising a secondary analysis of the interview data from six states that would rely on the software program Ethnograph (Qualis Research Associates, 1987) as a tool and that would elaborate the theory derived from early analysis. The funding could be low, because no new data collection was required.

Months later, the reviewers came back. One reviewer said, "This proposal breaks fresh and important ground in the political field." Another noted that "using qualitative data in a systematic way and employing computers in data management are innovative techniques well worth development." A third, however, said, "The proposal is to apply qualitative analysis to the interview materials. Perhaps that term has some [other] understood connotation in other research traditions, but so far as I could fathom what it means is the investigator would read/listen to interview materials and file them on a micro computer." The proposal was rejected.

Overcoming frustration, Marshall decided to revise and resubmit her proposal. In the new proposal, she made these important changes. First, in the theoretical framework, related literature, and significance, she created a chart, tracing the precise place where assumptive worlds fit with other political science and education policy theory and literature. Second, although retaining the section explaining the traditions of qualitative research, she connected this directly to quotations in which political scientists had called for more theory building with comparable case studies and in which they had bemoaned the fact that political scientists are good at identifying structures, but they need to get behind the scenes and into the ways in which the values of the policy culture affect policy outcomes. Third, she retained the table (see Table 6.5) that demonstrated the promise, derived from the preliminary analysis, of the theory. Narratively, she described its significance for understanding the policy culture. Finally, and perhaps most important, following a section on the philosophy of qualitative methodology and a section on the use of microcomputers with qualitative data, she wrote the following step-by-step description.

> Qualitative data analysis and the development of grounded theory (Glaser & Strauss, 1967) seem to be mystical processes to those accustomed to statistical analysis. However, the goal of both methodologies is the same: to identify clear and consistent patterns of phenomena by a systematic process. I will follow the following steps:
>
> 1. Transcribe data in Ethnograph files, using categories from preliminary analysis and from literature review, noted earlier.
>
> 2. Develop hypotheses on assumptive world effects on policy outcomes from field notes and interview data, based on analytic notes regarding assumptive worlds (already started with West Virginia and Pennsylvania data).

**Table 6.5  Functions of the Operative Principles of Assumptive Worlds**

| Action Guide Domains and Operational Principles | Maintain Power and Predictability | Promote Cohesion |
|---|---|---|
| Who has the right and responsibility to initiate? | | |
| The prescription for the CSSO role | x | |
| The prescription for the SDE role | x | |
| Legislative-SDE role | x | |
| Variations in initiative in legislature | x | |
| What policy ideas are deemed unacceptable? | | |
| Policies that trample on powerful interests | | x |
| Policies that lead to open defiance | | x |
| Policies that defy tradition and dominant interests | | x |
| Policy debates that diverge from the prevailing value | | x |
| Untested, unworkable policy | | x |
| What uses of power in policy-making activities are appropriate? | | |
| Know your place and cooperate with the powerful | x | |
| Something for everyone | x | |
| Touch all the bases | x | |
| Bet on the winner | x | |
| Limits on social relationships | x | |
| Constraints on staffers | x | |
| Work with constraints and tricks | x | |
| Policy actors' sponsorship of policy issue network | | x |
| Uses of interstate comparison | | x |
| What are the special state conditions affecting policy? | | |
| Cultural characteristics | | x |
| Geographic, demographic characteristics | | x |

SOURCE: C. Marshall, grant proposal to National Science Foundation, 1988.
NOTE: CSSO = Chief State School Officer; SDE = State Department of Education.

3. Test these hypotheses about assumptive worlds by examining all computer files with relevant descriptors. For example, when identifying patterns of behavior in legislative-state board relations, call up all files under the descriptor "state board" or, when identifying constraints on legislative staffers, call up all field notes and quotations under that label.

4. Obtain field notes and taped interviews from Wisconsin, Illinois, Arizona, and California.

5. Content-analyze all six states' data to (a) identify any additional patterns of behavior or belief not evident from the initial analysis and (b) identify redefinitions of domains and operational principles.

6. Reanalyze the file data using the alterations of assumptive world domains and operational principles.

7. Continue to reorder the six states' files until clear, mutually exclusive, and exhaustive categories of behavior and belief systems are identified that organize the data descriptions of the policy environment.

Such detailed description, she had learned, was required.

\*    \*    \*    \*    \*

Vignette 31 demonstrates that experienced qualitative researchers understand the labor intensiveness of qualitative data analysis and that it requires time and money. Those more attuned to traditional research, however, may need explicit details before they will provide support for that labor. Funding agencies, pressed by the needs of many eager researchers and guided by the peer review process, will not provide resources unless everyone involved can see clearly how the money will be converted into knowledge. Even small requests for a graduate assistant or a computer program will be denied if the research sounds like a mystical process or if it sounds like simple filing. Anyone who has ever done qualitative data analysis knows better, but those with the funds need explicit guidance so they can see how the expenditure is justified. Vignette 31 shows the need to fit explanations to the knowledge bases and predilections of reviewers by walking them through the steps to be followed and thereby providing assurances that the researcher can produce something meaningful on their terms.

This chapter has displayed the recursive processes of planning sufficient resources to support the conduct of a qualitative research project. Vignette 29 could aptly be retitled "Planning in a Context of Largess" because the study was conceived in the midst of adequate financial resources. The major problem for that study was paring down the ideal design to conform to those budget parameters.

Vignette 30 portrays some of the unique problems associated with planning dissertation research, in which financial resources are largely unavailable and where time and personal support systems become critical. Each type of project has unique challenges when the researcher is designing the proposal. Consideration of these issues strengthens the proposal by demonstrating that the researcher is aware of and sensitive to the many challenges that may arise during the conduct of the study. Finally, Vignette 31 reminds us that even low-budget studies will be criticized if they cannot lead the reviewers to an understanding of the resources needed for qualitative analysis. Attention to these considerations helps strengthen the overall proposal and makes its positive evaluation more likely.

Throughout this book, we have presented considerations for building clear, thorough, and thoughtful proposals for qualitative research. In the final chapter, we make these considerations more explicit by describing them as a set of criteria.

## Further Reading

Morse, J. M. (1994). *Designing funded qualitative research.* In N. K. Denzin & Y. S. Lincoln (Eds.), *Handbook of qualitative research* (pp. 220-235). Thousand Oaks, CA: Sage.

Tripp-Riemer, T., & Cohen, M. Z. (1991). Funding strategies for qualitative research. In J. M. Morse (Ed.), *Qualitative nursing research: A contemporary dialogue* (pp. 243-256). Newbury Park, CA: Sage.

# 7

## Defending the Value and Logic
## of Qualitative Research

Writers of qualitative research proposals must develop a sound rationale for the choice of methodology. Although this must be demonstrated for any research proposal, with qualitative proposals the need may be especially acute. Developing a logic that will solidly defend the proposal entails three large domains: (a) responding to criteria for the overall soundness of the project, (b) demonstrating the usefulness of the research for the conceptual framework and research questions, and (c) showing the sensitivities and sensibilities to *be* the research instrument. Careful consideration of each will help the proposal writer develop a logic in the support of the proposal.

### Criteria of Soundness

All research must respond to canons of quality—criteria against which the trustworthiness of the project can be evaluated. These canons can be phrased as questions to which all social science research must respond (Lincoln & Guba, 1985). First, how credible are the particular findings of the study? By what criteria can we judge them? Second, how transferable and applicable are these findings to another setting or group of people? Third, how can we be reasonably sure that the findings would be replicated if the study were conducted with the same participants in the same context? And fourth, how can we be sure that the findings reflect the participants and the inquiry itself rather than a fabrication from the researcher's biases or prejudices? Postmodern and feminist challenges to traditional research assert that all discovery and truths emerge from the researcher's prejudgments and predilections. Those espousing these positions argue that such predispositions should be *used* "as building blocks . . . for acquiring new knowledge" (Nielson, 1990, p. 28). Qualitative researchers, however, still need to argue that their research will meet the more traditional criteria of soundness.

Lincoln and Guba (1985) refer to these questions as establishing the "truth value" (p. 290) of the study, its applicability, consistency, and neutrality. Every systematic inquiry into the human condition must address these issues. Although Lincoln and Guba match these terms to the conventional positivist paradigm—internal validity, external validity, reliability, and objectivity— they then demonstrate the need to rework these constructs for naturalistic or qualitative inquiry. Too, researchers now recognize the politics of knowledge—the ways certain knowledge is privileged (often that of the powerful and dominant groups) and gains credence, thereby marginalizing other forms or sources of knowledge (frequently those historically oppressed or excluded from power arenas). Although not reassuring to the novice researcher, this essentially contested nature of criteria of soundness is part of the current methodological scene. Thus, proposals for qualitative research are constantly devising alternative strategies for judging the soundness of research (Lather, 1991; Marshall, 1997; Scheurich, 1997).

Lincoln and Guba (1985) propose four alternative constructs that more accurately reflect the assumptions of the qualitative paradigm. The first is *credibility,* in which the goal is to demonstrate that the inquiry was conducted in such a manner as to ensure that the subject was accurately identified and described. The inquiry then must be "credible to the constructors of the original multiple realities" (p. 296).

The strength of a qualitative study that aims to explore a problem or describe a setting, a process, a social group, or a pattern of interaction will rest with its validity. An in-depth description showing the complexities of processes and interactions will be so embedded with data derived from the setting that it cannot help but be valid. Within the parameters of that setting, population, and theoretical framework, the research will be valid. A qualitative researcher should therefore adequately state those parameters, thereby placing boundaries around the study.

The second construct Lincoln and Guba propose is *transferability,* in which the researcher must argue that his findings will be useful to others in similar situations, with similar research questions or questions of practice. Here, the burden of demonstrating the applicability of one set of findings to another context rests more with the researcher who would make that transfer than with the original researcher. Kennedy (1979) refers to this as the second decision span in generalizing. That is, the first decision span allows the researcher to generalize the findings about a particular sample to the population from which that sample was drawn (assuming adequate population specification and random selection of the sample). The second decision span occurs when another researcher wants to apply the findings about the population of interest to a second population believed or presumed to be sufficiently similar to the first to warrant that application. This second decision span entails making judgments about and an argument for the relevance of the initial study to the second setting.

A qualitative study's transferability or generalizability to other settings may be problematic. The generalization of qualitative findings to other populations, settings, and treatment arrangements—that is, its *external* validity—is seen by traditional canons as a weakness in the approach. To counter challenges, the researcher can refer to the original theoretical framework to show how data collection and analysis will be guided by concepts and models. By doing so, the researcher states the theoretical parameters of the research. Then those who make policy or design research studies within those same parameters can determine whether or not the cases described can be generalized for new research policy and transferred to other settings. In addition, the reader or user of specific research can see how research ties into a body of theory.

For example, a case study of the implementation of a new staff development program in a high school can be tied into theory of implementation of innovations in organizations, leadership, personnel management, and adult career socialization theory. The research can then be used in planning program policy and further research in a variety of settings—not just the high school, school organizations, and staff development. It can be included with research about organizations; it can contribute to the literature on organizational theory.

One additional strategic choice can enhance a study's generalizability: triangulating multiple sources of data. Triangulation is the act of bringing more than one source of data to bear on a single point. Derived from navigation science, the concept has been fruitfully applied to social science inquiry (see Denzin, 1978; Jick, 1979; Rossman & Wilson, 1985, 1994). Data from different sources can be used to corroborate, elaborate, or illuminate the research in question (Rossman & Wilson, 1994). Designing a study in which multiple cases, multiple informants, or more than one data-gathering method are used can greatly strengthen the study's usefulness for other settings.

The third construct is *dependability,* in which the researcher attempts to account for changing conditions in the phenomenon chosen for study and changes in the design created by an increasingly refined understanding of the setting. This represents a set of assumptions very different from those shaping the concept of reliability. Positivist notions of reliability assume an unchanging universe where inquiry could, quite logically, be replicated. This assumption of an unchanging social world is in direct contrast to the qualitative/ interpretive assumption that the social world is always being constructed and that the concept of replication is itself problematic.

The final construct, *confirmability,* captures the traditional concept of objectivity. Lincoln and Guba stress the need to ask whether the findings of the study could be confirmed by another. By doing so, they remove evaluation from some inherent characteristic of the researcher (objectivity) and place it squarely on the data themselves. Thus, the qualitative criterion is, do the data help confirm the general findings and lead to the implications? This is the appropriate qualitative criterion.

A qualitative research proposal should respond to concerns that the natural subjectivity of the researcher will shape the research. Again, the researcher should assert the strengths of qualitative methods by showing how she will develop an in-depth understanding, even empathy, for the research participants to gain entry into their worlds. The researcher's insights increase the likelihood that she will be able to describe the complex social system being studied. She should, however, build into the proposal strategies for limiting bias in interpretation. Such strategies could include the following:

- Planning to use a research partner or a person who plays "devil's advocate" and critically questions the researcher's analyses.
- Building in time to search for negative instances.

▓ Describing how analysis will include checking and rechecking the data and a purposeful examination of possible alternative explanations.

▓ Providing examples of judgment-free note taking; planning to take two sets of notes, one with more objective observation and another with tentative categories.

▓ Citing previous researchers who have written about bias, subjectivity, and data quality.

▓ Planning to conduct an audit of the data collection and analytic strategies. (see Lincoln & Guba, 1985)

The qualitative researcher should be familiar with the issues in data quality control and analysis and should display an ability to develop strategies appropriate to the research.

Clearly, criteria of goodness for qualitative research differ from the criteria developed for experimental and positivist research. Still, it is helpful to articulate the parallels and differences. Qualitative research does not claim to be replicable. The researcher purposefully avoids controlling the research conditions and concentrates on recording the complexity of situational contexts and interrelations as they occur naturally. The researcher's goal of discovering this complexity by altering research strategies within a flexible research design, moreover, cannot be replicated by future researchers, nor should it be attempted.

Qualitative researchers can respond to the traditional social science concern for replicability, however, by taking the following steps. First, they can assert that qualitative studies by their nature (and, really, all research) cannot be replicated because the real world changes. Second, by planning to keep thorough notes and a journal or log that records each design decision and the rationale behind it, researchers allow others to inspect their procedures, protocols, and decisions. Finally, by planning to keep all collected data in well-organized, retrievable form, researchers can make them available easily if the findings are challenged or if another researcher wants to reanalyze the data.

Marshall (1985a, 1990) recommends additional criteria for assessing the value and trustworthiness of qualitative research. These criteria were developed to apply to written reports of qualitative research; we have adapted them here for proposal development. Attention to these standards helps ensure a sound and reasonable research proposal; proposal writers should design, conduct, and report their studies with these criteria in mind. The standards are discussed in the sections that follow, drawing from Marshall (1990, pp. 193-195).

### The Design and Methods Are Explicitly Detailed

The researcher explicates the design and methods in detail so the reader can judge whether they are adequate and make sense. This includes a rationale for qualitative research generally and the specific genre in which the study is situated. The anticipated methods for attaining entry and managing role, data collection, recording, analysis, ethics, and exit are discussed. There is description of how the site and sample will be selected. Data collection and analysis procedures will be made public, not magical.

The researcher states clearly any assumptions that may effect the study. Biases are expressed, and the researcher engages in some preliminary self-reflection to uncover personal subjectivities. She articulates, often drawing on the work of others, how she will be a finely tuned research instrument, whose personal talents, experiential biases, and insights will be used consciously. She argues that she will be careful to be self-analytical and recognize when she is becoming overly subjective and not critical enough of her interpretations. As part of this process, she analyzes the conceptual framework for theoretical biases. Furthermore, the researcher articulates how she will guard against value judgments in data collection and in analysis—for example, how she will exercise caution to distinguish between descriptive field notes saying "the roofs had holes and missing tiles" and judgmental field notes saying "many houses were dilapidated."

The researcher writes about her tolerance for ambiguity, how she will search for alternative explanations, check out negative instances, and use a variety of methods to ensure that the findings are strong and grounded (i.e., triangulation). Methods are proposed for ensuring data quality (e.g., informants' knowledgeability, subjectivities, and candor) and for guarding against ethnocentric explanations by eliciting cross-cultural perspectives.

The researcher describes preliminary observations, a pilot study, or "first days in the field," demonstrating how the research questions have been generated from observation, not merely from library research. The researcher is careful about sensitivity of those being researched: Ethical standards are maintained. She argues that people in the research setting will likely benefit in some way (ranging from an hour of sympathetic listening to feeling empowered to take action to alter some facet of their lives).

### Research Questions and the Data's Relevance
### Are Made Explicit and Rigorously Argued

The researcher discusses how there will be abundant evidence from raw data to demonstrate the connection between those data and her interpretations. She shows how data will be presented in readable, accessible form, perhaps aided by graphics, models, charts, and figures. The preliminary research questions are stated clearly, and the researcher argues that the data collected will allow her to respond to those questions and generate further questions. The relationship between the proposed study and previous studies is explicit. The researcher discusses how the study will be reported in a manner accessible to other researchers, practitioners, and policymakers. She argues that she will be able to make an adequate translation of findings so that others will be able to use the findings in a timely way.

### The Study Is Situated in a Scholarly Context

The proposal acknowledges the limitations of generalizability while assisting the readers in seeing the potential transferability of findings. The study is tied into "the big picture." The researcher will look holistically at the setting to understand linkages among systems and will trace the historical context to understand how institutions and roles have evolved.

Definitions of central concepts are provided, with reference to previously identified phenomena, but the researcher argues that this research will go beyond established frameworks—challenging old ways of thinking.

### Records Will Be Kept

The researcher describes how the data will be preserved and available for reanalysis. Any in-field analysis will be documented. Furthermore, there is explicit mention of a running record of procedures, perhaps an audit trail that will be included in an appendix to the final written report.

Attention to these criteria ensures a solid qualitative proposal that displays concern for issues of trustworthiness and shows how knowledgeable the proposal writer is regarding these several issues. Many issues are addressed

in the body of the proposal; others may be discussed in the meeting to defend
the proposal or in response to the queries of funding agencies. (See Marshall,
1985b, 1990, for a discussion of the evolving set of "criteria of goodness" that
cut across scholarly and political debates.)

Increasingly, feminist, postmodern, and critical theorists demand that
research have liberatory potential. They seek to discover and create, often
collaboratively, knowledge that benefits those usually marginalized from the
mainstream. Thus, emerging criteria lend special credence and value to
proposals that challenge dominant (and *dominating*) practice or include participants whose meaning making was overlooked in previous policy and
research (Carspecken, 1996; Harding, 1987; Lather, 1991; Marshall, 1997:
Scheurich, 1997). And increasingly, the practical utility of research is becoming a valued criterion, especially for action research and when immediate
pressing problems need research-based recommendations (Hammersley,
1990).

Finally, researchers need to allay the fears (both their own and those of their
reviewers) that they might "stay in the field" or become stalled when faced
with analyzing the data. They need to demonstrate their ability to move from
data collection to analysis and interpretation to writing. Again, a pilot study,
a hypothesized model, or an outline of possible data analysis categories can
be appended to the proposal. The qualitative researcher should always caution
that such models, outlines, and categories are primarily heuristic—tentative
guides—from which to begin observation and analysis. They are reassuring,
however, to those who have low tolerance for ambiguity.

## Defending the Qualitativeness of the Study

Frequently, in an attempt to make a proposed design efficient and conform
to traditional research, reviewers recommend alterations in the original design. They may argue that the time for exploration is wasteful; they may try
to change the nature of the study from ethnographic exploration and description to a more traditional design. They may worry that the design is not "tight."

The following vignettes show how two different researchers developed
rationales for their work. Vignette 32 describes how a proposal writer anticipated a funding agent's challenge to the usefulness of qualitative research.
Vignette 33 shows how a doctoral student successfully withstood challenges

to his right to alter the design during fieldwork if it became necessary or prudent.

*   *   *   *   *

### Vignette 32

*Justifying Time for Exploration*

The proposal to conduct three in-depth case studies of high schools undergoing change (Rossman, Corbett, & Firestone, 1984) had received favorable internal review, although one administrator made his standard objections about the value of qualitative research. The proposal had been transmitted to Washington, where it would receive close scrutiny as a major portion of the group's work scope over the next 5 years.

As the research team sat on the train heading south, they pondered the type of questions they would be required to answer. Surely their sampling plan would be challenged: The criterion of "improvement" would have to be quite broadly construed to locate the kinds of high schools they wanted. The notion of studying a school's culture was new to many in the research community, never mind Washington bureaucrats. The team anticipated questions about the usefulness of that concept, as well as the presentation of theoretical ideas on cultural change and transformation.

It struck the researchers as prudent to develop a rationale grounded in the applied research of others rather than relying on anthropological constructs. As they reviewed that logic, three points seemed most salient. First, the research proposal assumed that change in schools could not be adequately explored through a "snapshot" approach. Rather, the complexity of interactions among people, new programs, deeply held beliefs and values, and other organizational events demanded a long-term, in-depth approach. Second, at that time, little was known about change processes in secondary schools. Most of the previous research focused on elementary schools and had been generalized, perhaps inappropriately, to secondary schools. The proposed research was intended to fill the gap. Finally, much had been written about teachers' resistance to change. The rationale for and significance of the study would be in uncovering some of that construct, in delving beneath the surface and exploring the meaning perspectives of teachers involved in profound change.

The proposal called for long-term engagement in the social worlds of the three high schools selected for study. The team anticipated a challenge to that time allocation and decided to defend it through the rationale presented above as well as with the idea that complex processes demand adequate time for exploration, that interactions and changes in belief systems occur slowly.

After the 2-hour hearing, the team felt it had done a credible job but realized that the funding agent had not yet come to accept the longer time frame of qualitative research. In the negotiations, the research team had to modify the original plan to engage in participant observation over the course of a school year. To save the project from rejection, they had agreed to 6 months of data collection, over the winter and spring terms.

*   *   *   *   *

In the vignette above, the researchers had developed a sound logic for the major aspects of the study. Justification for the substantive focus grew from the conceptual framework and the significance of the study. The major research approach—long-term engagement in the social world—could best be justified through demonstrating the need for exploration. This is the hardest aspect to convince the critic about and crucial aspect of qualitative research. The next vignette shows how a doctoral student in economics successfully countered challenges to the need for design flexibility.

*   *   *   *   *

## Vignette 33

### Defending Flexibility[1]

Katz had been fascinated with families' financial decisions long before he first took a course in microeconomics as a college sophomore. That exposure to theory crystallized his interest and gave it an intellectual home. During his doctoral course work, however, he had pursued this interest from a cross-cultural perspective, enrolling in as many anthropology courses as his adviser would permit.

Katz's interest in families' fiscal decision making grew as he read case studies of families in other cultures. Quite naturally, he became interested in the methods anthropologists used to gather their data; they seemed so very different from econometrics or even economic history methods. As he immersed himself in these methods, his fascination grew. Now, about to embark on his dissertation, he had convinced one committee member to support his proposal to engage in a long-term, in-depth study of five families in very different socioeconomic circumstances. As he prepared for a meeting with the other two committee members, he reviewed the strengths of his proposal.

First, he was exploring the inner decision-making processes of five families—something no economics research had as yet done. The value of the research would rest, in part, on the contribution this would make to understanding the beliefs, values, and motivations of certain financial behaviors. Second, he was contributing to methodology because he was approaching a topic using new research methods. He could rely on the work of two or three other qualitative economists—well-established scholars in their fields—to demonstrate that others had undertaken such risky business and survived!

Third, he had thoroughly combed the methodological literature for information that would demonstrate his knowledge of many of the issues that would arise: The design section of the proposal was more than 60 pages long and addressed every conceivable issue. He had not attempted to resolve them all but, rather, to show that he was aware that they might arise, knowledgeable about how others had dealt with them, and sensitive to the trade-offs represented by various decisions.

During the committee meeting, the thoroughness and richness of the design section served him well. The fully documented topics and sensitive discussion revealed a knowledge and sophistication not often found in doctoral students. What Katz had not anticipated, however, was the larger question brought up by one committee member: With such a small sample, how could the research be useful?

Fortunately, Katz recalled the argument developed by Kennedy (1979) about generalizing from single case studies. He had conceptualized his study as a set of family life histories from which would be drawn analytic categories, with relationships among them carefully delimited. Not unlike a multisite case study, Katz's proposal could be evaluated from that perspective. This logic proved sufficiently convincing that Katz's committee approved his proposal.

\*   \*   \*   \*   \*

In the foregoing vignettes, each proposal demanded a well thought-out, thorough, logical defense. When considered as an argument in support of the proposal, the need to develop a clear organization, build documentation for major design decisions, and demonstrate the overall soundness of the study as conceived becomes more clear. Following the advice we provide here will help the qualitative research proposal writer to think through the conceptual and methodological justifications and rationales for the proposed study. In planning a defense of the proposal, we suggest that the researcher anticipate questions that may come from a funding agency or from a dissertation committee. Having well-prepared and rehearsed answers will facilitate the defense. Tables 7.1 and 7.2 present types of questions that we have encountered. Those in Table 7.1 come from reviewers with little experience with qualitative methods; those in Table 7.2 are from those who are familiar with the methods and seek justifications for the decisions in the proposal.

Although some of these questions may never be articulated, they may be present in the minds of foundation officials or dissertation committee members. Building a logic in support of the proposed qualitative study will help reassure skeptics and strengthen the argument.

## A Final Word

The process of developing a qualitative research proposal—the revisions necessitated by the interrelatedness of the sections—will create a final product that convinces readers and develops a rationale for the researcher's own guidance. It will justify the selection of qualitative methods and demonstrate the researcher's ability to conduct the study. The writing and creating processes will help the researcher to develop a logic and a plan that will guide and direct the research. The time, thought, and energy expended in writing a proposal that is theoretically sound, methodologically ethical, efficient, and thorough and that demonstrates the researcher's capacity to conduct the research, draw sound, credible, and convincing conclusions, and write the final report will reap rewards throughout the research endeavor.

## Note

1. This vignette is fictitious.

**Table 7.1 Questions From Reviewers With Little Qualitative Experience**

"I don't know why everybody's getting on this qualitative bandwagon. Explain it to me . . ."

"Well, why don't you just do surveys?"

"Where's the logic? I'm used to numbers."

"What will be your control group?"

"How can this be generalized?"

"You're the one collecting *and* analyzing the data. How will we know you are right?"

"How can you be objective?"

"Do you expect me to believe those findings?"

"Just what is 'grounded theory'?"

"What's this about emergent sampling? Emergent data analysis?"

"How can you call stories 'data'?"

"How can you start *research* when you don't even know what you're looking for?"

"Is any of this ### stuff useful?"

---

**Table 7.2 Questions From Reviewers Attuned to Qualitative Methodology**

"Nice—but what's the significance?"

"How have you made a good match of topic and qualitative or quantitative approaches?"

"Do you *really* believe you can finish that in a year?"

"What processes will you go through to categorize data?"

"How do you handle validity and reliability in qualitative research?"

"Could you give me an example of going from concepts to data collection? Going from interpretations to generalizable findings? Other naturalistic inquiries? Dealing with negative instances? Emergent sampling?"

"What if you don't get access? What if people won't talk to you?"

"What is the final product going to look like?"

"Can you give me some examples of comparable work?"

"How can you get qualitative research published in 12-page journal articles?"

"How can you make time in your life to focus on this?"

"How are you going to get policymakers or practitioners to make use of this?"

"Are you going to go out 'in the field' never to be seen again?"

"How will you know when to stop collecting data?"

# References

Alvarez, R. (1993). *Computer mediated communications: A study of the experience of women managers using electronic mail.* Unpublished manuscript, University of Massachusetts at Amherst.

Alvarez, R. (1998). *Organizational information systems implementation: An empirical study of the influence of innovation factors and institutional forces.* Unpublished Ph.D. proposal, University of Massachusetts at Amherst.

Anderson, E. (1976). *A place on the corner.* Chicago: University of Chicago Press.

Anderson, G. (1989). Critical ethnography in education: Origins, current status, and new directions. *Review of Educational Research, 59,* 249-270.

Anderson, G. L., & Herr, K. (1993). The micro-politics of student voices: Moving from diversity of voices in schools. In C. Marshall (Ed.), *The new politics of race and gender* (pp. 58-68). Washington, DC: Falmer.

Anthony, P. G., & Rossman, G. B. (1990). *Restructuring for the integration of all students* (Evaluation proposal). Malden: Massachusetts Department of Education, Office of Planning, Research, and Evaluation.

Argyris, C., & Schön, D. A. (1974). *Theory in practice.* San Francisco: Jossey-Bass.

Argyris, C., & Schön, D. A. (1991). Participatory action research and action science compared: A commentary. In W. F. Whyte (Ed.), *Participatory action research* (pp. 85-96). Newbury Park, CA: Sage.

Atkinson, P., Delamont, S., & Hammersley, M. (1988). Qualitative research traditions: A British response to Jacob. *Review of Educational Research, 58,* 231-250.

Bargar, R. R., & Duncan, J. K. (1982). Cultivating creative endeavor in doctoral research. *Journal of Higher Education, 53,* 1-31.

Becker, H. S., & Geer, B. (1969). Participant observation and interviewing: A comparison. In G. J. McCall & J. L. Simmons (Eds.), *Issues in participant observation: A text and reader* (pp. 322-331). Reading, MA: Addison-Wesley.

Benbow, J. T. (1994). *Coming to know: A phenomenological study of individuals actively committed to radical social change.* Unpublished doctoral dissertation, University of Massachusetts at Amherst.

Berelson, B. (1952). *Content analysis in communication research.* Glencoe, IL: Free Press.

Birdwhistell, R. L. (1970). *Kinesics and content: Essays on body motion communication.* Philadelphia: University of Pennsylvania Press.

Bloom, L. R., & Munro, P. (1995). Conflicts of selves: Non-unitary subjectivity in women administrators' life history narratives. In J. A. Hatch & R. Wisniewski (Eds.), *Life history and narrative* (pp. 99-112). London: Falmer.

Bowen, E. S. (1964). *Return to laughter.* Garden City, NY: Doubleday.

Brantlinger, E. A. (1997, April). *Knowledge, position, and agency: Activism and inward gaze as a natural next step in local inquiry.* Paper presented at the annual meeting of the American Educational Research Association, San Diego, CA.

Brice Heath, S., & McLaughlin, M. (1993). *Identity and inner-city youth: Beyond ethnicity and gender.* New York: Teachers College Press.

Bronfenbrenner, U. (1980). Ecology of childhood. *School Psychology Review, 9,* 294-297.

Burrell, G., & Morgan, G. (1979). *Sociological paradigms and organisational analysis.* London: Heineman.

Campbell-Nelson, K. (1997). *Learning the land: A local hermeneutic for indigenous education in West Timor, Indonesia.* Unpublished research proposal to the U.S. Information Agency, Fullbright-Hays Doctoral Support Program, University of Massachusetts at Amherst.

Cancian, F. M., & Armstead, C. (1992). Participatory research. In E. F. Borgatta & M. Borgatta (Eds)., *Encyclopedia of sociology* (Vol. 3, pp. 1427-1432). New York: Macmillan.

Carnoy, M. (1995, Winter). Why aren't more African Americans going to college? *Journal of Blacks in Higher Education,* pp. 66-69.

Carspecken, P. F. (1996). *Critical ethnography in educational research: A theoretical and practical guide.* New York: Routledge & Kegan Paul.

Castelloe, P., & Legerton, M. (1998). *Learning together: Children and caregivers getting ready for school.* A two-year report and evaluation for the Learning Together Project. Lumberton, NC: Center for Community Action.

Chaudhry, L. N. (1997). Researching "my people," researching myself: Fragments of a reflexive tale. *Qualitative Studies in Education, 10*(4), 441-453.

Chodorow, N. (1978). *The reproduction of mothering: Psychoanalysis and the sociology of gender.* Berkeley: University of California Press.

Christman, J. (1987). *Making both count: An ethnographic study of family and work in the lives of returning women graduate students.* Unpublished doctoral dissertation, University of Pennsylvania.

Clarricoates, K. (1980). The importance of being Ernest, Emma, Tom, Jane. In R. Deem (Ed.), *Schooling for women's work* (pp. 26-41). London: Falmer.

Clarricoates, K. (1987). Child culture at school: A clash between gendered worlds? In A. Pollard (Ed.), *Children and their primary schools* (pp. 188-206). London: Falmer.

Cole, R. E. (1991). Participant observer research. In W. F. Whyte (Ed.), *Participatory action research* (pp. 159-166). Newbury Park, CA: Sage.

Collins, P. H. (1990). *Black feminist thought: Knowledge, consciousness, and the politics of empowerment.* New York: Routledge & Kegan Paul.

Connelly, F. M., & Clandinin, D. J. (1990). Stories of experience and narrative inquiry. *Educational Researcher, 19,* 2-14.

Cooper, H. M. (1988). Organizing knowledge syntheses: A taxonomy of literature reviews. *Knowledge in Society, 1,* 104-126.

Corbett, H. D., Dawson, J. L., & Firestone, W. A. (1984). *School context and school change.* New York: Teachers College Press.

Cormier, D. T. (1993). *Gilligan's theory extended: A case study of organizational conflict.* Unpublished doctoral dissertation, University of Massachusetts at Amherst.

Crabtree, B. F., & Miller, W. L. (Eds.). (1992). *Doing qualitative research: Multiple strategies.* Newbury Park, CA: Sage.

Creswell, J. W. (1994). *Research design: Qualitative and quantitative approaches.* Thousand Oaks, CA: Sage.

Creswell, J. W. (1998). *Qualitative inquiry and research design: Choosing among five traditions.* Thousand Oaks, CA: Sage.

Crites, S. (1986). Storytime: Recollecting the past and projecting the future. In T. R. Sarbin (Ed.), *Narrative psychology: The storied nature of human conduct* (pp. 152-173). New York: Praeger.

Davis, A., Gardner, B. B., & Gardner, M. R. (1941). *Deep South: A social anthropological study of caste and class.* Chicago: University of Chicago Press.

Denzin, N. K. (1970). *The research act: A theoretical introduction to sociological methods.* New York: McGraw-Hill.

Denzin, N. K. (1978). *The research act: A theoretical introduction to sociological methods* (2nd ed.). New York: McGraw-Hill.

Denzin, N. K., & Lincoln, Y. (1994). *The handbook of qualitative research.* Thousand Oaks, CA: Sage.

DiMaggio, P. (1988). Interest and agency in institutional theory. In L. G. Zucker (Ed.), *Institutional patterns and organizations: Culture and environment* (pp. 3-22). Cambridge, MA: Ballinger.

Dobbert, M. L. (1982). *Ethnographic research: Theory and application for modern schools and societies.* New York: Praeger.

Dollard, J. (1935). *Criteria for the life history.* New Haven, CT: Yale University Press.

Doppler, J. (1998). *The costs and benefits of gay-straight alliances in high schools.* Unpublished dissertation proposal, University of Massachusetts at Amherst.

Douglas, J. D. (1976). *Investigative social research: Individual and team field research.* Beverly Hills, CA: Sage.

Edgerton, R. T., & Langness, L. L. (1974). *Methods and styles in the study of culture.* San Francisco: Chandler & Sharp.

Eisner, E. W. (1988). The primacy of experience and the politics of method. *Educational Researcher, 20,* 15-20.

Fals-Borda, O., & Rahman, M. A. (1991). *Action and knowledge: Breaking the monopoly with participatory action-research.* New York: Apex Press.

Fine, G. A., & Sandstrom, K. L. (1988). *Knowing children: Participant observation with minors.* Newbury Park, CA: Sage.

Firestone, W. A., & Rossman, G. B. (1986). Exploring organizational approaches to dissemination and training. *Knowledge: Creation, Diffusion, and Utilization, 7*(3), 303-330.

Fraser, N. (1997). *Justice interruptus: Critical reflections on the "postsocialist" condition.* New York: Routledge & Kegan Paul.

Friedan, B. (1981). *The second stage.* New York: Summit.

Friere, P. (1970). *Pedagogy of the oppressed.* New York: Seabury.

Gall, M. D., Borg, W. R., & Gall, J. P. (1996). *Educational research: An introduction* (6th ed.). White Plains, NY: Longman.

Geer, B. (1969). First days in the field. In G. McCall & J. L. Simmons (Eds.), *Issues in participant observation* (pp. 144-162). Reading, MA: Addison-Wesley.

Geertz, C. (1973). Thick description: Toward an interpretive theory of culture. In C. Geertz (Ed.), *The interpretation of cultures: Selected essays* (pp. 3-30). New York: Basic Books.

Gerstl-Pepin, C. I. (1998). *Cultivating democratic educational reform: A critical examination of the A+ schools program.* Unpublished doctoral dissertation, University of North Carolina at Chapel Hill.

Giele, J. L. (Ed.). (1982). *Women in the middle years: Current knowledge and directions for research and policy.* New York: John Wiley.

Gilligan, C. (1982a). Adult development and women's development: Arrangements for a marriage. In J. Z. Giele (Ed.), *Women in the middle years: Current knowledge and directions for research and policy.* New York: John Wiley.

Gilligan, C. (1982b). *In a different voice: Psychological theory and women's development.* Cambridge, MA: Harvard University Press.

Glaser, B., & Strauss, A. (1967). *The discovery of grounded theory.* Chicago: Aldine.

Goode, W. J. (1960). A theory of role strain. *American Sociological Review, 25,* 483-496.

Griffin, C. (1985). *Typical girls?* London: Routledge & Kegan Paul.

Greene, J. C., Caracelli, V. J., & Graham, W. F. (1989). Towards a conceptual framework for mixed-methods evaluation design. *Educational Evaluation and Policy Analysis, 11,* 255-274.

Greenwald, J. (1992). *Environmental attitudes: A structural developmental model.* Unpublished doctoral dissertation, University of Massachusetts at Amherst.

Grumet, M. R. (1988). *Bitter milk: Women and teaching.* Amherst: University of Massachusetts Press.

Guba, E. G. (1978). *Toward a methodology of naturalistic inquiry in educational evaluation* (Monograph 8). Los Angeles: UCLA Center for the Study of Evaluation.

Hall, E. T. (1966). *The hidden dimension.* Garden City, NY: Doubleday.

Hammersley, M. (1990). *Reading ethnographic research: A critical guide.* London: Longman.

Harding, S. (Ed.). (1987). *Feminism and methodology.* Bloomington: Indiana University Press.

Herriott, R. E., & Firestone, W. A. (1983). Multisite qualitative policy research: Optimizing description and generalizability. *Educational Researcher, 12,* 14-19.

Hoffman, B. (1972). *Albert Einstein: Creator and rebel.* New York: Viking.

Hollingshead, A. B. (1975). *Elmtown's youth and Elmtown revisited.* New York: John Wiley.

Hollingsworth, S. (Ed.). (1997). *International action research: A casebook for educational reform.* London: Falmer.

Home Box Office Project Knowledge. (1992). *Educating Peter* [Film]. New York: Ambrose Video Publishing (Distributors).

hooks, b. (1989). *Talking back: Thinking feminist, thinking black.* Boston: South End Press.

Jackson, B. (1978). Killing time: Life in the Arkansas penitentiary. *Qualitative Sociology, 1,* 21-32.

Jacob, E. (1987). Qualitative research traditions: A review. *Review of Educational Research, 51,* 1-50.

Jacob, E. (1988). Clarifying qualitative research: A focus on traditions. *Educational Researcher, 17,* 16-24.

Jick, T. D. (1979). Mixing qualitative and quantitative methods: Triangulation in action. *Administrative Science Quarterly, 24,* 602-661.

Jones, M. C. (1983). *Novelist as biographer: The truth of art, the lies of biography.* Unpublished doctoral dissertation, Northwestern University.

Joseph-Collins, B. G. (1997). *Perspectives on the persistence of African American males in higher education.* Unpublished manuscript, University of Massachusetts at Amherst.

Kahn, A. (1992). *Therapist initiated termination to psychotherapy: The experience of clients.* Unpublished doctoral dissertation, University of Massachusetts at Amherst.

Kahn, R., & Cannell, C. (1957). *The dynamics of interviewing.* New York: John Wiley.

Kalnins, Z. G. (1986). *An exploratory study of the meaning of life as described by residents of a long-term care facility.* Project proposal, Peabody College of Vanderbilt University, Nashville, TN.

Kanter, R. (1977). *Men and women of the corporation.* New York: Basic Books.

Kaplan, A. (1964). *The conduct of inquiry.* San Francisco: Chandler.

Keddie, N. (1971). Classroom knowledge. In M. F. D. Young (Ed.), *Knowledge and control* (pp. 133-160). London: Collier-Macmillan.

Kelly, D., & Gaskell, J. (Eds.). (1996). *Debating dropouts: Critical policy and research perspectives.* New York: Teachers College Press.

Kemmis, S., & McTaggart, R. (Eds.). (1982). *The action research reader.* Geelong, Victoria, Australia: Deakin University Press.

Kennedy, M. M. (1979). Generalizing from single case studies. *Evaluation Quarterly, 12,* 661-678.

Kiegelmann, M. (1997). *Coming to terms: A qualitative study of six women's experiences of breaking the silence about brother-sister incest.* Ann Arbor: University of Michigan Press.

Koski, K. (1997). *Interviewing.* Unpublished manuscript, University of Massachusetts at Amherst.

Krieger, S. (1985). Beyond subjectivity: The use of the self in social science. *Qualitative Sociology, 8,* 309-324.

Krueger, R. A. (1988). *Focus groups: A practical guide for applied research.* Newbury Park, CA: Sage.

Kwon, T. H., & Zmud, R. W. (1987). Unifying the fragmented models of information systems implementation. In R. J. Boland & R. Hirschheim (Eds.), *Critical issues in information systems research* (pp. 227-262). New York: John Wiley.

Lather, P. (1991). *Getting smart: Feminist research and pedagogy with/in the post modern.* London: Routledge & Kegan Paul.

Lather, P., & Smithies, C. (1997). *Troubling the angels: Women living with HIV/AIDS.* Boulder, CO: Westview.

Lawless, E. J. (1991). Methodology and research notes: Women's life stories and reciprocal ethnography as feminist and emergent. *Journal of Folklore Research, 28,* 35-60.

LeCompte, M. D. (1993). A framework for hearing silence: What does telling stories mean when we are supposed to be doing science? In D. McLaughlin & W. G. Tierney (Eds.), *Naming silenced lives: Personal narratives and processes of educational change.* New York: Routledge & Kegan Paul.

Lee, R. M. (1995). *Dangerous fieldwork.* Thousand Oaks, CA: Sage.

Lees, S. (1986). *Losing out.* London: Hutchinson.

Libby, W. (1922). The scientific imagination. *Scientific Monthly, 15,* 263-270.

Lincoln, Y., & Guba, E. (1985). *Naturalistic inquiry.* Beverly Hills, CA: Sage.

Locke, L. F., Spirduso, W. W., & Silverman, S. J. (1993). *Proposals that work: A guide for planning dissertations and grant proposals* (3rd ed.). Newbury Park, CA: Sage.

Lutz, F., & Iannaccone, L. (1969). *Understanding educational organizations: A field study approach.* Columbus, OH: Charles Merrill.

Maguire, P. (1987). *Doing participatory research: A feminist approach.* Amherst, MA: Center for International Education.

Mandelbaum, D. G. (1973). The study of life history: Gandhi. *Current Anthropology, 14,* 177-207.

Manning, P. K. (1972). Observing the police: Deviants, respectables, and the law. In J. Douglas (Ed.), *Research on deviance* (pp. 213-268). New York: Random House.

Marshall, C. (1979). *Career socialization of women in school administration.* Unpublished doctoral dissertation, University of California at Santa Barbara.

Marshall, C. (1981). Organizational policy and women's socialization in administration. *Urban Education, 16,* 205-231.

Marshall, C. (1984). Elites, bureaucrats, ostriches, and pussycats: Managing research in policy settings. *Anthropology and Education Quarterly, 15,* 235-251.

Marshall, C. (1985a). Appropriate criteria of trustworthiness and goodness for qualitative research on education organizations. *Quality and Quantity, 19,* 353-373.

Marshall, C. (1985b). The stigmatized woman: The professional woman in a male sex-typed career. *Journal of Educational Administration, 23,* 131-152.

Marshall, C. (1986). *Power language and women's access to organizational leadership.* Grant proposal to the University Research Council, Vanderbilt University, Nashville, TN.

Marshall, C. (1987). *Report to the Vanderbilt Policy Education Committee.* Vanderbilt University, Nashville, TN.

Marshall, C. (1990). Goodness criteria: Are they objective or judgment calls? In E. Guba (Ed.), *The paradigm dialog* (pp. 188-197). Newbury Park, CA: Sage.

Marshall, C. (1991). Educational policy dilemmas: Can we have control and quality and choice and democracy and equity? In K. M. Borman, P. Swami, & L. D. Wagstaff (Eds.), *Contemporary issues in U.S. education* (pp. 1-21). Norwood, NJ: Ablex.

Marshall, C. (1992). School administrators' values: A focus on atypicals. *Educational Administration Quarterly, 28,* 368-386.

Marshall, C. (1997). Dismantling and reconstructing policy analysis. In C. Marshall (Ed.), *Feminist critical policy analysis: A perspective from primary and secondary schooling* (Vol. 1, pp. 1-34), London: Falmer.

Marshall, C., Mitchell, D., & Wirt, F. (1985). Assumptive worlds of education policy makers. *Peabody Journal of Education, 62*(4), 90-115.

Marshall, C., Mitchell, D., & Wirt, F. (1986). The context of state level policy formulation. *Educational Evaluation and Policy Analysis, 8,* 347-378.

Matsuda, M. J., Delgado, R., Lawrence, C. R., & Crenshaw, K. W. (1993). *Words that wound: Critical race theory, assault speech, and the First Amendment.* Boulder, CO: Westview.

Maxwell, J. A. (1996). *Qualitative research design: An interactive approach.* Thousand Oaks, CA: Sage.

McKernan, J. (1991). *Curriculum action research: A handbook of methods and resources for the reflective practitioner.* London: Routledge & Kegan Paul.

McTaggart, R. (Ed.). (1997). *Participatory action research: International contexts and consequences.* Albany: State University of New York Press.

Meyer, A. D., & Goes, J. B. (1988). Organizational assimilation of innovations: A multilevel contextual analysis. *Academy of Management Journal, 31,* 897-923.

Meyer, J. W., & Rowan, B. (1992). Institutionalized organizations: Formal structure as myth and ceremony. In J. W. Meyer & W. R. Scott (Eds.), *Organizational environments: Ritual and rationality* (updated ed., pp. 21-44). Newbury Park, CA: Sage.

Meyer, J. W., Scott, R. W., & Deal, T. W. (1992). Institutional and technical sources of organizational structure: Explaining the structure of educational organizations. In J. W. Meyer & W. R. Scott (Eds.), *Organizational environments: Ritual and rationality* (updated ed., pp. 45-67). Newbury Park, CA: Sage.

Miles, M. S., & Huberman, A. M. (1994). *Qualitative data analysis: An expanded sourcebook* (2nd ed.). Thousand Oaks, CA: Sage.

Miller, J. L. (1990). *Creating spaces and finding voices: Teachers collaborating for empowerment.* Albany: State University of New York Press.

Mitchell, D., Wirt, F., & Marshall, C. (1986). *Alternative state policy mechanisms for pursuing educational quality, equity, efficiency, and choice* (Final report to the U.S. Department of Education, Grant No. NIE-G-83 0020). Washington, DC: U.S. Department of Education.

Mooney, R. L. (1951). Problems in the development of research men. *Educational Research Bulletin, 30,* 141-150.

Morgan, D. L. (1997). *Focus groups as qualitative research* (2nd ed.). Newbury Park, CA: Sage.

Mouffe, C., & LeClau, E. (1985). *Hegemony and socialist strategy: Towards a radical democratic politics.* New York: Verso.

Nielson, J. (Ed.). (1990). *Feminist research methods: Exemplary readings in the social sciences.* Boulder, CO: Westview.

O'Hearn-Curran, M. (1997). *First days in the field: Lessons I learned in kindergarten.* Unpublished manuscript, University of Massachusetts at Amherst.

Oliver, K. (1990). *The lives of mothers following the death of a child: Toward an understanding of maternal bereavement.* Unpublished doctoral dissertation, University of Massachusetts at Amherst.

Park, P., Brydon-Miller, M., Hall, B., & Jackson, T. (Eds.). (1993). *Voices of change: Participatory research in the United States and Canada.* Ontario, Canada: Ontario Institute for Studies in Education Press.

Patton, M. Q. (1980). *Qualitative evaluation methods.* Beverly Hills, CA: Sage.

Patton, M. Q. (1990). *Qualitative research and evaluation methods* (2nd ed.). Newbury Park, CA: Sage.

Pearsol, J. (1985, April). *Controlling qualitative data: Understanding teachers' value perspectives on a sex equity education project.* Paper presented at the annual meeting of the American Educational Research Association, Chicago.

Phaik-Lah, K. (1997). The environments of action research in Malaysia. In S. Hollingsworth (Ed.), *International action research: A casebook for educational reform* (pp. 238-243). London: Falmer.

Piotrkowski, C. S. (1979). *Work and the family system: A naturalistic study of working-class and lower-middle-class families.* New York: Free Press.

Pleck, E. (1976). Two worlds in one: Work and family. *Journal of Social History, 70,* 178-195.

Polsky, N. (1969). *Hustlers, beats, and others.* Garden City, NY: Doubleday Anchor.

Powdermaker, H. (1966). *Stranger and friend.* New York: Norton.

Punch, M. (1994). Politics and ethics in qualitative research. In N. K. Denzin & Y. S. Lincoln (Eds.), *Handbook of qualitative research* (pp. 83-97). Thousand Oaks, CA: Sage.

Qualis Research Associates. (1987). *The ethnograph* [Computer program]. Littleton, CO: Author.

Reason, P. (Ed.). (1994). *Participation in human inquiry.* Thousand Oaks, CA: Sage.

Reardon, K., Welsh, B., Kreiswirth, B., & Forester, J. (1993, Spring). Participatory action research from the inside: Community development practice in East St. Louis. *American Sociologist,* pp. 69-91.

Riessman, C. (1993). *Narrative analysis.* Newbury Park, CA: Sage.

Rosenau, P. M. (1992). *Post-modernism and the social sciences: Insights, inroads, and intrusions.* Princeton, NJ: Princeton University Press.

Ross, M., & Conway, M. (1986). Remembering one's own past: The construction of personal histories. In R. Sorrentino & E. T. Higgins (Eds.), *Handbook of motivation and cognition: Foundations of social behavior* (pp. 122-144). New York: Guilford.

Rossman, G. B. (1984). I owe you one: Notes on role and reciprocity in a study of graduate education. *Anthropology and Education Quarterly, 15,* 225-234.

Rossman, G. B. (1985, April). *Studying professional cultures in improving high schools.* Paper presented at the annual meeting of the American Educational Research Association, Chicago.

Rossman, G. B., Corbett, H. D., & Dawson, J. L. (1986). Intentions and impacts: A comparison of sources of influence on local school systems. *Urban Education, 21,* 86-106.

Rossman, G. B., Corbett, H. D., & Firestone, W. A. (1984). *Plan for the study of professional cultures in improving high schools.* Philadelphia: Research for Better Schools.

Rossman, G. B., Corbett, H. D., & Firestone, W. A. (1988). *Change and effectiveness in schools: A cultural perspective.* Albany: State University of New York Press.

Rossman, G. B., & Rallis, S. F. (1998). *Learning in the field: An introduction to qualitative research.* Thousand Oaks, CA: Sage.

Rossman, G. B., & Wilson, B. L. (1985). Numbers and words: Combining quantitative and qualitative methods in a single large-scale evaluation study. *Evaluation Review, 9,* 627-643.

Rossman, G. B., & Wilson, B. L. (1994). Numbers and words revisited: Being shamelessly eclectic. *Quality and Quantity, 28,* 315-327.

Rossman, G. B., Wilson, B. L., & Corbett, H. D. (1985). *A cultural perspective on the local implementation of state school improvement programs* (Research proposal submitted to Florida State University). Philadelphia: Research for Better Schools.

Ryave, A. L., & Schenkein, J. N. (1974). Notes on the art of walking. In R. Turner (Ed.), *Ethnomethodology* (pp. 265-274). Baltimore: Penguin.

Schatzman, L., & Strauss, A. (1973). *Field research: Strategies for a natural sociology.* Englewood Cliffs, NJ: Prentice Hall.

Schein, E. H. (1985). *Organizational culture and leadership.* San Francisco: Jossey-Bass.

Scheurich, J. (1997). *Research methods in the postmodern.* London: Falmer.

Seidman, I. E. (1998). *Interviewing as qualitative research: A guide for researchers in education and the social sciences* (2nd ed.). New York: Teachers College Press.

Shadduck-Hernandez, J. (1997). *Affirmation, advocacy, and action: Refugee/immigrant student education and community building in higher education.* Unpublished research proposal to the Spencer Foundation, University of Massachusetts at Amherst.

Sharp, R., & Green, A. (1975). *Education and social control.* London: Routledge & Kegan Paul.

Smelser, N. J., & Erickson, E. H. (1980). *Themes of work and love in adulthood.* Cambridge, MA: Harvard University Press.

Smith, J. K. (1988, March). *Looking for the easy way out: The desire for methodological constraints in openly ideological research.* Paper presented at the annual meeting of the American Educational Research Association, New Orleans.

Soloway, I., & Walters, J. (1977). Workin' the corner: The ethics and legality of ethnographic fieldwork among active heroin addicts. In R. S. Weppner (Ed.), *Street ethnography* (pp. 159-178). Beverly Hills, CA: Sage.

Sorenson, E. R. (1968). The retrieval of data from changing cultures. *Anthropological Quarterly, 41,* 177-186.

Spradley, J. S. (1979). *The ethnographic interview.* New York: Holt, Rinehart & Winston.

Spradley, J. S. (1980). *Participant observation.* New York: Holt, Rinehart & Winston.

Strauss, A., & Corbin, J. (Eds.). (1997). *Grounded theory in practice.* Thousand Oaks, CA: Sage.

Stringer, E. T. (1996). *Action research: A handbook for practitioners.* Thousand Oaks, CA: Sage.

Sutherland, E. H., & Conwell, C. (1983). *The professional thief.* Chicago: University of Chicago Press.

Taylor, S. J., & Bogdan, R. (1984). *Introduction to qualitative research: The search for meanings* (2nd ed.). New York: John Wiley.

Tesch, R. (1990). *Qualitative research: Analysis types and software tools.* New York: Falmer.

Thomas, W. I. (1949). *Social structure and social theory.* New York: Free Press.

Thompson, E. (Ed.). (1939). *Race relations and the race problem.* Durham, NC: Duke University Press.

Thorne, B. (1983). Political activists as participant observer: Conflicts of commitment in a study of the draft resistance movement of the 1960s. In R. Emerson (Ed.), *Contemporary field research: A collection of readings* (pp. 216-234). Prospect Heights, IL: Waveland.

Tierney, W. G., & Lincoln, Y. S. (Eds.). (1997). *Representation and the text: Re-framing the narrative voice.* Albany: State University of New York Press.

Titchen, A., & Bennie, A. (1993). Action research as a research strategy: Finding our way through a philosophical and methodological maze. *Journal of Advanced Nursing, 18,* 858-865.

Tong, R. (1989). *Feminist thought: A comprehensive introduction.* San Francisco: Westview.

Tsing, A. L. (1990). The vision of a woman shaman. In J. M. Nielsen (Ed.), *Feminist research methods* (pp. 147-173). San Francisco: Westview.

Tucker, B. J. (1996). *Teachers who make a difference: Voices of Mexican-American students.* Unpublished thesis proposal, Harvard University Graduate School of Education.

Van Maanen, J. (1988). *Tales of the field: On writing ethnography.* Chicago: University of Chicago Press.

Villenas, S. (1996). Chicana ethnographer: Identity, marginalization, and co-optation in the field. *Harvard Educational Review, 66*(4), 711-731.

Viney, L. L., & Bousefield, L. (1991). Narrative analysis: A method of psychosocial research for AIDS-affected people. *Social Science and Medicine, 23,* 757-765.

Wax, R. (1971). *Doing fieldwork: Warnings and advice.* Chicago: University of Chicago Press.

Webb, E., Campbell, D. T., Schwartz, R. D., & Sechrest, L. (1966). *Unobtrusive measures: Nonreactive research in the social sciences.* Chicago: Rand McNally.

Weick, K. E. (1976). Educational organizations as loosely coupled systems. *Administrative Science Quarterly, 21,* 1-19.

Weitzman, E. A., & Miles, M. B. (1995). *Computer programs for qualitative data analysis.* Thousand Oaks, CA: Sage.

Westley, W. A. (1967). The police: Law, custom, and morality. In P. I. Rose (Ed.), *The study of society* (pp. 766-779). New York: Random House.

Whyte, W. F. (1980). *The social life of small urban spaces.* Washington, DC: Conservation Foundation.

Whyte, W. F. (1984). *Learning from the field: A guide from experience.* Beverly Hills, CA: Sage.

Wilson, S. (1977). The use of ethnographic techniques in educational research. *Review of Educational Research, 47,* 245-265.

Wiseman, F. (1969). *High school* [Film]. Boston: Zippora Films.

Yablonsky, L. (1965). *The tunnel back: Synanon.* Baltimore: Penguin.

Yin, R. K. (1984). *Case study research: Design and methods.* Beverly Hills, CA: Sage.

Young, M. F. D. (Ed.). (1971). *Knowledge and control.* London: Collier-Macmillan.

Zaltman, G., Duncan, R., & Holbeck, J. (1973). *Innovations and organizations.* New York: John Wiley.

Zelditch, M. (1962). Some methodological problems of field studies. *American Journal of Sociology, 67,* 566-576.

Ziller, R. C., & Lewis, D. (1981). Orientations: Self, social and environmental precepts through auto-photography. *Personality and Social Psychology Bulletin, 7,* 338-343.

# Author Index

# Subject Index

# About the Authors

**Catherine Marshall** is Professor in the Department of Educational Leadership at the University of North Carolina at Chapel Hill. She received her Ph.D. from the University of California, Santa Barbara, benefited from a postdoctoral fellowship at UCLA, and served on the faculty of the University of Pennsylvania and Vanderbilt University before taking her current position at North Carolina. The ongoing goal of her teaching and research has been to use an interdisciplinary approach to analyze cultures of schools, state policy systems, and other organizations. She served as the editor of the *Peabody Journal of Education* and has published extensively about the politics of education, qualitative methodology, women's access to careers, and the socialization, language, and values in educational administration.

She is also author or editor of numerous other books. These include *Feminist Critical Policy Analysis* (Vols. 1 and 2), *Culture and Education Policy in the American States,* with Douglas Mitchell and Frederick Wirt; *The Assistant Principal: Leadership Choices and Challenges; The New Politics of Gender and Race* (editor); and *The Administrative Career: Cases for Entry, Equity, and Endurance,* with Katharine Kasden. Early in her scholarly career, while conducting qualitative research on policy and teaching literally hundreds of doctoral students how to adopt and adapt the qualitative approach into workable proposals, she recognized a need and began to develop this book.

**Gretchen B. Rossman** is Professor of Education at the University of Massachusetts at Amherst. She received her Ph.D. in education from the University of Pennsylvania with a specialization in higher education administration. She has served as Visiting Professor at Harvard University's Graduate School of Education. Prior to coming to the University of Massachusetts, she was Senior Research Associate at Research for Better Schools in Philadelphia. Her research has focused on the local impact of changes in federal, state, and local policy. Her current domestic research interests include studying school-based restructuring efforts to include students with disabilities and those from refugee and immigrant families. Internationally, she serves as Research and Evaluation Specialist for a U.S. Agency for International Development project on strengthening the education of girls in India.

She has coauthored three books based on her research: *Change and Effectiveness in Schools: A Cultural Perspective,* with Dick Corbett and Bill Firestone; *Mandating Academic Excellence: High School Responses to State Curriculum Reform,* with Bruce Wilson; and *Dynamic Teachers: Leaders of Change,* with Sharon Rallis. She has recently published an introductory qualitative research text, *Learning in the Field: An Introduction to Qualitative Research,* with Sharon Rallis. In addition to her teaching and research responsibilities, she consults regularly on restructuring in schools and serves as a qualitative evaluation specialist to several educational organizations.